Lecture Notes in Computer Science 8844

Commenced Publication in 1973
Founding and Former Series Editors:
Gerhard Goos, Juris Hartmanis, and Jan van Leeuwen

More information about this series at http://www.springer.com/series/7409

Guido Brunnett · Sabine Coquillart
Robert van Liere · Gregory Welch
Libor Váša (Eds.)

Virtual Realities

International Dagstuhl Seminar, Dagstuhl Castle
Germany, June 9–14, 2013
Revised Selected Papers

 Springer

Editors
Guido Brunnett
TU Chemnitz
Chemnitz
Germany

Sabine Coquillart
Inria Rhône-Alpes
Saint Ismier Cedex
France

Robert van Liere
CWI - Amsterdam
Amsterdam
The Netherlands

Gregory Welch
The University of Central Florida
Orlando, FL
USA

Libor Váša
Technische Universität Chemnitz
Chemnitz
Germany

Videos to this book can be accessed at
http://www.springerimages.com/videos/978-3-319-17042-8

ISSN 0302-9743   ISSN 1611-3349   (electronic)
Lecture Notes in Computer Science
ISBN 978-3-319-17042-8   ISBN 978-3-319-17043-5   (eBook)
DOI 10.1007/978-3-319-17043-5

Library of Congress Control Number: 2015935045

LNCS Sublibrary: SL3 – Information Systems and Applications, incl. Internet/Web and HCI

Springer Cham Heidelberg New York Dordrecht London

Printed on acid-free paper

Springer International Publishing AG Switzerland is part of Springer Science+Business Media
(www.springer.com)

Preface

Virtual Reality (VR) is a multidisciplinary area of research aimed at interactive human computer mediated simulations of artificial environments. An important aspect of VR-based systems is the stimulation of the human senses - usually sight, sound, and touch - such that a user feels a sense of presence in the virtual environment. Sometimes it is important to combine real and virtual objects in the same real or virtual environment. This approach is often referred to as Augmented Reality (AR), when virtual objects are integrated into a real environment. Research in VR and AR encompasses a wide range of fundamental topics, including: 3D interaction, presence, telepresence and tele-existence, VR modeling, multi-model systems, and human factors. Typical VR applications include simulation, training, scientific visualization, and entertainment, whereas typical AR applications include computer-aided manufacturing or mainte-nance, and computer-aided surgery or medicine.

During the week of June 9–14, 2013 the Schloss Dagstuhl Leibniz Center for Informatics held a second seminar in the area of Virtual Reality. The main goal of the seminar was to bring together leading international experts and promising young researchers to discuss current VR and AR challenges and future directions. The organization built on the experiences from the previous seminar "Virtual Realities 2008." The format included sessions with standard presentations as well as parallel breakout sessions devoted to "hot-topics" in VR and AR research. Plenary sessions were also scheduled to allow the working groups to report and discuss their findings.

This book comprises a collection of research and position papers presented at this seminar. All papers were subject to a peer-review process by at least two reviewers per manuscript. The manuscripts selected for this book have been structured into the four chapters: VR environments, Interaction and User Experience, Virtual Humans, and Tele-existence.

June 2013

Guido Brunnett
Sabine Coquillart
Robert van Liere
Gregory Welch
Libor Váša

Contents

Tele-Existence

VR Environments

Live Will Never Be the Same!

How Broadcasting Might Influence the Acceptance and Widespread Usage of Augmented Reality

Wolfgang Broll[1]([⊠]) and Jan Herling[2]

[1] Virtual Worlds and Digital Games Group, TU Ilmenau,
Ehrenbergstr. 29, 98693 Ilmenau, Germany
wolfgang.broll@tu-ilmenau.de
http://www.tu-ilmenau.de/vwdg
[2] fayteq AG, Erich-Kaestner-Str. 1, 99094 Erfurt, Germany
jan.herling@fayteq.com
http://www.fayteq.com

Abstract. While anticipated in Hollywood movies and sci-fi literature, a perfect artifical reality – i.e. the ultimate VR environment – will probably not become real within the next couple of years. However, using Augmented Reality (AR) technologies in order to seamlessly embed artificial content into the real environment, might be a much more feasible way to remove the clear border between reality and virtuality. In this paper we will look into lately developed AR technologies and how they relate to recent trends in movie and TV productions. We will further anticipate what this will mean to live broadcasts and which implications this might have for a widespread individual usage of sophisticated AR technology.

Keywords: Augmented Reality (AR) · Diminished Reality · Broadcasting · Postproduction · Compositing · Advertising · Seamless integration

1 Introduction

If you would just ask an arbitrary person on the street what she thinks VR is, she would probably answer: the Matrix or maybe the Holodeck. Another possibility to express this would be to say: what would make a virtual environment undistinguishable from real life? Obviously, there is no easy and no immediate answer to this question. However, if we look at Augmented Reality (AR), it seems that we are already much closer to a situation, where it becomes impossible or at least very difficult for an individual to distinguish between real and artificial (virtual) content. Recent works in the area of Diminished Reality and AR with real lighting reveal that the remaining steps in this area might be much smaller than usually estimated. The main advantage of AR settings compared to VR environments is that reality – perfect as it is – is already there and only rather small parts have to be added or removed. While virtual worlds have to

© Springer International Publishing Switzerland 2015
G. Brunnett et al. (Eds.): Virtual Realities, LNCS 8844, pp. 3–15, 2015.
DOI: 10.1007/978-3-319-17043-5_1

provide a complete perfect or at least very convincing impression, AR applications may already provide a perfect illusion when still restricted to particular settings. Limitations such as not being capable to deal with correct lighting or occlusions in arbitrarily complex scenes in realtime hence can easily be avoided. Therefore, the current limitation is rather with respect to the overall complexity of the scenario and application then the quality of the augmentation. Adding live virtual content is already well established in the area of broadcasting. Further, we can observe a rapidly growing market for digital product placement, providing the necessary driving force. Thus, perfectly integrated sophisticated (live) virtual content will probably quite soon become a standard element within movies and broadcasts. On the one hand, live transmissions will contain additional unreal content, while on the other hand, real elements are discarded – not recognizable for the observer. Combined with recent advances in see-through display technologies we should not be surprised to already see individually adapted environments undistinguishable from (pure) reality within a couple of years. As already explained, this seems feasible as in contrast to VR most of the content observed will still be real and (selected) virtual content can be adapted to the real one much easier than creating an entire convincible artificial world. As with the Matrix and the Holodeck, this raises the question, how such a development will influence our daily life with respect to communication, interaction, and the reception of our environment.

In this paper we will show how recent technological developments will influence our perception of the environment, in particular regarding the manipulation of content in live broadcasts. The paper is structured as follows: in section two we will provide an overview of the current types of usage of digital video manipulation. In section three we will review recent approaches and developments in Diminished Reality and advanced lighting for AR. In the fourth section the implications of these approaches on broadcasting – in particular live broadcasts – as well as our perception of the environment will be discussed. We will then conclude in the final section of the paper.

2   Digital Video Manipulation

In this section we will review some existing application areas of AR related technologies in broadcasting. While the first application area makes immediate usage of (simple) AR technology, more advanced visual effects are currently still restricted to compositing. Compositing is a major step in the postproduction of most movies, allowing for seamlessly combining different video sources, in particular digital content with real video footage. Nowadays, even experts can no longer clearly distinguish the real and the artificial parts of a scene. However, achieving such a perfect illusion is an elaborate and time-consuming process. Actually, a range of types for video editing and manipulation exists. Each of them combines or composes real and virtual content, and requires some kind of camera tracking for registering the artificial content. Further, they all require some means to adapt lighting to seamlessly integrate the digital content. In order to discriminate between the different types of video effects (VFX) and AR, we would like to introduce the following scheme:

– **Video Compositing:** this typically includes the usage of chroma keying (green screen, blue screen) video footage, video compositing tools, image editing, and involves plenty of manual editing. The scene composition may be arbitrarily complex. This process often takes several months and by that is feasable for feature films only.
– **Video Manipulation (offline):** this relates to standard video footage enhanced during post production using video compositing or image editing tools, still involving a significant amount of manual editing. The complexity of this kind is fair. The time frame nowadays is from a few days to a few weeks and is used for daily soaps and other TV productions.
– **Realtime Video Manipulation:** this refers to directly adding (or removing) content of video stream immediately before broadcasting them. It requires sophisticated realtime capable tools and often includes special hardware for tracking and/or well-known camera viewpoints. Nevertheless complexity is restricted to rather simple settings for now. The time available is between a few milliseconds up to a few seconds (as even *live* broadcasts are typically delayed by a few seconds). This is currently mainly used for certain types of sport broadcasts.
– **Augmented Reality:** while using the same underlying technologies as direct video manipulations, AR additionally allows the user to freely change her viewpoint, moving around in the augmented scene, and enables him to interact with the real and virtual content. However, existing examples often provide a rather limited tracking and by that registration quality. Additionally they often neglect visual integration.

2.1   Virtual Content in Sports Broadcasts

Sports broadcasts were the first area to establish an extensive usage of AR techniques for overlaying the real video feed by virtual information. Early examples included the overlay of a virtual touchdown line in American football games or the virtual goal distance line for penalty shots in soccer. More advanced examples also included moving representations of all-time records and/or a comparison with competitors in racing, running, cycling, and swimming competitions. However, the virtual content added is still rather simple as it is typically restricted to simple 2D or even 1D objects such as lines, circles, text, and sometimes images (Fig. 1). In fixed settings such as the playing field in soccer or football this was also already occasionally used to add virtual advertising (see also next subsections).

2.2   Digital Product Placement

Product placement has a very long tradition in major Hollywood productions. One of the oldest and best-known examples is probable James Bond driving

Fig. 1. Using simple augmentation in sport broadcasts (image adapted from [20] for illustration)

an Aston Martin. However product placement was previously often considered as covered advertising and by that has not been allowed as part of TV broadcasts for a long time in many countries including e.g. Germany. After recent law adjustments, product placement has meanwhile become a well-established form of advertisement and is common in most countries. Traditional product placement however, has one big disadvantage compared to standard TV advertising spots: the decision regarding the advertisement has to be made before the actual production of the movie, daily soap, or show. As such productions typically happen several months or at least weeks before their actual broadcast, and in contrast to this, the decision on advertising budgets is a rather short-term decision (a few weeks or even days before), traditional product placements provide a limited flexibility and by that market potential. Digital product placements partially overcome these limitations as they can be added to the scene afterwards. Their origin also trace back to feature films where they were added as part of the video compositing. This work however, is quite time-consuming and elaborate, and by that costly. Thus, it is not suitable or affordable for most productions, and for that reason may not be applied to advertisings for most commercial products. Digital product placement meanwhile has become quite common in certain TV formats such as the CBS production "How I met your mother".

2.3 Digital Advertising

Beside this, traditional forms of advertising as used in live events such as soccer games or car races become increasingly interesting for digital enhancements.

This refers for example to the advertising on shirts of players and drivers, or on cars as well as perimeter advertising. When broadcasting such events this local advertising is automatically transmitted as well. Looking for instance at international soccer matches we currently still see the situation that individual ads are used for the perimeters on each side. Having two almost independent camera teams filming the match from each side allows for country-specific ads. However, as such matches are usually also watched in several other countries or regions, a significant amount of the advertising does not reach the intended audience. Therefore, companies such as Supponor have started to enhance perimeters and cameras with appropriate sensor devices to detect these areas within the recorded video stream. This then allows for replacing the image area covered by the perimeter ads by custom-tailored content. Thus, individual ads can be applied and broadcasted to reach a specific audience. While such hardware and labor intensive approaches are currently still the only possibility to apply realtime modifications, cost pressure will eventually quicken the deployment of software solutions.

2.4 Object Removal

An airplane in the sky above Troy, a building visible through the window of the Titanic: original footage often contains undesired content, not matching to the current scene or the anticipated era. Thus, removing undesired objects from video sequences is a major issue in the postproduction of movies and films. Often supporting rigs, dollies, wires, people, buildings, microphones, etc. are either directly or indirectly (in some mirroring surfaces) visible and have to be removed from the original footage for the final cut. Existing tools provide rather limited support for this task. Therefore, objects are typically removed manually by standard image editing tools, which is very cumbersome and time-consuming, and by that a costly process. For this reason, in undesired objects are either just left where they are or the entire scene is removed in productions without the budget of feature films.

3 Related Work

In this section we will have a look at related work. We will focus on approaches and technologies, which may not necessarily be part of the ongoing developments currently, but which will or might influence them significantly in the future.

3.1 Diminished Reality

While Augmented Reality (AR) enhances reality by artificial (virtual) content, Diminished Reality (DR) is exactly the opposite of it. Diminished Reality means removing real content seamlessly and invisible from the reality. In the context of audio this meanwhile represents a standard technology: noise cancelation earphones, allowing for removing environmental audio sources and replacing them by different (displayed) content are an off-the-shelf commercial product. From a technological point of view, Diminished Reality for video uses a totally different approach. Removing real content from a video stream requires an object removal on each individual frame. We can distinguish between two generally different approaches. The first approach removes objects by revealing the real background covered by the object to be removed. The second approach does not try to discover the real background, but rather tries to generate a coherent and by that convincible image. We will introduce both approaches below.

Regarding the first approach, two different methods exist. One method is to use multiple cameras. Thus, while the background of an occluding object is covered for one camera, it is still visible by another camera. Knowing the transformation between the individual cameras, the transformed real background image can be inserted into the original video frame, effectively removing the undesired real object. This method was e.g., used by Zokai et al. [23], and Enomoto and Saito [5]. Another possibility to remove objects is when either the object or the camera or both move within the video sequence and the occluded background is revealed in one of the other frames. Based on the camera movement the transformed real background can again be inserted into the appropriate video frame. This method originally was introduced by Wexler et al. [21]. Similar methods are meanwhile already available in a couple of video editing resp. compositing tools, e.g. Nuke or Mocha. In contrast to the first method, the second method is not very suitable for real-time usage, as it requires searching for matching image patches in previous or subsequent video frames. In order to allow for real-time or close to real-time processing the search has to be restricted to a small number of preceding frames. Nevertheless processing time remains a critical issue here.

The second approach is based on image inpainting methods. Image inpainting aka content-aware fill is a technique where a certain (masked) area of an image is filled with synthetic content based on the remainder of the image. While this meanwhile has become a standard tool in image editing software, its application to video editing is still in its infancy. While image inpainting approaches such as one by Simakov et al. [19] or Barnes et al. [2] usually search for suitable image patches in the remainder of the image, filling the mask with patches ensuring coherency throughout the entire image, video inpainting additionally requires coherency among subsequent video frames. In order to apply video inpainting to a live video stream, the inpainting process additionally has to be real-time capable. A real-time capable video inpainting approach was first presented in our previous work [9] and further enhanced in our more recent approaches [10,12]. It allows for generating an artificial content, coherent with the surrounding image throughout the entire video sequence (Fig. 2). This even allows for removing objects, which could not be removed in reality.

One challenging task in video inpainting approaches is the identification or specification of the undesired image content. The specification can be done either in a pre-precessing step training the application for detecting the undesired object automatically or by a user-interaction in the moment the undesired image content becomes visible (see [10,13]). An automatic detection can be realized by

Fig. 2. Real-time removal of objects from a video sequence in real-time while generating a coherent stream.

Fig. 3. User-defined selection of undesired image content by definition of a rough object contour on a tablet device.

applying visual patterns as used by Gordon and Lowe [7], our descriptorless approach [11], or by the application of geometric CAD models as used by Reitmayr and Drummond [17] or Wuest and Stricker [22]. However, if the undesired object is not known in advance the object needs to be selected by the user manually. Several individual interaction techniques are conceivable. The selection of the object's contour is one of the most intuitive ways defining the undesired object (Fig. 3). Nevertheless, masking of the entire undesired image content with a brush or mask tool may also be appropriate.

All approaches to video inpainting require some kind of tracking. Either the location of the object to be removed has to be tracked or the movement of the camera, or both. Traditional tracking techniques as used e.g., for AR are only of limited usability for this task. While putting traditional black and white markers on objects to be removed does not represent a feasible solution, most other (feature-based) tracking approaches such as those introduced by Gordon and Lowe [7] or Bay et al. [3] will fail as well. One reason is, that objects to be removed often do not provide suitable features, or features change due to camera or object movements, and new features cannot clearly be assigned either to belong to the object or the background. Further, besides detecting the movement of the camera in relation to the scene and/or the object, it is also necessary to clearly separate the object to be removed from the background. This image segmentation is the by far most difficult task of DR-related tracking. An approach applying fingerprints may be found in our previous work [10] allowing for the segmentation of undesired object in real-time. However, if more accurate segmentation is required (e.g., applying sub-pixel accuracy) more time consuming segmentation approaches like those used by Rother et al. [18] or Arbelaez et al. [1] may be more appropriate. An additional difficulty is the fact that objects to be removed may partially or even temporarily completely become out of sight at the video image border. Even worse, other scene content, such as moving people, cars, etc. may partially or temporarily completely occlude the objects to be removed, making a proper segmentation difficult up to impossible.

3.2 Advanced Lighting for Seamless Integration

In order to seamlessly integrate artificial virtual content into a real-life environment or video footage, proper lighting is an important issue. In order to achieve a good integration, mutual influence of lighting has to be considered. On the one hand, environmental light influences the appearance of augmented virtual content. On the other hand, this virtual content might also influence its (real) environment. In order to model the environmental lighting influence on artificial objects the light distribution in the scene has to be estimated. Traditional methods applied sphere maps or cube maps received from fisheye lenses or multiple cameras, or used spheres placed in the real scene in order to detect highlights on them [4]. By applying for instance shadow maps and irradiance volumes [8] or light propagation volumes [6] such methods provide surprisingly realistic renderings of virtual objects within real environments. However, they allow for simulating the captured light sources only and become less accurate when virtual objects are rendered at other locations. While placing spheres or cameras within a scene is often not feasible, they provide live information of the lighting situation. Spheres however have the disadvantage that they can only detect light sources shining more or less in same direction as the observer is looking.

For an appropriate modeling of the global illumination of the real scene, the actual geometry resp. the surface normal of each surface is required. The acquisition of the scene geometry can for instance be done using 3D laser scanners. This however, restricts the information to static scenes. As soon as the environment contains any dynamic items, the scene information and by that the resulting lighting will become incorrect. Another possibility to gather the required scene information are SLAM (simultaneous localization and mapping) approaches [14], which allow to create a 3D model of the environment while simultaneously tracking the movement of the camera within it. Finally, depth cameras provide another

Fig. 4. Influence of light reflected from virtual objects on real environment.

possibility to capture the scene information. While typically providing a rather rough resolution, their RGBD image allows for reconstructing surfaces and by that surface normals. In order to do so, the depth image has to be smoothed, outliers have to be removed and holes have to be filled. Depth cameras typically use infrared light and are either based on regular patterns projected onto the environment (e.g. Kinect) or use the time-of-flight (ToF) principle (e.g. Mesa or Kinect II). Approaches applying such information in order to seamlessly integrate virtual content into a real environment include Kinect Fusion [15,16].

As stated above, another issue is the influence of the artificial content on the real environment. This includes direct and indirect lighting of the real environment by artificial (virtual) lights, casting of shadows of virtual objects onto real objects, and real lighting reflected from virtual objects back to real objects (Fig. 4). These aspects of mutual lighting always require a 3D model of the real environment to be applied realistically. If neither information about the light sources nor the geometry of the environment from scanners or depth sensors is available, e.g. in a (2D) video stream, a proper estimation of the real lighting is difficult up to impossible. However, when replacing flat surfaces in a scene (i.e. billboards), the lighting (including its changes throughout multiple frames) may (roughly) be extracted and applied to a 2D replacement. If the camera is moved, SLAM approaches, as introduced above, may also be used.

4 Applications and Implications

4.1 Adding Desired Content

We may now apply AR technologies for frame-to-frame tracking of objects such as billboards or perimeters. By overlaying the real content by artificial digital content, ads, or other types of information can be added right into the scene as if they already have been there during the original shoot. Suddenly this will no longer be restricted to feature films. Integration of such technologies into postproduction tools will offer a new generation of powerful mechanisms for billboard replacement, digital product placement, etc. This will allow adding digital content even in low budget productions as this may then be done as part of the regular video editing rather than a separate compositing step during the postproduction. However, this will also require looking into additional aspects, typically not considered in standard AR applications. Those include aspects such as blurring due to objects being out of focus, or due to fast moving objects or cameras. In contrast to traditional AR environments, the digitally added virtual content will have to be adapted according to the visual parameters in the original footage. Further, lighting aspects will not be limited to those described above. In particular dynamic shadows and highlights may frequently occur and will have to be transferred to added digital content in order to achieve a believable output.

4.2   Removing Undesired Content

By applying DR technology for the removal of undesired content in videos, a much wider usage than with traditional postproduction techniques can be achieved. Using DR technology allows for easily removing undesired content with minimal or even without manual effort. The technology not only allows for removing undesired objects, but also provides means for removing content due to legal demands. Thus, e.g. product placement has to be discarded for broadcasts on children channels (at least in some countries), certain content has to be removed before a movie may be shown aboard of airplanes (airplane editing). Further, this approach may also be used to remove station logos and captions from material received from other stations.

4.3   Real-Time Application for Broadcasting

As the technologies presented in section two already showed, their application is generally not restricted to offline tasks as part of the postproduction process. In fact they provide the basis for applying the above scenarios even to live broadcast. Similar to the usage within sports broadcasts today, the addition of digital (virtual) content, and the removal or the replacement of real content will become common even in live broadcasts in the near future. Software based technologies currently do not provide the necessary robustness to be used to this kind of scenario. In order to be used for live broadcasts, they have to be absolutely fail-safe. As discussed before, partial and/or temporal occlusions lead to complex tracking issues, which require to be solved before. Very dynamic scenes (imagine for instance a car race) imply further challenges due to the very small number of frames where an object to be modified might be visible. Applications will include the removal of unlawful content. Broadcast of tobacco ads for example is illegal in Europe, while ads for alcoholic beverages might not be allowed in some Islamic countries. As those advertisements might still be allowed in the real setting, real-time DR and AR approaches will provide a convenient and efficient solution preventing the broadcast of this content by removing or replacing undesired ads on player shirts. However, while anticipating those opportunities, a clear labeling of modified content (as it is currently already required for (digital) product placement in some countries), will be important to make people aware of the fact that every content they observe might be manipulated.

4.4 Implications on Usage and Acceptance of AR

A general availability of a certain technology is often based on general developments not directly related to the original product. 3D graphics adapters for example were very expensive and available in high-end workstations only unless they were put at reasonable prices in every personal computer to enable it for gaming. The same applies to AR technology when it comes to smartphones and tablets. While the processing power, the graphics, the camera, and the sensors required made creating an AR system a cumbersome and costly adventure, almost everything necessary nowadays is available within a standard smartphone or tablet. What currently is missing from the device side is an appropriate head-worn display. However, with the currently ongoing developments (such as Google's Glass, Epson's Moverio, and Laster's SeeThru) it is quite likely that affordable wearable displays will be available shortly. Although their first generation might still lack the required field-of-view or brightness required for full outside AR and DR, their general availability and usage will lead to frequent updates and improvements (similar to the other developments mentioned here). When mobile phones became widespread, it took some time until one got used to people walking around and talking (in particular when using a head set). The same process will probably take place with head-worn displays. However, being used to the fact that even a live transmission may be enhanced by additional content, while other content might have been discarded, will achieve a higher acceptance than confronting people directly with the possibilities of the new technologies. Nevertheless, this will also open up a new field for empirical studies in the area of social sciences to study the implications of a widespread usage of such technologies. Looking at the implications of smartphones one might assume that arising social implications shall be pretty serious. With the broadcasting and advertising industry driving the development of convincing life-like real-time AR and DR, and the general availability of the necessary hardware for a significant fraction of the population, it seems reasonable to assume that highly sophisticated AR/DR undistinguishable from pure reality - might become common within a couple of years.

5   Conclusion and Future Work

In this paper we presented our vision towards a fundamental change of the reception of our environment. Due to the rapid development of new technologies for seamlessly integrating virtual content into real scenes as well as removing real content from them, our perception of live broadcast transmissions will fundamentally change compared to what we are currently used to. Moreover, once established for live broadcasts, the technology will also quickly become affordable and sufficiently robust for individual usage. In combination with current and upcoming hardware this will even change the perception of our real surrounding. Thus, a live view will truly no longer be the same as we were used to. However, in order to achieve this step there are still a couple of problems to solve, in particular when it comes to automatic segmentation, tracking, and analysis of lighting conditions. Further, such scenarios come along with a whole bunch of ethical and social implications, to be investigated by social scientists. Further, security issues in particular due to differences between the individual reception and the physical reality represent an important issue requiring further attention.

References

1. Arbeláez, P., Maire, M., Fowlkes, C., Malik, J.: Contour detection and hierarchical image segmentation. IEEE Trans. Pattern Anal. Mach Intell. **33**(5), 898–916 (2011)
2. Barnes, C., Shechtman, E., Finkelstein, A., Goldman, D.B.: Patchmatch: a randomized correspondence algorithm for structural image editing. In: SIGGRAPH, pp. 1–11. ACM, New York (2009)
3. Bay, H., Ess, A., Tuytelaars, T., Van Gool, L.: Speeded-up robust features (surf). Comput. Vis. Image Underst. **110**(3), 346–359 (2008)
4. Debevec, P.: Rendering synthetic objects into real scenes: bridging traditional and image-based graphics with global illumination and high dynamic range photography. In: Computer Graphics, pp. 189–198. ACM (1998)
5. Enomoto, A., Saito, H.: Diminished reality using multiple handheld cameras. In: ACCV 2007 Workshop on Multidimensional and Multi-view Image Processing (2007)
6. Franke, T.A.: Delta light propagation volumes for mixed reality. In: Proceedings of 2013 IEEE International Symposium on Mixed and Augmented Reality (IEEE ISMAR 2013). IEEE Computer Society, Piscataway (2013)
7. Gordon, I., Lowe, D.G.: What and where: 3D object recognition with accurate pose. In: Ponce, J., Hebert, M., Schmid, C., Zisserman, A. (eds.) Toward Category-Level Object Recognition. LNCS, vol. 4170, pp. 67–82. Springer, Heidelberg (2006)
8. Grosch, T., Eble, T., Mueller, S.: Consistent interactive augmentation of live camera images with correct near-field illumination. In: Proceedings of the 2007 ACM Symposium on Virtual Reality Software and Technology (ACM VRST 2007), pp. 125–132. ACM, New York (2007)
9. Herling, J., Broll, W.: The ocean framework: providing the basis for next-gen MR applications. In: Proceedings of the IEEE Virtual Reality 2010 Workshop, 3rd Workshop on Software Engineering and Architectures for Realtime Interactive Systems, SEARIS 2010 (2010)
10. Herling, J., Broll, W.: PixMix: a real-time approach to high-quality diminished reality. In: 11th IEEE International Symposium on Mixed and Augmented Reality, ISMAR 2012, USA, pp. 141–150. IEEE, November 2012

11. Herling, J., Broll, W.: Random model variation for universal feature tracking. In: Proceedings of the 18th ACM Symposium on Virtual Reality Software and Technology, VRST 2012, pp. 169–176. ACM, New York (2012)
12. Herling, J., Broll, W.: High-quality real-time video inpainting with pixmix. IEEE Trans. Vis. Comput. Graph. **20**(6), 866–879 (2014)
13. Kawai, N., Sato, T., Yokoya, N.: Diminished reality considering background structures. In: 2013 IEEE International Symposium on Mixed and Augmented Reality (ISMAR), pp. 259–260, October 2013
14. Klein, G., Murray, D.: Parallel tracking and mapping for small AR workspaces. In: Proceedings of ISMAR 2007, Washington, DC, USA, pp. 1–10 (2007)
15. Lensing, P., Broll, W.: Instant indirect illumination for dynamic mixed reality scenes. In: Proceedings of the 11th IEEE International Symposium on Mixed and Augmented Reality (ISMAR). IEEE Computer Society, Piscataway (2012)
16. Newcombe, R.A., Davison, A.J., Izadi, S., Kohli, P., Hilliges, O., Shotton, J., Molyneaux, D., Hodges, S., Kim, D., Fitzgibbon, A.: Kinectfusion: real-time dense surface mapping and tracking. In: Proceedings of the 10th IEEE International Symposium on Mixed and Augmented Reality, pp. 127–136. IEEE Computer Society, Piscataway, October 2011
17. Reitmayr, G., Drummond, T.: Going out: robust model-based tracking for outdoor augmented reality. In: Proceedings of the 5th IEEE and ACM International Symposium on Mixed and Augmented Reality, ISMAR 2006, pp. 109–118. IEEE Computer Society, Washington, DC (2006)
18. Rother, C., Kolmogorov, V., Blake, A.: "grabcut": interactive foreground extraction using iterated graph cuts. In: SIGGRAPH, pp. 309–314. ACM, New York (2004)
19. Simakov, D., Caspi, Y., Shechtman, E., Irani, M.: Summarizing visual data using bidirectional similarity. In: CVPR, IEEE (2008)
20. Tomasland: American football sample scene "jake delhomme goes deep" (2009). https://www.flickr.com/photos/tomasland/3965511917/, available under cc 2.0. https://creativecommons.org/licenses/by/2.0
21. Wexler, Y., Shechtman, E., Irani, M.: Space-time completion of video. IEEE Trans. Pattern Anal. Mach. Intell. **29**(3), 463–476 (2007)
22. Wuest, H., Stricker, D.: Tracking of industrial objects by using cad models. JVRB J. Virtual Reality Broadcast. **4**(1) (2007). URN: urn:nbn:de:0009-6-11595
23. Zokai, S., Esteve, J., Genc, Y. Navab, N.: Multiview paraperspective projection model for diminished reality. In: Proceedings of the 2nd IEEE/ACM International Symposium on Mixed and Augmented Reality, ISMAR 2003, USA, pp. 217–226. IEEE (2003)

Four Metamorphosis States in a Distributed Virtual (TV) Studio: Human, Cyborg, Avatar, and Bot – Markerless Tracking and Feedback for Realtime Animation Control

Jens Herder[✉], Jeff Daemen, Peter Haufs-Brusberg, and Isis Abdel Aziz

Department of Media, FH Düsseldorf, University of Applied Sciences,
Josef-Gockeln-Str. 9, 40474 Düsseldorf, Germany
herder@fh-duesseldorf.de
http://vsvr.medien.fh-duesseldorf.de

Abstract. The major challenge in virtual studio technology is the interaction between actors and virtual objects. Virtual studios differ from other virtual environments because there always exist two concurrent views: The view of the TV consumer and the view of the talent in front of the camera. This paper illustrates the interaction and feedback in front of the camera and compares different markerless person tracking systems, which are used for realtime animations. Entertaining animations are required, but sensors usually provide only a limited number of parameters. Additional information based on the context allows the generation of appealing animations, which might be partly prefabricated. As main example, we use a distributed live production in a virtual studio with two locally separated markerless tracking systems. The production was based on a fully tracked actor, cyborg (half actor, half graphics), avatar, and a bot. All participants could interact and throw a virtual disc. This setup is compared and mapped to Milgram's continuum and technical challenges are described in detail.

Keywords: Markerless tracking · Virtual studio · Avatars · Virtual characters · Interaction feedback

1 Introduction

While today's TV and video productions got used to the benefits of virtual studio technology, the interaction between actors and virtual objects inside a virtual world remains challenging. This contribution offers deep insights to actor tracking in virtual studios and their advantages for live productions. Different solutions as well as approaches with their strengths and weaknesses are compared

Electronic supplementary material The online version of this chapter (doi:10.1007/978-3-319-17043-5_2) contains supplementary material, which is available to authorized users. Videos can also be accessed at http://www.springerimages.com/videos/978-3-319-17042-8.

© Springer International Publishing Switzerland 2015
G. Brunnett et al. (Eds.): Virtual Realities, LNCS 8844, pp. 16–32, 2015.
DOI: 10.1007/978-3-319-17043-5_2

Fig. 1. The cyborg was created by partly overlaying the real, tracked actor with computer generated graphics within the green box.

to each other. Major functionalities were evaluated in exemplary productions at the Fachhochschule Düsseldorf, University of Applied Sciences.

The interaction control as well as multiple interfaces of a virtual set environment have been discussed and classified in [1]. An overview about the origin of virtual set environments and an introduction to virtual studios can be found in [2]. Virtual studio's developments were accompanied by experiments with distributed live productions using virtual studios and avatars all along [3]. The EU-funded Origami project addressed the interaction challenge within virtual sets by capturing the actor's volume and projecting feedback on a retro-reflective background [4].

Virtual studios allow the realtime combination of camera images and virtual elements, which brings advantages in flexibility and efficiency by using virtual scenery. Through keying techniques (e.g. chroma keying [5]) a separation of actors or objects and background can be accomplished. For this purpose a possible approach is the green- or blue-screen compositing technique, which requires a chroma keyer and a concolorous background. The separated background is replaced by a virtual environment, which must be rendered in realtime. This is done with the help of a high-performance computer system and special rendering software. Apart from the virtual background image, the render engine transmits a matte-out signal, the so-called external key signal, to the keyer. It allows displaying virtual objects in front of the camera image. In order to provide realistic virtual camera perspectives and orientations in a virtual scenery, the camera's position and setup has to be tracked. The determination of that information, as well as the rendering of the virtual environment requires a small amount of time, by which the camera image has to be delayed. To ensure a smooth production flow, this offset must not exceed the length of 8 frames. Nowadays, most commercial virtual studios use a similar configuration as just described. An operator in the control room manages the virtual set. Newer approaches give the actor the possibility to control the set by using tablets, smartphones or computer-displays in the speaker's desk. More intuitive ways of control are gestures or a scene, which reacts on the actors' movements. This can be accomplished by tracking the actor's position or even his full skeleton. Because this should be done unobtrusive, only markerless tracking is suitable. In Sect. 2 different methods of markerless actor tracking are described. The determination of the actor's position has to be taken into account when setting the video delay. If the delay surpasses the value needed to accommodate the camera tracking determination, the camera tracking data has to be delayed additionally. This applies in reverse as well. Figure 2 describes the signal and data-flow in a virtual studio, using actor tracking. The render engine processes the tracking data, renders the background and external key signal, and transmits them to the chroma keyer. The delayed video signal and the virtual background get combined regarding the external key signal to display parts of the virtual image in front of the camera image.

2   Markerless Talent Tracking

Nowadays actor tracking is successfully used for movie and game productions, as well as for medical applications. The applied systems often require markers, which can have a disturbing influence in some situations. In virtual studio productions for example, the audience shall not notice, that the actor is tracked, so only markerless actor tracking is suitable. In medical applications, a reasonable compromise between precision and interference for the patients has to be found. Markerless tracking would be absolutely unpersuasive but less precise. Because of the significant accuracy improvements of markerless motion capturing systems, they are suitable for the study of the biomechanics of human movement like e.g. gait analysis [6]. There are different approaches to determine the position and orientation of people or even of their whole skeletons. Some systems use depth cameras, to some extent in combination with colour or monochrome image streams, to identify body parts and determine their spatial position. With the aid of a 2D Laser-scanner, the position of people's feet can be located. Other systems analyse the images of multiple cameras, which capture the tracking area from different perspectives. In the following Section, several tracking methods are described, followed by a comparison of some commercially available systems.

In virtual studios, actor tracking can be used for an automatic occlusion handling[1], interactions with virtual objects are possible and the motions of the

---

[1] Display virtual elements in front or behind the actor, dependent on her/his tracked position.

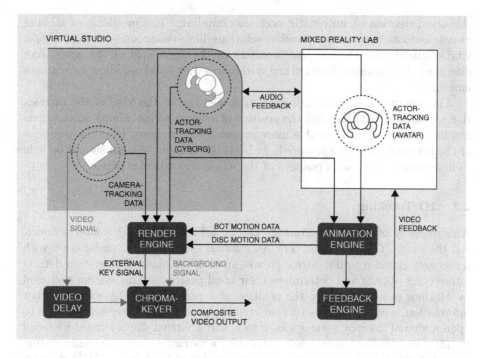

Fig. 2. System layout for the distributed live production with actor, avatar (controlled from separate locations), cyborg and bot.

tracked actors can control avatars. Mammoth Graphics and Kenziko developed an interactive control system for virtual studio sets for the broadcasting of the Olympic Games in London by *BBC* using the *Microsoft Kinect* [7,8]. The anchor was able to display a menu of virtual objects, navigate through them and make a choice just by gestures. Price et al. presented the Prometheus Project, where an MPEG-4 stream of a virtual 3D-production was transmitted [9]. An auxiliary camera, attached at the edge of the studio's ceiling identified the silhouette of the actor, which was used to determine the position of the actor's feet on the floor. In an example, the actor was mapped as a texture of a plane in the virtual set. The position of that plane was adapted to the position of the actor's feet. As a result, the occlusion was handled automatically.

Gibbs et al. described the idea of virtual actors in virtual studios and gave the example of Hugo, a German game show where a hobgoblin-like character was controlled by a human actor outside the set using an improvised cyber suit [10]. In the experimental production described in Sect. 3, markerless actor tracking was used to control different types of virtual characters.

Kim et al. [11] proposed a 3D system enabling natural-looking interactions of actors with synthetic environments and objects. A stereo camera was used to capture a 3D environment. The image and the spatial position of an actor were captured by a multiview camera. A realtime registration and rendering software processed and combined all information. Several examples of applications of the proposed approach were illustrated, e.g. direct interaction, enabled through collision detection or automatic occlusion handling. The problems of missing visual feedback, as well as possible solutions like background-coloured props, vibrotactile display devices and monitors in the sight field of the actor were discussed. The main weakness of the system was that it did not allow any camera movement.

The amount of tracking information is decisive for the level of the interaction's complexity. By knowing the position of a whole person, simple interactions can be accomplished. To enable more precise interactions, at least the positions of the person's hands are required. At best, the tracking system should be able to determine every joint's position of the whole skeleton of a person.

2.1   2D Tracking

A simple way of 2D person tracking can be achieved by using a laser scanner, e.g. the *radarTOUCH* system [12]. An infrared laser beam in combination with a precisely timed rotating mirror creates an invisible plane. The system detects intersecting objects and determines their areal positions. This system was used by Marinos et al. to acquire the position of a person's feet. By means of that information, a virtual interactive set could be controlled. A person was able to open a virtual door by getting closer to it and a virtual display could be faded in [13]. *Orad Hi-Tec Systems* had announced a markerless actor tracking system named *X-PLORO*. This system has been developed by *Xync*, a GMD start-up company, which was bought by *Orad*. Two overhead cameras on the studio's ceiling or walls capture the actor in the scene. By analysing both image streams, the actor can be identified and located in the 2D area, which allows an automatic occlusion handling.

2.2   3D Tracking

Because 2D position information only allow very simple interactions, 3D tracking is much more attractive for the application in virtual studios. Different systems using depth cameras, as well as multi-camera systems, which capture the scene from several perspectives, are distinguished.

Depth-Based. The different depth cameras vary in the techniques to determine the depth map of their field of view. Some systems consist of infrared or visible light sources combined with sensors, whereas others require a specific illumination of the environment. The depth values, often in combination with the colour- or brightness information of additional sensors, have to be analysed to identify the person or its body parts, where then a depth value can be assigned to. Common methods[2] to acquire depth maps are the passive stereo technique (e.g., *Point*

---

[2] Comparison of 3D imaging technologies issued by Texas Instruments can be found on http://www.ti.com/ww/en/analog/3dtof/.

Grey Bumblebee), structured light coding (e.g., *Microsoft Kinect* 1) and the time of flight method (e.g., *Microsoft Kinect* 2). A middleware like *SoftKinetic iisu* allows tracking the full body of up to four people using the depth map. Systems like the Microsoft Kinect 1 or 2 allow skeleton tracking within their own SDK. Time-of-flight cameras were already used to gather the position of a whole person or even of some of its body parts in a virtual studio. Using the monochromatic image, which the time-of-flight camera provides additionally to the depth map, the distance between camera and actor could be determined by finding the 2D-position of the head in the monochromatic image and combining that information with the depth value. Automatic occlusion handling was possible with this technique [14]. Flasko et al. used an auxiliary HD-studio camera to track the position of the head and the hands of a person, to allow interaction in a virtual studio [15]. The skeleton information, acquired by a *Microsoft Kinect*, was used by Hough et al. [16] to handle the occlusion of virtual objects in a virtual studio. Because one position information for a whole person is not sufficient for advanced occlusion handling, especially the hand's positions were added.

Multiple Camera Images. Carranza et al. [17] describe an approach to reconstruct a 3D geometry of a person by means of camera images, captured with far distance between each other. In addition, the applied method allows determining the movements of multiple people's skeletons. This requires the camera's imaging properties, as well as their relative position to each other, to be known. This information can be established by a system calibration. By means of the silhouettes of the people in the tracking area, their individual visual hull can be determined, in which a skeleton model is fitted in. The *OpenStage* system by Organic Motion is the first commercially available tracking system, which uses multiple camera images to track people's motions. Table 1 shows a comparison of the properties of the *OpenStage* 2, *Microsoft Kinect* 1 and 2. The *Kinect* 2 delivers the largest number of additional parameters including biometric identity, activities, leaning, appearances, expressions, engagement, and heart rate.

Comparison of Systems. The different approaches shown in the previous Sections offer very different possibilities and features. All systems possess very different strengths and weaknesses depending on the lighting conditions. This means, after evaluation of the environment, an appropriate system has to be chosen. The lighting conditions do not only depend on the illumination of a virtual studio, for some systems, e.g. infrared based, the wavelength of light has to be considered as well. Sunlight for example might influence the quality of tracking.

Systems which capture the scene from only one perspective (e.g. *Microsoft Kinect* 1&2) do not allow a full 360° tracking. Motions, which cannot be seen by the sensor, e.g. body parts which occlude others, can be estimated to a certain extent, but mostly lead to tracking errors. Combining multiple sensors can solve

Table 1. Comparison of commercially available full body tracking systems.

	Organic Motion OpenStage 2	Microsoft Kinect 1	Microsoft Kinect 2
Method	Multiple camera images	Structured Light Coding	Time-of-Flight
Tracking volume	Up to approx. $100\,m^3$ $6\,m \times 6\,m \times 3\,m$ for 18 camera system	Up to approx. $16\,m^3$ full body tracking: $1.8\,m$–$4\,m$ distance & $57\,° \times 43\,°$ field of view	Up to approx. $45\,m^3$ full body tracking: $1.8\,m$–$4.5\,m$ distance & $70\,° \times 60\,°$ field of view
Calibration effort	A few minutes	Pre-calibrated	Pre-calibrated
Sampling rate	60–120 fps	30 fps	30 fps
Latency	25 ms–50 ms	150 ms–250 ms	ca. 60 ms
Max. number of tracked people	5	2	6
Skeleton model	21 joints	20 joints	25 joints
Parameters:			
Head orientation	No	No	Yes
Foot orientation	Yes	No	Yes
Hand orientation	Limited	No	Yes
Hand state	No	No	Open/Closed/Lasso (Pointing with two fingers)
Additional parameters	No	Voice Recognition	Voice Recognition Person-related Parameters
References	[18, 19]	[18, 20]	[21]

this issue, but some sensors do not work perfectly when using them simultaneously. The *Microsoft Kinect* 1, which projects infrared patterns on the environment to determine the depth map, produces errors, when the pattern of a second *Kinect* interferes with the other one. On the contrary, there are no problems occurring when combining multiple *Microsoft Kinect* 2 sensors.

As shown in Table 1, the *OpenStage* system does not allow head and hand tracking. To enhance the *OpenStage* tracking data, it can be combined with the information of the head's orientation and the state of the hands, collected by the *Kinect* 2. The realisation of such an approach is discussed in Sect. 6.

2.3 Benefits of Markerless Actor Tracking

Markerless actor tracking offers a wide variety of new possibilities for virtual studios, medical applications, and virtual simulations. The key benefits of markerless actor tracking are the fast and easy operation. Compared to marker based tracking systems, no markers have to be attached to the actors. The actor is allowed to enter the tracking area and being recognised without any special preparations. In the context of virtual studios, marker based tracking systems influence the actor's behaviour as well as the audience's suspension of disbelief. Markers might interrupt the illusion of plausibility, produced in the virtual studio. By controlling the virtual set by the motions of the actors, for example the applications mentioned in Sect. 3, interactions can appear more natural and realistic. Moreover, markerless actor tracking enables new kinds of interaction, which could lead to new TV formats.

2.4   Limitations

Besides many advantages of markerless tracking in comparison to marker-based approaches, there are still some limitations. Depending on the system and lighting conditions, the precision, as well as the reliability can be insufficient. During live broadcasting, accurate tracking has to be provided permanently. However, the stability of today's systems is not good enough to guarantee this. Most systems are limited to track humans, which is sufficient for most applications. Sometimes, the tracking of objects or animals could be advantageous. For experimental use, systems like the *OpenStage* 2 allow the definition of new kinds of skeleton models, like animals or simple objects (e.g. Sticks). Another crucial problem is the missing feedback in a virtual environment, which will be discussed in Sect. 5.

3   Use Cases – Experimental Production

The simple story is based on three players, cyborg, avatar, and bot, who throw a disc to each other. All players are located within a virtual arena. A judge oversees the game and is played by a human. Every character represents one of the four metamorphosis states: Human, Avatar, Bot, and Cyborg as seen in Fig. 3. The cyborg is shown in Fig. 1. A tracked actor is partly overlaid with graphics, assembling an armour. The generated mask from the render engine was slightly larger than the armour graphics to compensate alignment errors and tracking noise. The armour was mapped to the exact position and orientation of every joint provided by the markerless tracking system. A human skeleton divided in 21 different joints can precisely be covered with virtual elements. The avatar's motions are controlled via a remote *OpenStage* markerless motion capture system. The bot's motions are controlled by an animation engine (*Unity3D*).

In a previous work [22], necessary software (plugin) was developed to receive and process *OpenStage*'s motion data within a commercial virtual studio renderer from Vizrt. The production took place at the FH Düsseldorf's virtual studio with an *OpenStage* system, using 18 cameras. The avatar was controlled by a second *OpenStage* system with 10 cameras in the separate Mixed Reality lab. The system layout and data flow is shown in Fig. 2. Beside the renderer, an animation engine (*Unity3D*) was used for controlling the bot and the disc's flight. The disc's target was chosen based on the situation e.g. the cyborg's or avatar's tracked hand or the wall/floor. This means that the disc is automatically catched by the avatar or cyborg, which ensures perfect story flow without special training for the talents

Fig. 3. Four metamorphosis states in a distributed virtual (TV) studio: Human, Cyborg, Avatar (controlled from a separate location), and Bot.

in the virtual environment. But still their movements had to match in time. The bot's arm was controlled with inverse kinematics to catch and throw the disc. Other behaviour of the bot was based on pre-recorded motions. For skeleton data Organic Motion's SDK was used. For other communications, messages using Open Sound Control (OSC) were applied.

The final video and some pictures from the production can be found online[3]. The tracking accuracy was good enough for wide shots.

4   Classification: Yet Another Continuum

The classification from Milgram et al., showing a continuum from reality to virtuality [23], requires another dimension for expressing the amount of control a user in our case actor has over avatars and virtual characters (see Fig. 4). Mixed control is necessary because input devices do not capture all parameters, required to animate an avatar. For example the current version of the *OpenStage* does not capture head or hand rotations. For a good animation those parameters have to be generated or captured by other means. In case of synthetic generated parameters, the instant control is reduced. If a reduced number of parameters is

---

[3] http://vsvr.medien.fh-duesseldorf.de/productions/vron2013/

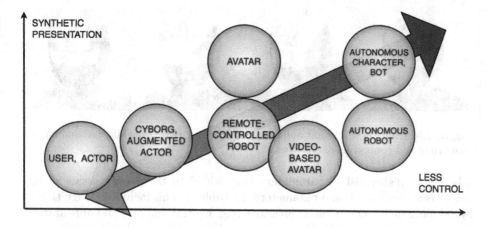

Fig. 4. User – Avatar – Virtual Character Continuum with different levels of control.

in use, the classification is deferred to the area of bots. For social interaction with systems, Holz et al. organised different incarnations (robots and social agents) in a continuum, which is also inspired by Milgram [24]. In principle, the bot in this article corresponds to the social agents. Also the listed mixed reality agents share the mixing of real and virtual images with the cyborg, but are not driven by a human.

4.1 Reduction and Expansion: Limited Data, but Extensive Animations

Organic objects, for instance humans, animals or plants are usually in constant motion. Complex characteristics – reduced to simple features – are hard to transfer to 3D animations in a natural and fluent way. Continuity is the key factor in this matter. Only then it is possible for the viewer to get the impression of realistic dynamics. Movements of animated beings are very complex processes. To be easily understood from computer programs they have to be reduced to a very basic type of data. This reduction can take different forms. In virtual studios for example recognising or tracking the body of a person can be interpreted by the render engine, as described earlier in Sect. 2, into a more or less rudimental skeleton which then can be used to control different kinds of animation in realtime. To give a rough example: 18 cameras record the moving actor, with an output of millions of pixels, which then form a huge volume with voxels, which are then converted into only 21 skeleton joints (as described in Sect. 2.2). These limited values may suggest that the animation itself has to be broken down to a very simple state, but this is not true. Even if the involved software receives only a very finite number of data, it can still be instructed to display a continuous and logical visualisation of the animation, so to speak expanding again after being reduced.

As mentioned in Sect. 2.2 the *Kinect 2* is one of the commercially available full body tracking systems, but besides making the skeleton of a person available,

Fig. 5. Eye Animation: closing animation of left and right eye; idle eye animation, using time and context as parameters

other more distinguished parameters were added to the newer version of the sensor (see also "additional parameters" in Table 1). This includes recognition of eyelid movements, emotional expressions (e.g. neutral, happy), and appearances (e.g. wearing glasses). Activities are left eye closed, right eye closed, mouth open, mouth moved and looking away. To be more concrete, the camera is going to identify two conditions of the eyes. These simple and reduced commands can be integrated in the virtual environment in a more complex way than it may seem at first sight. Instead of just animating the shutting of the left and right eye (see Fig. 5) it is possible to extend this motion beyond the actual restricted data. This could mean, for example, letting the 3D character have a random look around throughout the area while in an idle state (see Fig. 5). So even if the sensor does not send out usable data, the avatar is able to behave autonomous.

One other new and very useful feature of the *Kinect* 2 is the implemented face tracking, which delivers an emotional state. This offers the chance to recognise human expressions, which can then be translated to a synthetic avatar with a smooth transition between different moods or can be used to trigger custom animations according to the mood of the person in front of the camera.

In certain cases a completely precise tracking is not always possible. To avoid visible inconsistencies in the animation it can be helpful to interpret variables providing information about the current tracking quality. If the sensors in the camera cannot operate correctly, the respective state needs to be estimated. In this case the value is not necessarily Boolean, but could be referred to as a maybe, an interference, or even a percentage figure for the accuracy. This can be used to prioritise different data sources inside the render engine and prefer better working sensors (see explanation for sensor fusion, Fig. 6) or using a default animation. Another important aspect regarding realistic interactions between different scene objects or the actor and the 3D animations is a context-based reaction. This means that the respective object responds in accordance with another, for example a real-life actor during a realtime recording. The control of the virtual character was put into practice through a remote rendering scenario, where actors were in charge of the movement and voice response of the 3D animation [10]. In the case of the animated bot (Fig. 5) a context related interaction could mean letting it follow another entering 3D object or person with both eyes depending on the object's movement.

If one wants to focus the user's attention on a specific object, e.g. an animated character, automatic light and camera control will become crucial. As described

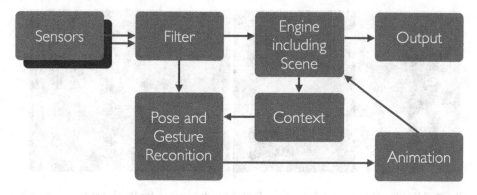

Fig. 6. Filtered sensor data and gesture/pose detection drive the animations, influenced by application context, which is mostly derived from the scene (graph).

by Herder et al. [25] the context, meaning the scene, can be used to trigger certain animations, which focus the user's attention on specific parts in the scene. In this scenario a server was integrated that captured relevant data from the scene and user and then decided, which object needed most of the viewers attention. In that case a lighting animation got this input from the server and highlighted the according objects.

Figure 6 gives an overview of the correlation between the actual animation, the scene context and the influence it has on the pose and gesture recognition using sensors. The illustration deliberately indicates that the virtual scene can be dependent on more than one sensor. The *Kinect*, for example, has not just a depth camera to capture the person's position, but can also acquire additional tracking data through the integrated microphone array. For sensor fusion, multiple sensors are combined for gaining better tracking results.

5   Talent Feedback

One major problem is the orientation inside the virtual studio. Virtual objects visible for the audience are invisible for the actor and do not allow reliable orientation. This problem is especially affecting precise actor tracking to determine interaction between the actor and virtual objects. This includes touch interactions with small virtual objects inside the virtual scenery. Very common techniques to provide some kind of feedback are displays and identification marks on the floor. These techniques provide a reliable orientation for the actor. Depending on the kind of production and virtual environment, these techniques for actor feedback have a serious disadvantage in influencing the actor's behaviour and bias. In the succeeding Sections, various kinds of feedback are described in detail and a connection to the experimental production is shown.

5.1   Visual Feedback

Any kind of visual feedback is only recommended, if the actor is not influenced in a noticeable manner or the production does not need the actor's real appearance.

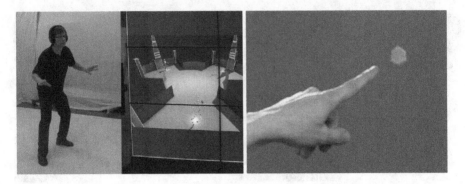

Fig. 7. Mixed reality lab with powerwall and headphone as feedback for the animator of the avatar (left & middle); Invisible props as visual feedback (right).

This for example means that actor tracking is only used to determine motions for virtual characters without any real world elements. A very reasonable approach is the utilisation of non-visible markers on the floor and mounted on transparent fishing lines, e.g. a green coin as shown in Fig. 7 (right). These invisible props are very efficient and less cost-intensive. In the experimental production mentioned in Sect. 3 visual feedback was an integral part and required to make a distributed live production possible. As a result of the different states (Human, Avatar, Bot, and Cyborg) very different kinds of visual feedback were in use. For example, the avatar was fully animated and only controlled by a tracked person. This offered the full attention of the person to a feedback-engine providing information about the actors positions and a robust scheduling for motions like throwing a virtual disc. The Feedback-Engine was based on a *Unity3D* scene providing detailed real time information about all tracked actors and their position in a virtual scene. This information was mirrored to a powerwall (see also Fig. 7, left).

Monitors and Projections in Green. Another quite common approach to provide some kind of feedback and orientation for the actor are displays placed in the studio. Those displays are not visible to the audience and show the mirrored camera output. The camera output can also be projected into the green or blue areas of the virtual studio. The advantage is that the audience does not recognise any special behaviour of the actor because of the projection is placed within the actor's natural field of view. In a production captured at the virtual studio of the FH Düsseldorf in 2012, a touchscreen was coated with a green semi-transparent tissue (see Fig. 8). The actor was able to identify the content on the touchscreen and could interact with it. Because of the keying process in the virtual studio, the screen was not visible in the final video output.

5.2 Vibrotactile Feedback

A waist-belt with vibrotactile elements can help to determine the orientation inside a virtual studio. Depending on the distance between the actor and specific virtual objects, signals can be sent to the vibrotactile elements to signalise the

Fig. 8. Green monitor with infrared touch frame for interaction and feedback.

distance to the object. This technique can be used in very different contexts and provides solid information without any noticeable influence on the actor. This means that safe and exact interactions and motions can be performed. Different forms of vibrotactile feedback/patterns were evaluated by Vierjahn et al. [26,27].

5.3 Acoustic Feedback

In contrast to visual feedback, acoustic feedback is not in sight of the audience. Depending on the kind of production acoustic feedback can provide precise and inconspicuous help for the actor. Acoustic feedback can either be audible to all actors and participants in the virtual studio or it can be realised with not visible in-ear headphones exclusive for the actor. Acoustic feedback can provide simple feedback if the actor enters a certain area of the studio or touches a virtual object. For a more precise feedback, head-related transfer functions can be used to give directional and distance cues of virtual objects [28]. In the experimental production mentioned in Sect. 3, acoustic feedback was used to coordinate the actors placed in different locations. To harmonise closely spaced movements like throwing a disk between Human, Avatar, Bot, and Cyborg, acoustic feedback is of great help.

6 Conclusions and Future Development

The clear progress and acceptance of virtual studios in nowadays TV productions offer enormous potential for further development and new approaches. For a lot of TV productions an enhancement in interactivity enabled by precise markerless actor tracking could lead to new TV formats and shows. Although there are a lot of exemplary productions and approaches, there is still a lot of research and improvement needed to maximise its deployment. We showed new ways of interaction using markerless talent tracking in a virtual studio and combined it with a game engine for physics and inverse kinematics. Major issues like robust tracking and instant feedback still remain.

For an evaluation of markerless actor tracking for virtual (TV) studio applications [22], several experts experienced in the field of virtual studios were asked about their opinion. Most of the experts reported concerns connected to newscasts and recommended the far more possibilities of interactivity connected to game shows or alike. They mentioned subtle effects like raising dust or virtual footprints as reasonable applications of markerless actor tracking. The feedback considering the new type of actor composed of real and virtual elements was also quite positive.

The story in the production illustrates the user avatar virtual characters continuum diagram. Having all metamorphosis states in one distributed real-time system is challenging. The problems and solutions were addressed. Future development needs to focus on the actor's feedback in virtual environments. While head mounted displays might be used for actors controlling an avatar, this is not an option for actors in a green box. The use of virtual acoustics might be a solution [28].

As already mentioned in Sect. 4.1, the combination of different tracking systems can enhance the stability and quality of the tracking data, as well as the amount of available information. In order to be able to combine multiple data flows, which often follow different logics, a mutual way of transfer, as well as unified messages have to be defined. By respecting a predefined dictionary for the joints' names and the naming of additional information, the data of different systems can be processed within one framework (e.g. OscCalibrator[4] by Marinos).

Acknowledgments. The authors thank Jose Burga, Sascha Charlie Djuderija, Maren Gnehr, Sven Hartz, Mohammed Ibrahim, Nikolas Koop, Laurid Meyer, Antje Müller, Björn Salgert, Richard Schroeder, and Simon Thiele who helped to implement the "VRON" example production. The music was composed by Lars Goossens. Christophe Leske contributed as actor. Christoph Postertz, Tobias Mönninger, and Julian Thiede run the example production with the green touch screen in Fig. 8. Some work was carried out within the "IVO [at] hiTV - Interaction with virtual objects in iTV productions" project, supported by the "FHprofUnt" program of the Federal Ministry of Education and Research (BMBF), Germany (grant no. 17010X10).

References

1. Herder, J.: Interactive content creation with virtual set environments. J. 3D-Forum Soc. **15**(4), 53–56 (2001). Japan
2. Gibbs, S., Arapis, C., Breiteneder, C., Lalioti, V., Mostafawy, S., Speier, J.: Virtual studios: an overview. IEEE Multimedia **5**(1), 18–35 (1998)
3. Bunsen, O.: Verteilte Virtuelle TV-Produktion im Gigabit-Testbed West. Abschließender Bericht, Laboratory for Mixed Realities, Institut an der Kunsthochschule für Medien Köln, GMD Forschungszentrum Informationstechnik GmbH Institut für Medienkommunikation, February 2000

---

[4] https://github.com/fubyo/osccalibrator.

4. Grau, O., Pullen, T., Thomas, G.: A combined studio production system for 3-d capturing of live action and immersive actor feedback. IEEE Trans. Circuits Syst. Video Technol. **14**(3), 370–380 (2004)
5. Ray, A., Blinn, J.F.: Blue screen matting. In: SIGGRAPH'98, Conference Proceeding, pp. 259–268 (1996)
6. Corazza, S., Mndermann, L., Chaudhari, A., Demattio, T., Cobelli, C., Andriacchi, T.: A markerless motion capture system to study musculoskeletal biomechanics: visual hull and simulated annealing approachD. Ann. Biomed. Eng. **34**(6), 1019–1029 (2006)
7. Vizrt: Kenziko and mammoth graphics at IBC 2012: Kinetrak 2012. http://www.vizrt.com/news/newsgrid/35347/Kenziko_and_Mammoth_Graphics_at_IBC_2012
8. Mammoth Graphics and Kenziko Ltd.: Kinetrak (2014). http://www.kinetrak.tv
9. Price, M., Thomas, G.A.: 3d virtual production and delivery using mpeg-4. In: International Broadcasting Convention (IBC). IEEE (2000)
10. Gibbs, S., Baudisch, P.: Interaction in the virtual studio. In: SIGGRAPH Computer Graphics, vol. 30, pp. 29–32. ACM Press, New York, November 1996. ISSN:0097-8930
11. Kim, N., Woo, W., Kim, G., Park, C.M.: 3-d virtual studio for natural inter-"acting". IEEE Trans. Syst. Man Cybern. Part A: Syst. Hum. **36**(4), 758–773 (2006)
12. Wöldecke, B., Marinos, D., Pogscheba, P., Geiger, C., Herder, J., Schwirten, T.: radarTHEREMIN - creating musicalexpressionsin a virtual studio environment. In: Proceeding of ISVRI 2011 (International Symposium on VR Innovation), Singapore, pp. 345–346 (2009)
13. Marinos, D., Geiger, C., Herder, J.: Large-area moderator tracking and demonstrational configuration of position based interactions for virtual studios. In: 10th European Interactive TV Conference, Berlin (2012)
14. Herder, J., Wilke, M., Heimbach, J., Göbel, S., Marinos, D.: Simple actor tracking for virtual tv studios using a photonic mixing device. In: 12th International Conference on Human and Computer, Hamamatsu / Aizu-Wakamatsu / Düsseldorf, University of Aizu (2009)
15. Flasko, M., Pogscheba, P., Herder, J., Vonolfen, W.: Heterogeneous binocular camera-tracking in a virtual studio. In: 8. Workshop Virtuelle und Erweiterte RealitLt der GI-Fachgruppe VR/AR, Wedel (2011)
16. Hough, G., Athwal, C., Williams, I.: Advanced occlusion handling for virtual studios. In: Lee, G., Howard, D., Kang, J.J., Skezak, D. (eds.) ICHIT 2012. LNCS, vol. 7425, pp. 287–294. Springer, Heidelberg (2012)
17. Carranza, J., Theobalt, C., Magnor, M.A., Seidel, H.P.: Free-viewpoint video of human actors. ACM Trans. Graph. **22**(3), 569–577 (2003)
18. Brooks, A., Czarowicz, A.: Markerless motion tracking: Ms kinect & organic motion openstage. In: 9th International Conference on Disability, Virtual Reality and Associated Technologies, vol. 9, ICDVRAT and The University of Reading, pp. 435–437 (2012)
19. Organic Motion Inc.: Openstage 2.0 technical overview, June 2014. http://www.organicmotion.com/openstage-2-0-technical-overview/
20. Livingston, M., Sebastian, J., Ai, Z., Decker, J.: Performance measurements for the microsoft kinect skeleton. In: Virtual Reality Short Papers and Posters (VRW), pp. 119–120. IEEE (2012)
21. Microsoft: Kinect for windows sdk documentation, July 2014

22. Daemen, J., Haufs-Brusberg, P., Herder, J.: Markerless actor tracking for virtual (tv) studio applications. In: International Joint Conference on Awareness Science and Technology & Ubi-Media Computing, iCAST 2013 & UMEDIA 2013. IEEE (2012)

23. Milgram, P., Takemura, H., Utsumi, A., Kishino, F.: Augmented reality: a class of displays on the reality-virtuality continuum. Proc. SPIE **2351**, 282–292 (1995)

24. Holz, T., Dragone, M., O'Hare, G.: Where robots and virtual agents meet. Int. J.Soc. Robot. **1**(1), 83–93 (2009)

25. Herder, J., Cohen, M.: Enhancing perspicuity of objects in virtual reality environments. In: CT'97 – Second International Cognitive Technology Conference on IEEE, pp. 228–237. IEEE Press, August 1997. ISBN 0-8186-8084-9

26. Vierjahn, T., Wöldecke, B., Geiger, C., Herder, J.: Improved direction signalization technique employing vibrotactile feedback. In: 11th Virtual Reality International Conference, VRIC'2009 (2009)

27. Wöldecke, B., Vierjahn, T., Flasko, M., Herder, J., Geiger, C.: Steering actors through a virtual set employing vibro-tactile feedback. In: TEI 2009: Proceedings of the 3rd International Conference on Tangible and Embedded Interaction, pp. 169–174. ACM, New York (2009)

28. Ludwig, P., Büchel, J., Herder, J., Vonolfen, W.: InEarGuide - a navigation and interaction feedback system using in ear headphones for virtual tv studio productions. In: 9. Workshop Virtuelle und Erweiterte Realität der GI-Fachgruppe VR/AR, Düsseldorf (2012)

VELOS - A VR Environment for Ship Applications: Current Status and Planned Extensions

A.I. Ginnis[1], K.V. Kostas[2], C.G. Politis[2], and P.D. Kaklis[3(✉)]

[1] School of Naval Architecture and Marine Engineering (NAME),
National Technical University of Athens (NTUA), Athens, Greece
[2] Department of Naval Architecture (NA),
Technological Educational Institute of Athens (TEI-A), Athens, Greece
[3] Department of Naval Architecture, Ocean and Marine Engineering (NAOME),
University of Strathclyde, Glasgow, Scotland
panagiotis.kaklis@strath.ac.uk

Abstract. *Virtual Environment for Life On Ships* (VELOS) is a multi-user Virtual Reality (VR) system that supports designers to assess (early in the design process) passenger and crew activities on a ship for both normal and hectic conditions of operations and to improve the ship design accordingly [10]. Realistic simulations of behavioral aspects of crowd in emergency conditions require modeling of panic aspects and social conventions of inter-relations. The present paper provides a description of the enhanced crowd modeling approach employed in VELOS for the performance of ship evacuation assessment and analysis based on the guidelines provided by IMO's Circular MSC 1238/2007 [20].

1 Introduction

Under the impact of a series of events involving large number of fatalities on passenger ships [33], the International Maritime Organization (IMO) has developed regulations for new and existing passenger ships, including ro-ro passenger ships, requiring escape routes to be evaluated by an evacuation analysis described in IMO's Circular MSC 1238/2007, entitled Guidelines for evacuation analysis for new and existing passenger ships [20]. It is worth mentioning that, although the evacuation scenarios in [20] address issues related to the layout of the ship and passenger demographics, they do not address issues arising in real emergency conditions, such as unavailability of escape arrangements (due to flooding or fire), crew assistance in the evacuation process, family-group behavior, ship motions, etc. To heal such deficiencies, [20] adopts the mechanism of safety factors.

Much effort has been devoted to the development of sophisticated models for performing advanced evacuation analysis of passenger ships. As a result, around twenty such models and tools are available as reported in [21, 25]. A not-necessarily complete list should include the following tools:

© Springer International Publishing Switzerland 2015
G. Brunnett et al. (Eds.): Virtual Realities, LNCS 8844, pp. 33–55, 2015.
DOI: 10.1007/978-3-319-17043-5_3

1. AENEAS [32], a fast-performing simulation tool, allowing for large passenger populations.
2. Maritime-EXODUS [8], a customization of the evacuation platform EXODUS that makes use of proprietary trial data for the behavior of passengers under conditions of list and heel.
3. IMEX [27], a ship evacuation model combining dynamics and human behavior model.
4. Evi [34,35], a multi-agent evacuation simulation software package, utilizing the mesoscopic approach.
5. EVAC [7], a mustering simulation program that adopts the microscopic approach and utilizes data and knowledge stemming from EU-funded projects.
6. BYPASS [22], a simple cellular-automaton based model.

Crowd simulation is a complex task with issues related to collision avoidance, considering a large number of individuals, path planning, trajectories and so forth. Depending on the application, other requirements such as real-time simulation is needed to populate virtual environments in VR systems. Moreover, in order to provide a tool to simulate behavioral aspects of crowd in emergency conditions, panic aspects and social conventions of inter-relations are needed, [14,31]. In general, three approaches are used to model crowd motion. The *Fluid* model, where fluid equations, such as Navier Stokes equations, are used to model crowd flow [15,17,18]. The *Cellular Automata* (CA) model, which are discrete dynamic systems whose behavior is characterized by local interactions. Each CA is made up of a regular lattice of cells and at each unit of time the state of each cell is recalculated by the application of a set of rules to neighboring cells [3,9]. The majority of crowd simulations employ the *Particulate* approach, which is also called the *atomic* approach. This is also the approach for crowd modeling used in VELOS and it is briefly presented in Sect. 2.1. The first pioneer work on this area was that of Reynolds [29] who worked on simulations of flocks of birds, herds of land animals and schools of fish. A later work of the same author [30] extends these concepts to the general idea of *autonomous characters* with an emphasis on animation and games applications. A *Social force model* for crowd simulation was introduced by Helbing and Molnár in [16]. They suggest that the motion of pedestrians can be described as if they are subject to social forces - Acceleration, Repulsion and Attraction- which measure the internal motivation of individuals to perform certain actions. By combining these three forces they produce an equation for pedestrian's *total motivation* and finally the *social force model*. In [14] the social force model was applied to the simulation of building escape panic, with satisfactory results.

The paper is structured as follows: Sect. 2 presents VELOS's base: VRsystem, along with its major components and functionalities including a brief description of the employed crowd modeling approach for the performance of ship evacuation assessment & analysis, while Sect. 3 is devoted to our proposed additions in steering behaviors and crowd modeling allowing their usage in ship evacuation analysis. Section 4 includes the presentation of ship evacuation test cases investigating the effects of crew assistance, passenger grouping and fire incidents.

Furthermore, an additional test case demonstrating the effects of ship motions on passengers movement is also included. The last section is devoted to our ongoing work extending grouping behavior with dynamic characteristics.

2   The VELOS System

VELOS is based on *VRsystem* [10], a generic multi-user virtual environment, that consists of mainly two modules, the server and client modules connected through a network layer. Figure 1 provides a schematic overview of the VRsystem architecture. As depicted in this figure, users' participation in the virtual environment is carried out through the CLIENT module in the form of AVATARS enabling them to be immersed in the virtual world and actively participate in the evacuation process by interacting with agents and other avatars. On the other hand, system administrator utilizes the SERVER module for creating the virtual environment, setting all properties and rules for the scenario under consideration, e.g., scheduling of fire/flooding events, and awaits participants to connect to the system. Administrator's interaction may also take place during simulation phase.

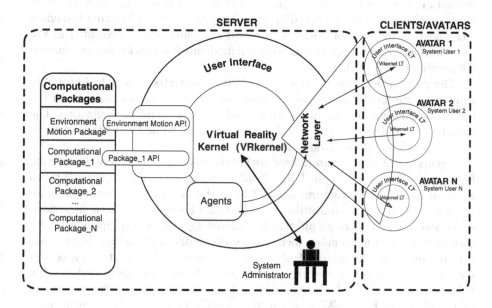

Fig. 1. The VRsystem architecture

The server module comprises two major components, namely the VRkernel and the User-Interface, while the client module has a similar structure and comprises customized versions of them, referred to as VRkernelLT and User-InterfaceLT; see again Fig. 1. VRkernel is the core component of VRsystem platform in the server module. It can be thought of as a library of objects and functions suitable for materializing the synthetic world with respect to geometric representations, collision detection, crowd modeling, motion control and simulation, event handling and all other tasks related to visualization and scene organization. The core functionalities of VRkernel are provided by Open Inventor, an OpenGL based library of objects and methods used to create interactive 3D graphics applications.

2.1 Crowd Modeling for Ship Evacuation

Crowd Modeling is a major part of VRkernel and, in view of VELOS areas of interest (evacuation, ergonomics, comfortability), it could be considered as the most significant of its components. It is based on agents, avatars, scene objects (such as obstacles) and steering behaviors technology. The term agent in VRkernel is used to describe autonomous characters, which *"...combine aspects of an autonomous robot with some skills of a human actor in improvisational theater"*; see [30]. Avatars are the system users' *incarnation* within the virtual environment and their major difference from agents is their *controlling entity*: humans for avatars vs. computer for agents. Avatars may take any role in the simulation; however they are more commonly used for controlling crew members in evacuation scenarios presented in the subsequent sections. Steering behaviors technology is the core of VRkernel's crowd modeling and is presented in the following paragraphs while enhanced crowd modeling features for ship evacuation are presented in Sect. 3.

The motion behavior of an agent is better understood by splitting it into three separate levels, namely action selection, steering and locomotion. In the first level, goals are set and plans are devised for the action materialization. The steering level determines the actual movement path, while locomotion provides the articulation and animation details.

Agents' autonomy is materialized within the steering level, where the steering behaviors technology is applied. Specifically, agents' autonomy is powered by an artificial intelligence structure, referred to in the pertinent literature as mind; see, e.g., [13,30]. The mind utilizes a collection of simple kinematic behaviors, called steering behaviors, to ultimately compose agent's motion. Specifically, for each time frame, the agent's velocity vector is computed by adding the previous velocity vector to the mind-calculated steering vector. This vector is a combination of the individual steering vectors provided by each associated steering behavior in agent's mind. For example, in *Seek* behavior the steering vector can be calculated as $\mathbf{f} = w\frac{\mathbf{q}-\mathbf{p}}{\|\mathbf{q}-\mathbf{p}\|}$, where $\mathbf{p}$ is agent's position, $\mathbf{q}$ is the seek point and w is an appropriate weighting factor.

Nearly twenty steering behaviors have been so far implemented within VRkernel. These behaviors, based on the works by C.W. Reynolds [30] and R. Green [13], include: *Seek, Arrive, Wander, Separation, Cohere, Leader Follow, Obstacle Avoidance & Containment, Path-following, Pursuit, Flee, Evade, offset-{Seek, Flee, Pursuit, Evade, Arrive}*; see also [23,24].

In mind modeling we employ two different approaches for the steering vector calculation. The first and rather obvious one, used in simple mind, produces the steering vector as a weighted average of the individual ones. The second approach that takes into account priorities, called priority blending, is an enhanced version of the simple priority mind proposed in [30].

In simple mind, agent's velocity at each time frame is calculated as follows:

1. Compute steering vector f as a convex combination $f = \sum w_i f_i$, where f_i, with $\|f_i\| = 1$, are the individual steering vectors from each simple behavior included in agent's mind. Weight values are generally agent- and time-dependent with weights corresponding to "prime" behaviors (i.e., those affecting collision avoidance: *Obstacle Avoidance* and *Separation*) being relatively higher than the remaining ones; see a detailed description in [23,24].

2. New velocity is computed as:

$$v_{new} = c \cdot (v_{prev} + f), \text{ where } c = \min\left\{\frac{v_m}{\|v_{prev} + f\|}, 1\right\}, \qquad (1)$$

where, v_m is the agent's maximum allowable velocity.

3   Enhanced Features of Crowd Modeling

Crowd modeling, as described in [10] can be used to materialize a ship evacuation scenario adopting the advanced method of analysis proposed by IMO in circular [19,20]. Although this advanced method is more realistic than the simplified approach proposed in the same circulars, it is still subject to some restrictive assumptions and omissions as, e.g., ship motions, fire/smoke, crew assistance and passenger grouping effects which are collectively accounted via corrective safety factors. Aiming in the elimination of these restrictions, we herein enrich crowd modeling in VELOS with appropriate features, which are described in detail in the following sub-sections. These features include the introduction of new behaviors, as the *Inclination* behavior, modeling the effect of ship motions, the *Enhanced Cohere* behavior applied in passenger grouping, and the adoption of behavioral models and aids, such as the *Triggers* supporting crew assistance modeling. Finally, passenger's *health index* and ship's *space availability* are introduced for modeling smoke and/or fire influence on the evacuation process.

3.1   Modeling Ship Motions and Accelerations

VELOS provides several interfaces for the consideration of ship motions and accelerations. Specifically, there are modules that allow importing of precomputed ship responses either in the frequency or time domain. Furthermore, there is also functionality for importing time histories of linear velocities and accelerations for selected points aboard a ship that are recorded with the aid of accelerometers. Thus, ship accelerations can be either estimated via numerical differentiation of ship motions or acquired from the experimental measurements.

Generally, ship motions comprise time histories of the displacements of a specific point P of ship (usually ship's center of flotation) as well as time histories of ship rotational motions (pitch, roll and yaw). Using numerical differentiation we can calculate linear velocity (v_p) and acceleration ($\dot{v}_p$) of point P and angular velocity (ω_B) and acceleration ($\dot{\omega}_B$) of the ship. Then, using the following well-known relations from rigid-body kinematics we can calculate velocity and acceleration at every point Q on ship: $q = p + \omega_B \times r_{pq}$, $\dot{v}_q = \dot{v}_p + \omega_B \times (\omega_B \times r_{pq}) + \dot{\omega}_B \times r_{pq}$, where, r_{pq} is the vector formed by P and Q.

The effects of ship motions on passengers and crew aboard are modeled in two ways as it is presented in detail in the sequel. The first simplified approach is based on a kinematic modeling that utilizes the ship motions while the second approach takes into account the dynamic nature of the phenomenon and relies on the availability of ship accelerations.

Inclination Behavior. Advanced evacuation analysis in VELOS is combining the availability of ship motion data with the so-called *Inclination* behavior that has been introduced, as a first layer, for considering the effect of ship motion on agent's movement. Precomputed ship-motion history is imported in VELOS through a suitable series of interfaces. Inclination behavior resembles in definition and effect the influence of a gravity field that would hinder agent motion accordingly. Specifically, we consider a static global force-vector g normal to deck's plane in the upright position of the ship. If the deck deviates from its upright position (i.e., non zero heel, and/or trim, angles), the projection of g on it will obviously acquire a non-zero value g_p, which forms Inclination's steering vector as follows: $f_i = \lambda(\phi)\frac{g_p}{\|g_p\|}$, where $\lambda(\phi)$ is an appropriate weight function depending on the angle ϕ formed between g and the normal to the deck plane. Inclination behavior is active when ϕ lies between two threshold angles: the lower threshold is used to discard plane motions with negligible effect on agent's motion, while values above the upper threshold lead to movement inability, as the limit of agent's balancing capabilities is surpassed. Threshold angles and the weight function $\lambda(\phi)$ are defined via experimental data; see, e.g., [2,4,5].

Motion Induced Interruptions (MII). During certain weather conditions, i.e., rough weather, walking and even more working in the ship becomes difficult and even the most experienced sailors will experience events where they must stop their activity, be it a specific task or merely standing, and take suitable measures to minimize the risk of injury, or more generally change their stance so that balance can be retained; these events are called, in pertinent literature, *Motion-Induced Interruptions (MIIs)*. MIIs can be identified by considering the dynamic equations of motions of the person due to ship motion leading to the onset of loss-of-balance due to tipping or sliding. Baitis et al [1] and Graham et al [11,12] have proposed the following relations for the consideration of tips to port or starboard. Specifically, a tip to port will occur if: $T_{LATp} = \frac{1}{g}\left(\frac{1}{3}h\ddot{\eta}_4 - \ddot{D}_2 - g\eta_4 - \frac{l}{h}\ddot{D}_3\right) > \frac{l}{h}$, and analogously for tip to starboard. Similarly, the following tipping coefficients can

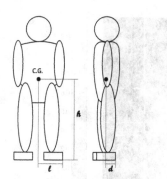

Fig. 2. Person C.G., half-stance and half-shoe width

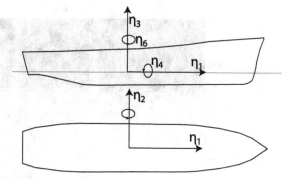

Fig. 3. Ship coordinate system

be derived when considering tips to the aft or fore part of the ship: $T_{LONa} = \frac{1}{g}\left(\ddot{D}_1 + \frac{1}{3}h\ddot{\eta}_5 - \frac{d}{h}\ddot{D}_3\right) > \frac{d}{h}$ and analogously for tip to fore.

In the above equations, η_1 (surge), η_2 (sway), and η_3 (heave) stand for the translational while η_4 (roll), η_5 (pitch) and η_6 (yaw) stand for the rotational components of ship motion along the $x-$, $y-$ and $z-$ axis of the ship-coordinate system, respectively, see Fig. 3. Furthermore, $D = (D_1, D_2, D_3) = (\eta_1, \eta_2, \eta_3) + (\eta_4, \eta_5, \eta_6) \times (x, y, z)$ denotes the displacement of point $P(x, y, z)$. Finally, symbols l, h and d denote the half-stance length, the vertical distance to person's center of gravity and half-shoe width respectively as shown in Fig. 2. Typical values for $\frac{l}{h}$ lie in the interval $(0.20, 0.25)$ while for $\frac{d}{h}$ lie in $(0.15, 0.17)$.

Taking into account the above discussion concerning tipping coefficients, the effect of ship motions on passenger movement is implemented in the following way:

1. Adjustment $\tilde{v}_m$ of the maximum allowable velocity v_m according to the following rule: $\tilde{v}_m = k \cdot v_m$, where

$$k = \begin{cases} 1, & \text{if } T_{LAT} < 0.20 \wedge T_{LON} < 0.15 \\ (-20T_{LAT} + 5), & \text{if } 0.20 < T_{LAT} < 0.25 \wedge T_{LON} < 0.15 \\ (-20T_{LAT} + 5)(-50T_{LON} + 8.5), & \text{if } 0.20 < T_{LAT} < 0.25 \wedge 0.15 < T_{LON} < 0.17 \\ (-50T_{LON} + 8.5), & \text{if } T_{LAT} < 0.20 \wedge 0.15 < T_{LON} < 0.17 \\ 0, & \text{if } T_{LAT} > 0.25 \wedge T_{LON} > 0.17 \end{cases}$$

$$(2)$$

The values of k are depicted graphically in Fig. 4.

2. Adjustment of w_i weight values in computation of the steering vector. A typical scenario would include a 10 % increase of the wander behavior contribution and a corresponding decrease in *Obstacle Avoidance* and *Separation* contribution.

3. Adjustment of the parameters of each individual steering behavior.

3.2   Passenger Grouping

Passenger grouping in VELOS, as presented in [24], is based on the *Enhanced-Cohere* behavior which constitutes an enhancement of the standard *Cohere*

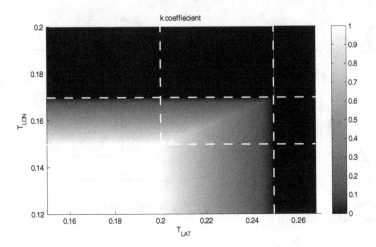

Fig. 4. Colorplot of k-coefficient values

behavior. *Enhanced-Cohere* behavior is responsible for keeping together agents that are not only geometrically close to each other (as in the standard *Cohere* behavior), but also belong to the same group, e.g., a family, a crew guided group, etc. For this purpose, each agent is endowed with an ID in the form of a common length binary representation and the new velocity vector of every agent is obtained by applying the standard *Cohere* calculations on the subset of the neighboring agents that belong to the same group. Our implementation of standard *Cohere* behavior, assuming an agent's position at point **p** and the remaining group members locations at $\mathbf{p}_i$, respectively, produces a steering vector along the direction of $\mathbf{s} - \mathbf{p}$ where **s** is calculated as:

$$\mathbf{s} = \frac{1}{\sum_i w_i} \sum_i w_i \mathbf{p}_i, \text{ where } w_i = \frac{1}{\|\mathbf{p} - \mathbf{p}_i\|}. \tag{3}$$

In this way, by blending properly the *Cohere* behavior we can produce different grouping levels which can be categorized as follows:

Grouping Level 0: In this level, grouping is formed indirectly, via a common short-term target for the *group* members, as, e.g., followers of the same leader, or through the usage of the standard *Cohere* behavior.

Grouping Level 1: The members of the group are endowed with an *ID* and the *Enhanced-Cohere* behavior described above. Group cohesion is maintained only among nearby agents (within *Cohere*'s neighborhood) sharing a common ID. However, if a member of the group gets out of the *Cohere* behavior's neighborhood, the remaining members will take no action.

Grouping Level 2: The members of the group are endowed with the same properties as in Level 1 and moreover at least one member (e.g., the group leader) has the responsibility of checking group's integrity. In this way, cohesion of the

group is maintained, since if a member of the group is lost the responsible agent
will take some corrective action, as to wait for the lost member to join the group
or to search for finding the lost member.

3.3   Crew Assistance

Crew-Assistance behavior [24] is materialized by affecting the *simple-* or *priority-
mind mechanism* in two ways, either by using *Triggers* or via the *Guide Operation*.

A *Trigger* attached to a crew agent is a scene object and at the same time
a scene area *(Trigger Neighborhood or TN)* that, when visited by a passenger
agent, a prescribed list of actions or property changes, the so called *Trigger
Actions or TAs*, are applied to the agent. A TA example could be the following:
if passenger density at the chosen TN exceeds a prescribed limit, the TA enables
the crew agent to redirect passengers towards the closest muster station along a
path different from the main escape route; see scenario 3 in Sect. 4.1.

Guide Operation is materialized through the *Enhanced-Cohere* behavior and
the basic *Leader-Follow* behavior. A *Guide-Operation* example could involve a
crew member that is ordered by the officer in charge to guide a group of passengers from a specific site to the closest muster station along a path different from
that provided by the evacuation plan; see scenario 2 in Sect. 4.1.

Furthermore improvement of *Crew Assistance* services could be provided by
properly combining *Triggers* with *Guide Operation*. An example of this combined
operation could involve a crew member that is charged to guide a group of
passengers blocked at a space where a fire event is evolved.

3.4   Influence of Smoke, Heat and Toxic Fire Products

VELOS offers the possibility to model a fire event during evacuation process
by permitting passengers/crew to be influenced by smoke, heat and toxic fire
products that are present in fire effluent. This is achieved by:

- importing precomputed time-series of fire products, according to different
  methods for calculating fire growth and smoke spread in multiple compart-
  ments; see, e.g., [26, 28],
- setting the time of fire or explosion (before, simultaneously or after the evacuation starting time),
- modeling the influence of fire products on the behavioral model of agents with
  the aid of the Function *Health_ Index* presented below,
- visualizing the fire products in the synthetic world.

Function Health_ Index: In order to model the influence of fire products on agents
we introduce the Health Reduction Rate function as follows:

$$HRR(t) = F(aT(t) + bC_{CO}(t)), \quad (Health\_units/sec) \quad (4)$$

where, F describes the used functional model, T is the temperature ($^\circ C$) and C_{CO} the carbon monoxide concentration (ppm) of the space where the agent is at the time t (see Sect. 4.2). We introduce now the *Health Index* function as follows

$$HI(t) = 1 - \int_0^t F(aT(t) + bC_{CO}(t))dt \qquad (5)$$

where, we have assumed that the initial Health Index of all agents is 1. When the Health Index of an agent becomes zero the agent is considered dead. Moreover, when the Health Index of an agent deteriorates this also affects, by a suitable law, its maximum speed (ability of walking).

Function Space_Availability: In a typical ship evacuation simulation, the path-finding module of VELOS computes the required path for each passenger to reach their designated muster station from their initial position. The employed algorithm is Dijsktra's shortest path algorithm [6] and is applied on ships topological graph where nodes correspond to ship spaces and edges to doors and/or passageways. Edge weighting between two connected nodes, in the simplest case, corresponds to the walking-distance between the two spaces' center points while this weighting scheme becomes more complex when space availability is considered. Specifically, ship spaces availability is connected and contribute to the edges' weighting implemented on the topology graph of ship spaces. For example, an increase of ambient temperature or CO concentration, or a visibility decrease in a certain space results in an increase of the weighting factors of the edges connected to the graph node representing this space. Consequently, paths passing through this particular space are less possible to be chosen by the path planning algorithm. Furthermore, when going beyond certain temperature, CO concentration and visibility thresholds, the corresponding space(s) is(are) rendered unavailable, i.e. removed from the topological graph.

4   Test Cases

In this section we use VELOS for performing evacuation analysis for a RO-RO passenger ship:

– with and without crew assistance and grouping behaviors, and
– with and without a concurrent fire event.

Furthermore, we also examine the effect of ship motions on passengers' movement in the test case described in Sect. 4.3.

4.1   Crew Assistance and Grouping

In the first test case examined, one hundred passengers are located in the cabins of Deck 5 (see Fig. 5) of the aft. vertical zone of a ship, while Muster Station is located on Deck 7. Population demographics are as proposed in [20]. For every simulation run we distribute randomly the population in the aforementioned

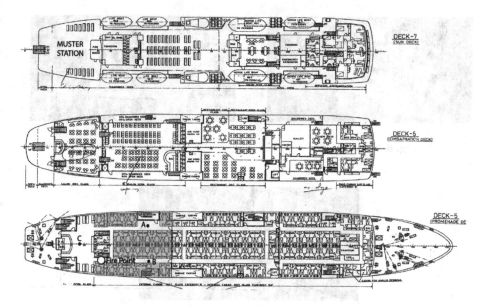

Fig. 5. General arrangement and passengers distribution at the aft. vertical zone

areas. Three variations of the above scenario are simulated 3000 times each. For each variation, we compute the *travel time* required for all passengers to reach Muster Station as well as *cumulative arrival time* corresponding to the percentage of passengers reaching Muster Station for each time unit.

In the first variation (Scenario 1), passengers follow the designated escape route without crew assistance; Fig. 6 provides a snapshot of the evacuation process. The other two variations involve crew assistance. In Scenario 2 passengers are directed by two crew members to follow two distinct routes (see Fig. 7), while in Scenario 3 a crew member monitors passengers' density at a specified place and, whenever congestion is likely to arise, he/she redirects a group of passengers towards a secondary escape route; see Fig. 8. In both cases, crew assistance is materialized through *Triggers*, which in Scenario 2 involves TAs applied to all passengers passing through the corresponding TN, while in Scenario 3 TAs are of dynamic character as a result of the attached density sensor.

Figure 9 depicts the average of the cumulative arrival time for each scenario. As it can easily be seen from this figure, Scenarios 2 and 3, based on crew-assistance & grouping, achieve a considerably better performance compared to Scenario 1. Among Scenarios 2 and 3, the latter is marginally better as a result of the dynamic crew-assistance policy adopted. Analogous conclusions can be drawn from Fig. 10, where the distributions of travel-time of the three scenarios are depicted. Average travel time for Scenarios 1, 2 and 3 are equal to 147 s, 112 s and 113 s, respectively. Moreover, in Scenarios 2 and 3 travel-time

Fig. 6. Scenario 1

Fig. 7. Scenario 2

Fig. 8. Scenario 3

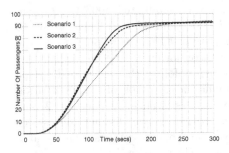

Fig. 9. Average cumulative arrival time for Scenarios 1, 2 and 3

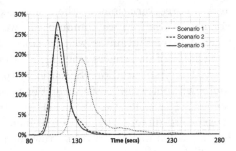

Fig. 10. Travel time distribution for Scenarios 1, 2 and 3

distribution is narrow-banded, which reflects the effectiveness of the adopted evacuation processes versus that of Scenario 1.

4.2   Fire Event

In this test case, we have the same arrangement and passenger distribution with the first test case; see Fig. 5. Population demographics are as proposed in [20]. A fire event occurs simultaneously with the beginning of the evacuation process. The initial fire site is located on deck 5 and depicted in Fig. 5. The fire propagation, along with temperature distribution, Carbon Monoxide (CO) concentration and visibility due to smoke has been precomputed [26] for all affected spaces on deck 5 and the time history of all corresponding quantities has been imported to VELOS. Fire and its products (temperature, CO concentration and visibility-degradation due to smoke) affect both the availability of ship spaces and the movement capabilities of passengers and their health. Space availability changes are implemented via the edge weighting mechanism described in Sect. 3.4.

For every simulation run we distribute randomly the population in the afore-mentioned areas. The fire scenario under consideration is simulated 360 times and for each run, we record the *travel time* required for all passengers to reach Muster Station and compute the *cumulative arrival time* corresponding to the percentage of passengers reaching Muster Station for each time unit. As illus-trated in Fig. 11 the passengers reaching muster station are around 30 % less when compared to the evacuation without the fire event. This is caused by the fire-blockage of passage ways and the resulting fatalities. Furthermore, the slight acceleration of the evacuation process depicted in the same figure for the fire-event example case is due to the fact that the effective evacuation population has been reduced due to the effects of the fire incident and thus the available spaces and pathways are used by less evacuating passengers.

4.3   Ship Motions' Effect

This last test case examines passengers' movement on Deck 5 of the same RO-RO passenger ship with and without ship motions' effect consideration. Specifi-cally, we simulate the movement of two groups of passengers (20 persons) from points A and B respectively, to point C (see Fig. 5) in still water, and at a sea state described by a wave spectrum with 4 m significant wave height, 11 s peak period and 90^0 ship heading (beam seas). Ship responses were pre-computed and imported into VELOS using the SWAN seakeeping software package. The cases examined have as follows:

- Still water (No Waves),
- (Sea state as described above): Kinematic modeling of motion effects through inclination behavior,
- (Same sea state): Dynamic modeling using tipping coefficients implementation.

Figure 12 depicts the average cumulative arrival time to point C for each of the three example cases. Each of the test cases has been simulated 500 times and the average travel times and arrival rates at point C have been collected. As it can easily be seen from this figure the time required for the prescribed passengers movement is the least when we are in still water. The effect of the wavy sea state, which induces ship motions and hinders passengers movement is illustrated with the right-shifting of the remaining two curves. The total travel time needed for both inclination behavior and tipping coefficient modeling is about the same (≈ 70 s) and considerably higher than the still water case (≈ 50 s), where, obvi-ously, no motion effect is considered. However the arrival rate (slope) for the tipping coefficient modeling is steeper than the slope of the curve corresponding to the kinematic approach.

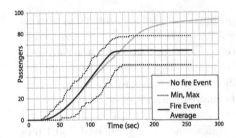

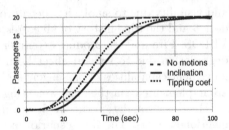

Fig. 11. Ship evacuation with and without a fire event

Fig. 12. Average cumulative arrival time for test cases 1, 2 and 3

5 Current Work - Dynamic Grouping

As the assumption that passengers have knowledge of the full route to muster stations is not realistic, we aim in further developing the grouping behaviors and guiding functionality within groups so that a more realistic path-finding can be accomplished. Towards this goal, we briefly present here the current development of *Dynamic Grouping*.

Dynamic Grouping extends the *Enhanced-Cohere* behavior described in Sect. 3.2. Additionally to group IDs, dynamic grouping uses the notion of a group leader which, obviously, shares the same ID with the corresponding group and possesses the leader tag. The steering vector, in this case, is a weighted average of the steering vector in Eq. 3 and the vector $\frac{l-p}{\|l-p\|}$, where l, p correspond to leader's and agent's positions respectively.

Dynamic grouping permits changes in group membership when the group leader is not "visible" to a group member. When a member stops seeing the leader, it loses its ID and thus, stops belonging to a specific group. After that, the "lost" individual scans within its neighborhood for other leaders, i.e., agents look in their "view area" for other agents and choose to follow the leader that most of them are following. If one is found, the individual acquires the group ID of the leader closer to its position. If none is found, it switches its *Enhanced-Cohere* behavior to the standard one as described in Sect. 3.2.

The following subsection demonstrates the current development of the Dynamic Grouping behavior for the case of two groups with leaders in a simple space arrangement. "Visibility" in this generic example is implemented as a circular disc with a prescribed radius centered at the agent's position.

5.1 Example Scenario

The test environment comprises 4 consecutive spaces ($7.5 \times 10\,\text{m}$ each) and two initial groups. The first group (black group) is initially positioned at space A while the second group (gray group) resides in space B as shown in Fig. 13. Black group comprises, excluding its leader (colored white with black outline), 18

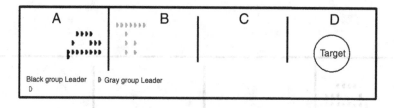

Fig. 13. Generic example: spaces and groups' arrangement

members and the gray group comprises 13 members. The target space for both groups is space D and only group leaders have knowledge of the required path. All group members are endowed with the following set of steering behaviors:

1. *Obstacle Avoidance,*
2. *Separation,*
3. *Wander,* and
4. *Dynamic Cohere*

Both group leaders are equipped with the above set of behaviors with the addition of the Path-Following steering behavior.

We demonstrate the dynamic grouping in a simple generic example for 5 test cases with different group leaders' velocities and/or initial positions along their predefined path towards the target space.

The first 3 test cases investigate the effect of leaders speed. In Figs. 14, 15 and 16 group members have maximum allowable speeds according to the statistical distributions prescribed in [20] while the black group leader has a speed equal to the black group members' average speed. In Fig. 14 the gray group leader has a maximum speed (1.2 m/s) lower than the average of its corresponding group. As a consequence its group members retain their membership (with the exception of a single slow individual) through the whole experiment. In Fig. 15 the gray group leader has a maximum speed (1.4 m/s) equal to the average of its corresponding group. In this case the slower members lose their group membership as their leader leaves their visibility area. Finally, in Fig. 16, the gray group leader is considerably faster (1.6 m/s) than the average speed leading to a significant reduction of its group size at route's halfway.

The second set of test cases comprises two experiments: One with leaders having initial position closer to their corresponding group while for the second test we have shifted the black group leader's position on the path towards the target space (see Fig. 18). In this experiment both leaders' speed is equal to their groups' average speed. In the first test case (Fig. 17), as expected, all members retain their group membership while in the second one both groups merge forming one group behind the gray group leader. There is an exception of a black individual that manages not to lose sight of its initial leader (see Fig. 18).

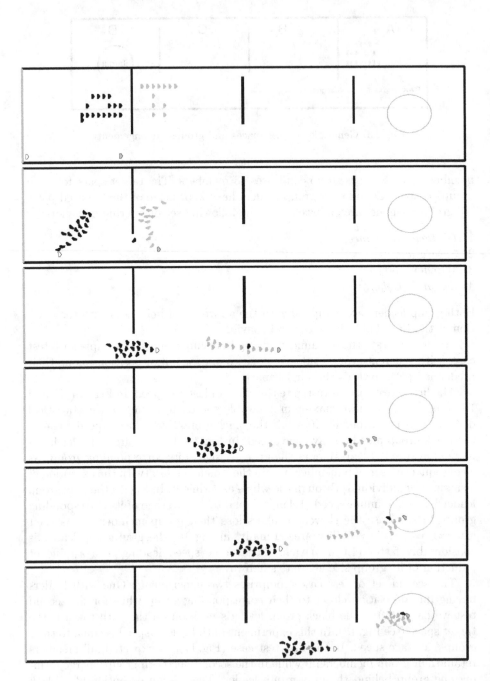

Fig. 14. Gray Group Leader: low speed, 1.2 m/s

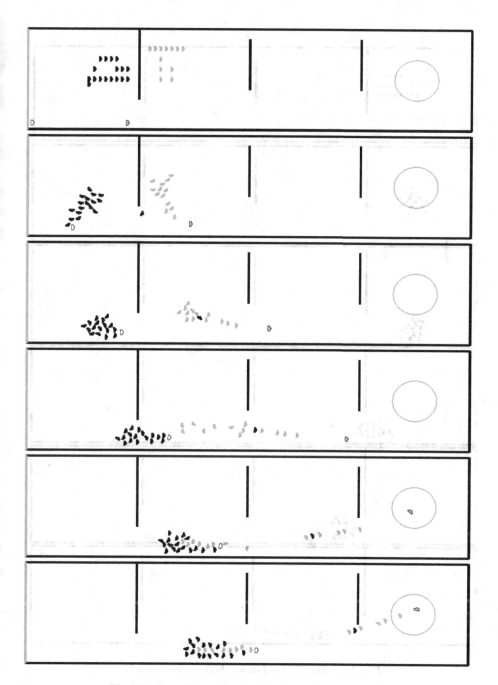

Fig. 15. Gray Group Leader: medium speed, 1.4 m/s

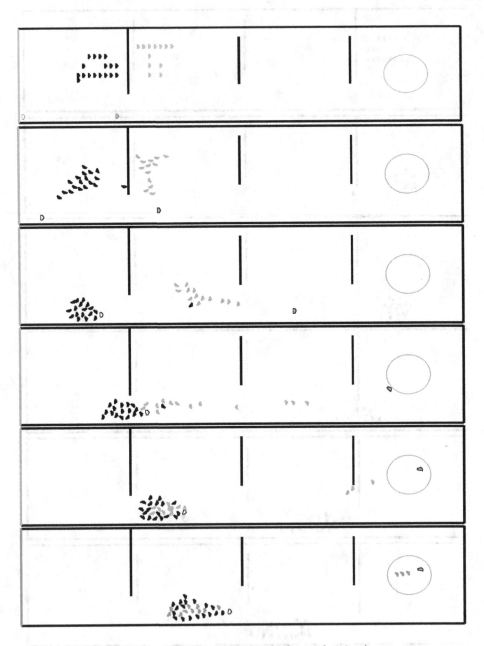

Fig. 16. Gray Group Leader: high speed, 1.6 m/s

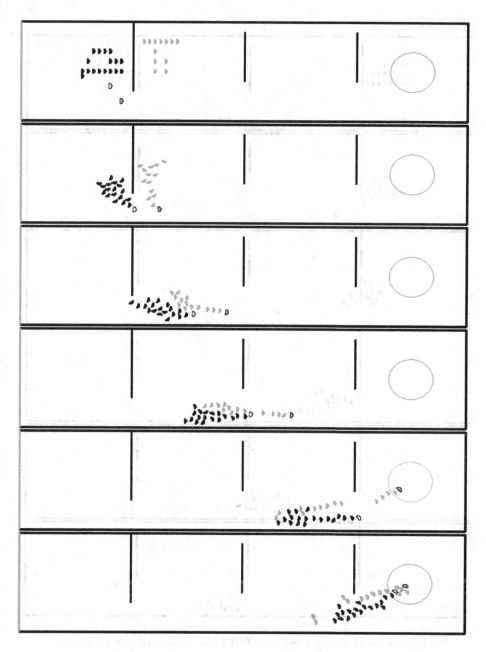

Fig. 17. Group Leaders: Close to their group

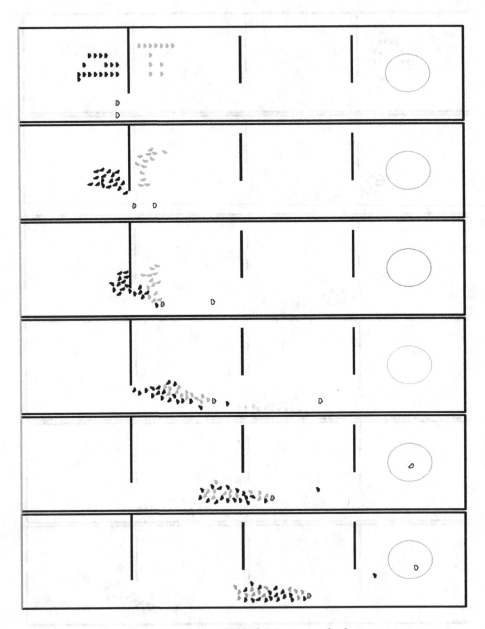

Fig. 18. Black Group Leader: Shifted 7.5 m towards the target space

6   Conclusion

The present paper provides a description of the enhanced crowd modeling app-roach employed in VELOS for the performance of ship evacuation assessment and analysis based on the guidelines provided by IMO's Circular MSC 1238/2007 [20]. Although the evacuation scenarios, proposed in [20] address issues related to the layout of the ship and passenger demographics, they do not touch issues aris-ing in real emergency conditions, such as unavailability of escape arrangements (due to flooding or fire), crew assistance in the evacuation process, family-group behavior, ship motions, etc.

We have presented VELOS' components and functionalities including a brief description of the employed crowd modeling approach for the performance of ship evacuation assessment & analysis. The VELOS novel features include: the modeling of ship motions & accelerations, passenger grouping and crew assis-tance and the influence of smoke, heat and toxic fire products. The examples presented include ship evacuation test cases investigating the effects of crew assistance, passenger grouping and fire incidents. Furthermore, an additional test case demonstrating the effects of ship motions on passengers movement is also included. Finally, our ongoing work extending grouping behavior with dynamic characteristics has been also presented.

As a concluding remark, we would like to note that an obvious next step in the development process is the inclusion and assessment of dynamic grouping in a more realistic ship test case. This, however, requires further development of the "visibility" mechanism and elaboration of the factors that affect members' group-changing decision.

Acknowledgments. We thank the three anonymous reviewers for their constructive comments, which helped us to considerably improve the manuscript. This research has been co-financed by the European Union (European Social Fund - ESF) and Greek national funds through the Operational Program *"Education and Lifelong Learning"* of the National Strategic Reference Framework (NSRF) - Research Funding Program: THALIS-UOA (MIS 375891).

References

1. Baitis, A.E., Holcombe, F.D., Conwell, S.L., Crossland, P., Colwell, J., Pattison, J.H.: 1991–1992 Motion Induced Interruptions (MII) and Motion Induced Fatigue (MIF) experiments at the Naval Biodynamics Laboratory. Techical report CRDKNSWC-HD-1423-01, Bethesda, MD: Naval Surface Warfare Center, Carde-rock Division (1995)
2. Bles, W., Nooy, S., Boer, L.: Influence of ship listing and ship motion on walking speed. In: Proceedings of the Conference on Pedestrian and Evacuation Dynamics (2001)
3. Blue, V., Adler, J.: Cellular automata microsimulation of bi-directional pedestrian flows. Transp. Res. Board **1678**, 135–141 (2000)

4. Crossland, P.: The influence of ship motion induced lateral acceleration on walking speed. In: Proceedings of the 2nd International Conference on Pedestrian and Evacuation Dynamics, Greenwich, (2003)
5. Crossland, P., Evans, M.J., Grist, D., Lowten, M., Jones, H., Bridger, R.S.: Motion-induced interruptions aboard ship: model development and application to ship design. Occup. Ergon. **7**(3), 183–199 (2007)
6. Dijkstra, E.W.: A note on two problems in connexion with graphs. Numerische Mathematik **1**, 269–271 (1959)
7. Drager, K., Orset, S.: Evac - the mustering and evacuation computer model resulting from the briteeuram project mepdesign. In: Proceedings of the Conference on Pedestrian and Evacuation Dynamics, Duisburg, pp. 355–368 (2001)
8. Galea, E., Lawrence, P., Gwynne, S., Sharp, G., Hurst, N., Wang, Z., et al.: Integrated fire and evacuation in maritime environments. In: Proceedings of the 2nd International Maritime Conference on Design for Safety, Sakai, Japan, pp. 161–170 (2004)
9. Gardner, M.: Mathematical games: Conway's game of life. Sci. Am. **407**, 487–490 (2000)
10. Ginnis, A.A.I., Kostas, K.V., Politis, C.G., Kaklis, P.D.: VELOS: a VR platform for ship-evacuation analysis. CAD **42**(11), 1045–1058 (2010). Special issue Computer Aided Ship Design
11. Graham, R.: Motion-induced interruptions as ship operability criteria. J. Naval Eng. **102**(2), 65–71 (1990)
12. Graham, R., Baitis, A.E., Meyers, W.: On the development of seakeeping criteria. J. Naval Eng. **104**(3), 259–275 (1992)
13. Green, R.: Steering behaviors. In: SIGGRAPH 2000 Conference Proceedings (2000)
14. Helbing, D., Farkas, I., Viscek, T.: Simulating dynamical features of escape panic. Nature **407**, 487–490 (2000)
15. Helbing, D., Molnar, P., Farkas, I., Bolay, K.: Self-organizing pedestrian movement. Environ. Plann. B: Plann. Des. **28**, 361–383 (2001)
16. Helbing, D., Molnár, P.: Social force model for pedestrian dynamics. Phys. Rev. E **51**, 4282–4286 (1995). http://link.aps.org/doi/10.1103/PhysRevE.51.4282
17. Henderson, L.: The statistics of crowd fluids. Nature **229**, 381–383 (1971)
18. Hughes, R.: The flow of human crowds. Annu. Rev. Fluid Mech. **224**, 120–123 (1970)
19. I.M.O.: Interim Guidelines for evacuation analyses for new and existing passenger ships, MSC/Circ. 1033, June 2002
20. I.M.O.: Guidelines for evacuation analyses for new and existing passenger ships, msc.1/circ. 1238 edn. 30 October 2007
21. Kim, H., Park, J.H., Lee, D., Yang, Y.S.: Establishing the methodologies for human evacuation simulation in marine accidents. Comput. Ind. Eng. **46**(4), 725–740 (2004)
22. Klupfel, H., Meyer-Konig, M., Wahle, J., Schreckenberg, M.: Microscopic simulation of evacuation processes on passenger ships. In: Bandini, S., Worsch, T. (eds.) Theoretical and Practical Issues on Cellular Automata, pp. 63–71. Springer, London (2000)
23. Kostas, K.: Virtual Reality Kernel with Support for Ship Life-cycle Modeling. Ph.D. thesis, Naval Architecture & Marine Engineering, NTUA (2006)
24. Kostas, K., Ginnis, A.I., Politis, C., Kaklis, P.: Use of VELOS platform for modelling and accessing crew assistance and passenger grouping in ship-evacuation analysis. In: Rizzuto, E., Guedes Soares, C. (eds.) Sustainable Maritime Transportation and Exploitation of Sea Resources, vol. 2, pp. 729–736 (2011)

25. Lee, D., Kim, H., Park, J.H., Park, B.J.: The current status and future issues in human evacuation from ships. Saf. Sci. **41**(10), 861–876 (2003)

26. McGrattan, K., Klein, B., Hostika, S.: Fire Dynamics Simulator. NIST (2007). maryland: NIST Special Publication 1019-5

27. Park, J., Lee, D., Kim, H., Yang, Y.: Development of evacuation model for human maritime casualty. Ocean Eng. **31**, 1537–1547 (2004)

28. Rein, G., Barllan, A., Fernandez-Pell, C., Alvares, N.: A comparison of three models for the simulation of accidental fires. Fire Prot. Eng. **1**, 183–209 (2006)

29. Reynolds, C.: Flocks, herds and schools: a distributed behavioral model. Comput. Graph. **21**(4), 25–34 (1987)

30. Reynolds, C.W.: Steering behaviors for autonomous characters. In: GDC 1999 (Game Developers Conference) (1999)

31. Thalmann, D., Musse, S.: Crowd Simulation. Springer, London (2007)

32. Valanto, P.: Time-dependent survival probability of a damaged passenger ship ii - evacuation in seaway and capsizing. Technical report 1661, Hamburg, HSVA (2006)

33. Vanem, E., Skjong, R.: Designing for safety in passenger ships utilizing advanced evacuation analyses - a risk based approach. Saf. Sci. **44**, 11–35 (2006)

34. Vassalos, D., Guarin, L., Vassalos, G., Bole, M., Kim, H., Majumder, J.: Advanced evacuation analysis - testing the ground on ships. In: Proceedings of the Conference on Pedestrian and Evacuation Dynamics, Greenwich (2003)

35. Vassalos, D., Kim, H., Christiansen, G., Majumder, J.: A mesoscopic model for passenger evacuation in a virtual ship-sea environment and performance-based evaluation. In: Proceedings of the Conference on Pedestrian and Evacuation Dynamics, Duisburg (2001)

Underwater Mixed Environments

Uwe Freiherr von Lukas[1]([✉]), John Quarles[2], Panagiotis Kaklis[3],
and Tim Dolereit[1,4]

[1] Maritime Graphics, Fraunhofer IGD, 18059 Rostock, Germany
uwe.von.lukas@igd-r.fraunhofer.de
[2] Department of Computer Science, University of Texas at San Antonio,
San Antonio, TX 78249, USA
[3] Department Naval Architecture, Ocean and Marine Engineering,
University of Strathclyde, Glasgow G1 1XQ, UK
[4] Institute for Computer Science, University of Rostock, 18059 Rostock, Germany

Abstract. In this chapter we give a systematic overview over Virtual
Reality (VR) and Augmented Reality (AR) in underwater settings and
suggest several future applications. Based on a novel classification scheme
we illustrate the broad range of available and future implementation
options. Whilst we find a variety of previous work on creating and using
virtual underwater worlds, quite few examples of real underwater settings exist up to now. Thus, we concentrate on this new category, sketch
attractive application areas that go beyond entertainment, and derive
requirements for Underwater Mixed Environments (UWME). Combined
with a short summary on relevant aspects of underwater optics, we formulate potential topics of future research to overcome current limitations
of UWME.

Keywords: Virtual Reality · Augmented Reality · Maritime technology · Rehabilitation · Ship Maintenance · Marine research

1 Introduction to Underwater Mixed Environments

1.1 Underwater Setting as an Example of an Unconventional Environment

There has been minimal research on the general aspects of unconventional Mixed
Environments [8]. In our context, conventional means that we are in a typical
lab or office environment - or even outside in the landscape. In any case we
have air as the surrounding medium for the display, the interaction devices and
the user. An example of an unconventional Mixed Environment would be an
underwater setting, where air is replaced by water. This environment creates
significant challenges for conventional mixed environment technologies, such as
optics, robust tracking, wireless communication, and user interaction.

There is a growing awareness that the seven seas will play a prominent role as
a source of energy, food and minerals. Even the deep sea areas are already subject

© Springer International Publishing Switzerland 2015
G. Brunnett et al. (Eds.): Virtual Realities, LNCS 8844, pp. 56–76, 2015.
DOI: 10.1007/978-3-319-17043-5_4

to intense usage by the oil and gas industry in some areas. This development leads to a number of research and business activities in sub-sea environments. As in other challenging environments, Mixed Reality could be a means to support the users via assistance, guidance or training applications.

1.2   Classification Scheme

We now present a classification scheme that allows us to distinguish different types of Underwater Mixed Environments (UWME). It is derived from analyzing the spectrum of available and future applications and uses the level of reality compared to a real-life underwater world as a second dimension. It reaches from a high degree of authenticity, i.e. the mixed reality equipment is used to mimic a typical underwater environment, over a mid level, where the real world is augmented, enhanced or maybe simplified to a minimum level, where we do not have any objects of an underwater world. The following Fig. 1 illustrates the classification scheme and gives examples for typical applications in the various categories. It is inspired by Milgrams well-known Virtuality Continuum [43] but using the specific distinction between real and virtual water on the x-axis.

		Wet environment	Dry environment
Natural underwater scene		• Extended aquarium for marine research	• Diver training • ROV training • Virtual aquarium for edutainment
Augmented underwater scene		• Diver assistance (e.g. ship maintenance and inspection) • ROV operation • Underwater AR experience	• Developing/testing marine technology • Archaeological research
No underwater scene		• Rehabilitation • Astronaut training	*Non-underwater application*

Fig. 1. Classification scheme for Underwater Mixed Environments

1.3   Previous Work on Virtual or Augmented Underwater Worlds

In the literature there are several examples for virtual underwater worlds designed for entertainment or education: Virtual Oceanarium [24], the SAP - Swimming Across the Pacific installation [15], the Virtual Exploration of Underwater Sites [14,29] or the immersive virtual aquarium installation [35]. They all present a virtual underwater world that can be explored with typical VR interaction.

The main focus is on a realistic experience of the scenery and specific aspects of interaction. The SAP project is the only one that reflects one important aspect of underwater environments: the lack of gravity that allows the user to float in the medium.

Similar work can be found in projects with a background in training for underwater operations in a virtual environment. The focus of the projects is set on a realistic (or at least plausible) behaviour of the technical objects or processes and a sound physical model of the operation. Typical work in this area is presented for underwater welding [62], for training of remotely operated vehicle (ROV) operators [22] or safety procedures for divers [36]. Sometimes those systems can also use real-time input of sensors and create a situational awareness for safe ROV operation [20, 26, 39]

We find a related focus in the group of VR systems that are used in the phase of product development for underwater equipment. Obviously we need a high level of physical correctness of the simulation and less visual quality. Representatives for this research work are [60] for a forward looking sonar or [61] dealing with virtual tests of autonomous underwater vehicles.

However, there are few systems actually being used in a real underwater environment. The following examples adapt Augmented Reality hardware to be used in an underwater setting for entertainment purposes: the DOLPHYN-based game [9], the AR-enriched tele-operation of a ROV [16], or the AREEF - Augmented Reality for Water-based Entertainment, Education and Fun [46].

The next section will introduce several application areas for what we call Underwater Mixed Environments. Those application areas cover a spectrum from diver assistance over astronaut training up to rehabilitation. After that we go into the technical aspects of UWME, summarize relevant physical basics and describe concrete challenges that arise from the liquid medium.

2   Driving Applications

As briefly touched upon in the first section, there are various applications that depend on Underwater Mixed Environments. We concentrate on three categories of the left column of Fig. 1 and present an important application area for each row: one biological (marine research), one industrial (ship inspection) and one medical (rehabilitation) in detail. Other useful application areas such as astronaut training, where the water simulates zero gravity are not discussed here but would lead to similar challenges.

2.1   Marine Research

Use Cases. While typical VR installations are designed for human users, there are also some examples for animal users. Empirical studies - especially in behavioral science - have been published for example with honeybees [1] or moths [27]. This kind of experiment is also useful in studying fish or other aquatic animals. For that purpose one or more displays are attached to an aquarium and camera systems are used to track and observe the animal in the underwater setting. Using the tracking information, the virtual world is updated according to the reaction of the animal. Those immersive virtual fish tank applications (from the perspective of the fish in the tank) should not be confused with the fish tank VR metaphor [63] defined as "a stereo image of a three dimensional (3D) scene viewed on a monitor using a perspective projection coupled to the head position of the observer".

A relatively simple setup has been used to study the startle response behavior of fish according to a visual stimulus [12]. It uses one screen displaying a growing ellipse as a simplified presentation of an approaching fish. A mirror was mounted at an angle to a side of the tank, so one camera could be used to compute the 3D position of the real fish in the tank (see Fig. 2). Similar work can be found studying the larval zebra fish prey capture [57].

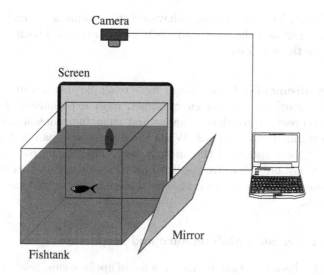

Fig. 2. Immersive VR setup for studying fish behavior [12]

A more elaborated underwater virtual environment, the Sub Sea Holodeck, uses seven displays with 14 megapixels to produce a high resolution visual aquatic environment [32] (see Fig. 3). The setup has been used in context of a project to study how cephalopods sense, respond to, and camouflage themselves in a marine environment.

The system can replay videos that are recorded with an omnidirectional underwater camera. This feature is used to copy real underwater scenarios to the VR environment. Alternatively, the surrounding screens and projectors can display the output of a rendering system to synthesize a controlled and reproducible visual environment.

We can summarize, that this kind of VR-enabled fish tank is a very flexible and powerful means to support research of marine biologists and neuro scientists.

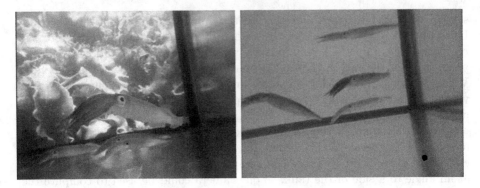

Fig. 3. The Sub Sea Holodeck with two different scenarios [32]

It allows the scientist to study the behaviour of the aquatic animals in a controlled environment and the setup can easily be instrumented with various sensors to measure the reaction.

Specific Requirements. Even though some examples use a quite elaborated model of the virtual underwater environment, most experiments show that a quite simple representation (basic shapes and changing ambient color) works quite well to stimulate the animals. While the presentation can be kept simple, the tracking of the response of the animals is the challenging part here: many experiments do not only measure the fish's position and orientation with a high frequency sometimes even eyetracking is used to characterize the reaction of the aquatic animals.

2.2   Underwater Ship Maintenance and Inspection

Use Cases. In this subsection we discuss a list of applications, related to Underwater Ship Maintenance and Inspection (UWSMI), which seem appropriate for challenging the concept of Underwater Mixed Environments (UWME). It is just one area of possible application of Mixed Reality in the maritime industry. Additional use cases not directly linked to the underwater setting are described for example in [40] or [59].

Our view is that UWSMI can be used for boosting the research in the areas of Virtual-, Augmented- and Mixed-Reality (VAMR) environments and, eventually, improving drastically the technological status and the quality of services provided in the context of this specific application with high industrial impact.

A non-exhaustive list of UWSMI activities may include:

– Underwater hull cleaning,
– Propeller polishing.
– Underwater welding.
– Applying adhesives suitable for underwater bonding.

- Materials underwater for both naval and commercial customers.
- Propeller crack detection.
- Plate thickness readings.
- Underwater surveys in lieu of dry docking.
- Impact damage inspection.
- Security inspections.
- Sea-valve inspections.
- Oil- and liquefied-gas-terminal jetty inspections.
- Hull-potential surveys.

The effect on the above activities in the operational and economic efficiency of a ship as well as its safety is important. For example, fuel saving is the major reason for making underwater hull cleaning an integral part of planned maintenance, especially in the era of (super)-slow-steaming. For example, marine engines manufacturer Wärtsilä [64], calculates that fuel consumption can be reduced by 58 % by reducing cargo ship speed from 27 knots to 22 knots while the large container ship Emma Maersk can save 4,000 metric tons of fuel oil on a Europe-Singapore voyage by slow steaming [34]. At a typical USD 600–700 per tonne, this works out to USD 2.4–2.8 million fuel savings on a typical one-way voyage.

In the maritime environment setting, concentration of marine fouling can lead to increased resistance, resulting in a detrimental impact on a vessel's hydrodynamic performance and hence the relationship between speed, power performance and fuel consumption. Fouling, particularly in the case of a prolific buildup of hard or shell fouling like barnacles or tubeworm, can cause turbulence, cavitation and noise, frequently affecting the performance of, e.g., sonars, speed logs and other hull-mounted sensors. Marine fouling is considered as a global-scale problem in marine systems, costing the U.S. Navy alone $1 billion per annum [13]. Ship-hull cleaning is performed in the dockyard when the ship has her official inspection each year or by divers underwater, while the ship docs at the port. Though the regular or intermediate inspections take place each year, it is desirable to have frequent ship hull cleaning in order to keep good fuel efficiency for securing lower transportation costs and CO_2 emission.

Analogously, the operational need for polishing a propeller stems from the fact that a super smooth surface is inhospitable to marine organisms as well as being beneficial to the efficiency of the propeller. In this connection, provided the service is done properly, the cost of the underwater propeller polish will only be a small proportion of the fuel savings.

UWME could be used for training divers in nearly realistic conditions by means of augmentation in their diving mask. Such an environment could be based on a towing-tank-like facility endowed with immersed physical mock-ups of full-scale parts of the ship hull and, if necessary, its propeller blades and appendages, as well as an AR interface capable to superimpose on them computer generated or photographic images. Such an installation would readily inherit from its physical counterpart, the surrounding medium and the effects of buoyancy, viscosity and free-surface waves while offering the trainees with a realistic perception of their working environment regarding its lighting (refraction, absorption and scattering by the water particles), water turbidity, spatial complexity and limitations (hull stern with its propeller), and the activities to be performed on it. One could bargain limited perception losses, e.g., buoyancy in fresh versus sea water, in favor of effective wireless communication, since it is known (see, e.g. [33]) that conventional RF propagation works poorly in sea water due to losses caused by its high conductivity (typically 4 S/m) versus that of fresh water (0.01 S/m).

In addition, UWME could be useful in the context of design, construction, testing and approval of mechanisms devised by the industry for supporting ship-hull maintenance and inspection [45].

On the basis of the above and the fact that VAMR technologies have been already acknowledged as a useful mediator for challenging maintenance services in maritime applications (see, e.g. [38,58]), one could reasonably expect that the current and emerging industrial needs should have already led to coordinated actions for testing the feasibility and efficiency of UWME for supporting UWSMI. Nevertheless, searching the pertinent literature the reader gets the impression that research in the area of UWME-for-UWSMI, with the exception of scarce high-quality attempts (e.g., [44]) has not yet grasped the threshold for being characterized as an emerging research area, even more, an emerging technological area.

Specific Requirements. For offering a realistic training environment, UWME should be enhanced with additional functionality regarding its physical components, enabling, e.g., the generation of currents, fluid rotation, turbulence effects, etc. Furthermore, the AR interface could be enriched with haptic devices for providing the user with a tactile feedback for improving the degree of realistic perception of activities that involve the operation of devices controlled by the user and acting on the underwater part of the ship hull and its appendages, e.g., operating a cleaning machine at the proper pressure level for removing mild or persistent fouling from a variety of coatings, including the new low-surface-energy coatings being introduced into service.

Furthermore, the following requirements can be derived from those industrial use cases for UWME:

- The systems must be robust enough to be used in the harsh environment of professional divers.
- The alignment of virtual objects and real objects (in an AR setup) must be highly accurate.
- The training environment should be easily adaptable to the concrete task and the necessary tools in order to cover a broad range of use cases.

2.3   Rehabilitation

Another of the main driving applications for UWMEs is rehabilitation. In this application there is a significant need for Virtual Environments (VEs) that work underwater. Water-based exercise is one of the primary physical therapist recommended rehabilitation approaches for many types of injuries and disabilities.

Background

Water-based Physical Therapy. Water-based (aka aquatic) Physical Therapy (WPT) has been used for many years to rehabilitate individuals with a variety of disabling problems. WPT utilizes the physical properties of water, such as providing resistance when moving through it. These properties enable a wide range of positive effects in therapy and exercise. The water offers buoyancy and hydrostatic pressure to provide additional support for the patient when performing the exercises and reduces the risk of falls. Thus, aquatic therapy and exercise can be of great benefit to balance impaired populations, such as the elderly [19]. Moreover, water can aid in the body's cooling process, which is especially important for MS patients [25], who commonly suffer from an exacerbation of symptoms due to overheating. Similarly, WPT has been used for many years to benefit individuals with other neurological problems, such as Parkinson's Disease [65].

Virtual Rehabilitation. Research suggests that VR and AR technology can offer new opportunities and methods for neurorehabilitation [17]. Typically VR or AR can be used to immerse a patient in a safe environment to practice rehabilitation exercises [54], such as hand [42,49] and motor [50] rehabilitation in stroke and gait rehabilitation in Parkinson's Disease [47].

For example in MS rehabilitation, rhythmic audio signals and a moving checker patterned floor [5] can be used effectively for feedback. Other researchers [53] focused on haptics for upper extremity rehabilitation in MS. These approaches had only preliminary evaluations and have never made it to market, but they were shown to improve movement while in use. This suggests that VR approaches could be effective in gait rehabilitation for MS, but none of the prior work has developed VR systems that could be used in conjunction with water-based therapies.

Rehabilitation Games. VR Rehabilitation games have not been completely incorporated into common therapy practice, but they do seem to have significant benefits to rehabilitation. For example, a VE is not subjected to the dangers and limitations of the real world [10,18], which expands the types of exercises that patients can practice, while still having fun. In general, research suggests that VR games have measurable benefits for rehabilitation effectiveness [18] and motivation [10].

There has been recent research on deriving design guidelines for VR rehabilitation games based on results of empirical studies. Alankus et al.'s [2] guidelines include: simple games should support multiple methods of user input, calibrate through example motions, ensure that users' motions cover their full range, detect compensatory motion, and let therapists determine difficulty. There is a need for more focused game design research and development for specific populations [23].

User Descriptions. In the context of rehabilitation we have to distinguish between two important user groups that have different roles in the rehabilitation sessions.

Patients: Since water-based exercise is recommended for many different injuries/ disabilities, the potential patient population for this application is widely diverse. Here, we will consider an example population - multiple sclerosis (MS) patients. MS is a degenerative neurological disease that affects 400,000 people in the U.S. and over 2.1 million worldwide [52].The most common form of MS is relapsing-remitting, in which patients experience acute attacks followed by periods of remission. During these remission periods, physical therapy has been shown to most effective in the remission periods and can help counter the residual effects of the attacks [51]. Therapists often augment the diminished proprioceptive feedback with other modalities of feedback, such as using mirrors to provide visual feedback [37].

Balance and gait (i.e. walking patterns) abnormality is one of the most prevalent symptoms that MS patients experience with 85 % of patients complaining of gait and balance [4]. Gait problems are exacerbated by other MS related symptoms such as fatigue, decreased reaction time, and attention deficits, especially in dual tasks such as walking while talking [28]. One of the most common issues experienced in MS is exacerbation of all MS symptoms when body temperature is increased. This makes rehabilitation and exercise significantly more difficult and reduces the benefits. To counter this overheating effect, therapists generally recommend water-based exercise, because it offers effective resistance training while keeping the body cool. It also reduces the risk of fall due to balance deficits, which are very common in MS.

Physical Therapist: For water-based rehabilitation, physical therapists are frequently present to help guide the patient and maximize the efficacy of the workout, especially at the beginning of a rehabilitation program. A physical therapist first creates a personalized set of exercises based upon the needs of a patient. Then they teach the patient to perform these exercises correctly, offering visual, auditory, and haptic feedback to the patients as needed. Therapists often rely both on patient history and visual assessment of the patients movement to drive their feedback. Thus, being able to visually assess patients in real time is critical for a physical therapist to effectively guide the patient and provide additional motivation.

Use Case. This use case considers a therapy session in which both the physical therapist and the patient are working together in the pool. The patient may be playing a game a rehabilitation game in a head mounted display, and is experiencing many virtual stimuli. To integrate exercise, the patient runs back and forth along the length of a lane while carrying water weights - large dumbbell shaped, air-filled objects that provide additional resistance when pushed through the water. The therapists aim is to assess the movements of the patient and provide corrective feedback through multiple modalities: verbal, visual, and haptic. Moreover, the therapist may also want to control some of the game events and difficulty level in order to tailor the game to the individual patients needs.

The therapist may need to be immersed and embodied inside the VE to provide effective multimodal feedback to the patient (i.e., otherwise the therapist would be unaware of what the patient was actually seeing). To facilitate this, the therapist will have a tracked egocentric view similar to the patient, but will also have a heads up display (HUD) that can provide additional information to the therapist. For example, the therapist can monitor the patients physiological data, such as heart rate. The periphery of the display may need to be unblocked due to the therapist's need to interact with the real world. For example, the therapist may wish to observe and correct the patients real movements outside of the VE. Moreover, depending on the patients progress and frustration level, the therapist may need to control the difficulty of the game or trigger events (e.g., boss fights).

Specific Requirements

Safety Requirements One of the primary concerns of any VE system for rehabilitation is user safety, which is arguably even more important in an underwater system. For a population with disabilities, who may have issues such as balance deficits or vertigo, there is an increased chance of falls, even in water. Considering the immersiveness of the system, the user may be surprised when they fall and their head is submerged in the water, which could result in an increased chance of aspirating water. Moreover, due to users potential vestibular deficits, users may have difficulty reorienting themselves to above the water line. Thus, the user may need additional visual and/or auditory feedback to help them reorient themselves. In general, it is advised for someone to follow behind or beside the user to ensure their safety and to help prevent falls. Mobile harnesses such as those used in gait rehabilitation, could be used, but they will need to be specifically designed for underwater usage or otherwise they could make fall recovery actually more difficult.

Whenever electronics are submerged in water, there is always the safety concern of electrocution. Thus, it is advisable to waterproof powered equipment and minimize active instrumentation of the user. For example, for optical tracking of the user, passive tracking markers or markerless tracking will be the safer choice because there is no chance of electrocution.

Real Environment Requirements. One potential requirement for the real environment - the pool - is its depth. The user should be able to stand in the pool with their head above water. Deeper pools would increase the danger caused by underwater disorientation if the users could not feel the bottom of the pool. Fortunately most gym pools are designed to be about 4 or 5 ft deep. If only a deep pool is available, the proposed UWME could be combined with a traditional pool lift - a powered mechanical arm with a seat on the end, which is strapped to users to safely lift them in and out of the pool.

Display Requirement

1. If a head mounted display is used, obviously it must be waterproof.
2. If the user is required to use the length of the pool, it should be untethered so that it does not interfere with the users movement. However, another potential approach is to use an endless pool, which is analogous to a treadmill in air-based exercise. The endless pool is small 15 ft pool with a wave generator on one side and sometimes a waterproof treadmill on the floor. This would enable them to run in place in one direction while they appear to be moving in the VE. The VE as described in the Serpents treasure use case would have to be changed to enable the user to always move in the same direction (e.g., one long hallway), unless the endless pool was modified with multiple wave generators, analogous to an omnidirectional treadmill. Another option is to use the aforementioned pool lift, which hypothetically could be modified to control orientation as well.
3. While not a strict requirement, it may be beneficial for the display to be see through. The purpose of this would be to give users more feedback about the water level, which would enable them to reorient themselves more effectively in the event of a fall. In many cases, there may be a trade-off between safety and the immersiveness of the system.

Interface Requirements

1. All interfaces must be waterproof.
2. Interfaces should not interfere with movement, unless intentionally designed for that purpose. E.g., it would be detrimental if an interface became tangled with the users legs. On the other hand, if the interface was integrated with the water weights, for example, it would technically interfere with movement, but for the purpose of increased resistance training.
3. Standard interfaces with buttons should be affixed to the user. If the user interacts with a handheld device and drops it, it would be potentially difficult to retrieve if it fell to the bottom of the pool or floated away.

3   Research Challenges

After looking in quite different usage areas we will now derive the research challenges that arise from those novel applications. There we distinguish between the technical challenges of the underwater setting and the human factor aspects.

3.1   Technical Challenges

Optics. With regard to the display of close to reality virtual underwater environments on screen, several aspects have to be considered, which strongly differ from conditions in air, especially optics and visibility. An additional aspect to be discussed is characteristic illumination artifacts.

The first aspect is the occurrence of refractive effects due to the different propagation speed of light in water and in air. This property of water can be best described by its refractive index. Water has to be considered as a transparent object in the rendering pipeline, altering the direction of light rays emanating from illuminated objects inside the water body.

In the following, the three main viewer locations are presented with regard to refraction. These comprise a viewer looking into water from outside the water body, vision in water and a viewer looking from inside the water body to above the surface. A light ray is refracted at every boundary between participating media with different refractive indexes on its way. This can be a direct contact of the viewer's eyeball with water or one of the more common cases of looking through the surface of the water itself or any kind of water-glass-air transition. The glass can be a waterproof protecting surface like a side of an aquarium or a divers diving goggles. As the refractive index of air is close to zero and the glass is optional and mostly thin, the most significant quantity is the refractive index of water. It is commonly known to be close to 1.33.

The computation of refraction can differ severely due to the complexity of the respective surface. Planar surfaces can be represented by a single surface normal. A planar refractive surface always leads to non-linear distortions with increasing incident angles towards this normal. The computation of close to reality distortions gets even severe if one is looking through a naturally wavy water surface. Such a more complex surface cannot be represented by a single surface normal for refraction computation. A commonly realizable refractive effect of water is a magnification of objects. This magnification is a result of objects being seen closer to the observer as they are in reality. For perspective projection this means that points on a virtual object, non-ambiguously related to points on the real object, seem to be mapped (see Fig. 4). This virtual location of object points is proposed to lie exactly on the refractive surface's normal through the real object point as partly stated in [7] and experimentally confirmed by [21].

A special phenomenon called Snell's window or optical manhole occurs, when the viewer is looking from inside the water body to above the surface [41]. In contrast to the aforementioned cases, the refractive index gets bigger at the transition from air to water. Hence, light rays get compressed to the circular region of a bottom of a view cone. Regions on the outside of this view cone are either dark or recognizable reflections of the underwater environment.

The second aspect differing from conditions in air is visibility underwater. Its peculiarity is comparable to haze in air with an additional characteristic color cast. The color cast is a result of the water's capability to absorb light wavelength-dependent. While longer wavelengths of visible light (red to yellow) are absorbed after reaching only a few meters in water, the shorter wavelengths (green to blue) penetrate the water body the most. This leads to the typical water color. Differences amount due to the local constituents of water. Besides the absorption capabilities of water itself, local constituents, with their own absorption capabilities, contribute to the overall absorption of the water body. Hence, locally different color casts arise, like the very blue water color in the

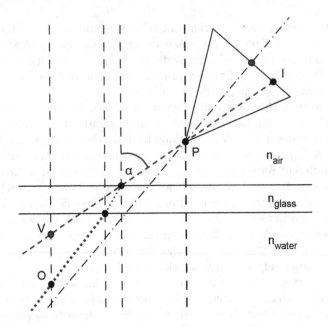

Fig. 4. Refraction of a light ray emanating from object point O on its way into the camera and the corresponding virtual point V (Color figure online)

Red Sea and on the contrary, the green color of the Baltic Sea. Some organic constituents lead to an observable, continuous flow called marine snow.

This restricted penetration of light in water is called attenuation. Besides absorption, attenuation is influenced by the scattering capabilities of the water body. It comprises diffraction and refraction. Scattering can be further divided into forward scatter and backscatter [31]. Its effects can be compared to using car headlights in fog. Following [31], image formation is a process of a linear superposition of backscatter, forward scatter and a direct component reaching the imaged objects from the light source. This model for image formation, or any other model considering all the aforementioned factors influencing underwater visibility, has to be taken as a basis for rendering close to reality underwater images.

The last aspect representing a difference to conditions in air is the appearance of characteristic illumination artifacts. Wavy water surfaces can lead to light refractions that converge and result in so called sunlight flicker on the bottom of the sea. These are bright light patterns in an irregular and fast varying arrangement.

Obviously, there are various factors that heavily influence the perception of images in underwater settings. We do not only have to take this in consideration for presenting virtual objects to the user but also when analyzing or interpreting underwater images - as we need it for example in the case of optical tracking.

Wireless Communication. In conventional virtual environments we find a variety of interaction concepts, such as gesture based interaction, flight sticks, Personal Interaction Panel or mobile devices (e.g., smartphones) for navigation and manipulation in the virtual world. Most of the techniques rely on 6 degrees of freedom (DOF) tracking of devices as an essential part of picking objects or describe gestures. In underwater settings, electromagnetic tracking will not work at all and optical tracking is much more difficult, as described in the previous section. Furthermore, Bluetooth will not work and WiFi signal strength is decreased due to the attenuation of the radio waves. One can easily verify this with a waterproof smart phone.

Tracking. Besides the limitations in wireless communication, we also have the problem of tracking. The positions of the Global Positioning System cannot be used and magnetic tracking systems may not work effectively. So we can only rely on optical or acoustic systems for tracking the user - with all the drawbacks of their robustness, fidelity and latency in underwater settings. Especially the robustness against changing light conditions remains a challenge for practical use in outdoor settings [46].

Harsh Conditions. If we put technical equipment underwater, we have to deal with some obvious technical challenges:

- We have to carefully shield the sensitive parts (especially all electric and electronic components) against the water. Equipment that is protected against the effects of continuous immersion in water is classified as International Protection Marking IPX8.
- According to the depth of the water, we have to safeguard the technical systems from the growing pressure.
- Equipment used in salty water has to be protected against corrosion.
- All materials that are exposed to (natural) water for a longer period will be subject to marine biofouling. This will not be relevant for most of the parts of the equipment but affects the optical parts such as displays or cameras.

3.2   Human Factors Challenges

Usability. Although usability guidelines for graphical user interfaces are very well defined and 3D user interfaces and VRs design guidelines are becoming more well defined, the usability of VEs underwater is not well understood. It is not clear if many of the guidelines used in air-based environments will still enable usable interfaces in an underwater environment. Consider that the usability of air-based VEs has been studied for over 30 years and is still being investigated as new interface and display technology is developed. Thus, the challenge here is the amount of empirical work it will take to derive usability guidelines for underwater VE interface design.

Ergonomics. As far as we know, there have not been any study of ergonomics for underwater applications of Mixed Reality so far. Similar to conventional MR environments there are several challenges when we try to (partially) replace the real world by a virtual world that does not have the same resolution and consistent behaviour. Due to the fact that especially the tracking problem is much harder to solve in an UWME and that wireless communication typically has more latency will make those studies even more important.

Relative to the study of healthy users in VEs, users with disabilities have always been significantly understudied. This is largely due to the variable nature of disabilities and the limited numbers of users with disabilities, making it difficult to conduct studies with a homogeneous population at an acceptable sample size. Moreover, it is unclear how users with disabilities would interact with an underwater VE. We already know that disabled persons may experience presence differently in an air-based VE. Thus, even if it was known how healthy persons interact with underwater VEs and we had derived the associated usability guidelines, it would be of minimal help towards understanding how many users with disabilities interact with VEs underwater. That is, the wide variability of disabilities will be a difficult challenge to overcome.

An additional challenge has been that VEs have traditionally been large installations, requiring the users with disabilities to come to a VE lab or rehabilitation clinic to use the equipment. This has begun to change with the advent of inexpensive VE hardware, such as the Microsoft Kinect and the Oculus Rift. However, with underwater VEs, regardless of the advances in hardware, most people do not have a pool in their backyard, which will require them to go to a local gym where the equipment can be used.

In a sense, the underwater VEs could be difficult to access installations, much like the high end VEs have been, thereby limiting their usage and study. Thus, the study of underwater VEs will be challenging, due to the logistical issues with being co-located with a pool.

4 Towards Implementation of UWME

4.1 Available Building Blocks

Controlling Color Cast. Depending on the setup and the application, we have the need to correct or simulate water-induced color cast in context of a UWME. This allows us to generate a realistic impression or improve the quality of acquired images, e.g. for optical tracking.

There are several algorithms to correct the color cast induced by the attenuation of the light depending on the different wave lengths. They go beyond a simple white balance and take into account the physical behaviour of light in underwater settings [30].

There a two possible solutions to integrate color cast correction in an UWME. First, it can be used as an amplifier for the display module. With a knowledge of the distance between underwater display and the user and some parameters of the medium we can especially raise the red and yellow frequencies. Second it could be used at the receptor side - either for a human being or a tracking system. Here we have to restore the attenuated frequencies of the spectrum to restore the original color distribution.

Distortion Correction. Distortion correction for underwater images differs severely from distortion correction in air. Distortion in air is a result of non-ideal projection capabilities of real lenses. It is dependent on the type of lens used, ranging from wide-angle, normal, to long-focus, all producing different amounts of distortion. Another factor is the quality of manufacturing of the single lens or respectively the lens-system. Distortion is most noticeable as radial effect producing pincushion to barrel distortions.

Besides radial distortion of real lenses, distortion in underwater imaging is additionally affected by a refractive interface. Light rays are refracted on their way into the camera (water-glass-air transition). This leads to noticeable distortions. The most common refractive interfaces are flat or domed ports. Flat interfaces lead to effects like radial distortion and the different refractive indexes of the participating media lead to an unintended magnification of objects in water. Domed ports are supposed to eliminate effects of flat interfaces, leaving just the magnification problem. The possible combination of lens type and interface type results in different non-linear distortions in underwater imaging.

Distortion underwater is additionally affected by the position of the camera to the refractive interface. For distortion correction, it is needed to compute the respective incidence angle of every pixel's ray. When this is known, a mapping with refractive distortion compensation should be possible. This mapping has to be a combination with in air distortion correction from camera calibration.

Underwater Communication. Wireless communication based on high frequency radio waves will not bridge more than 25 cm underwater due to the strong attenuation of the waves [48]. This means that wireless connections such as WiFi or Bluetooth will practically not work in an underwater setting. Acoustic waves have a long range in water but suffer from high latency and poor bandwidth. As described in [55] a short range underwater acoustic channel can only transfer 20–50 kbps with a latency of ∼300 ms. Furthermore, acoustic communication modems are error-prone in shallow waters. For usage in the context of coupling an interaction device with the Mixed reality system this would not be a good choice.

This makes optical connections the better choice. Although limited to short distances and depending on the turbidity of the water, especially in blue/green light wavelengths, offer an adequate alternative [3]. The light propagates much faster and by this avoids the high latencies. However, the optical communication needs a direct line of sight which cannot be assured in interactive scenarios.

Physical Protection. Protecting electrical, electronic or optical components for underwater operation is a standard offer of specialized suppliers. The traditional way of using waterproof housings for all the equipment to be used underwater is now complemented by the concept of pressure neutral systems, where the components are embedded in silicon. First research for this approach has been done in the 1970s [6] and it has a revival now for the lightweight design of underwater vehicles [56]. However, those housings make the technical equipment more expensive and sometimes difficult to handle.

4.2 Future Research

As already discussed, we see plenty of useful application areas for UWME. However, to exploit the potential of UWME for marine research, training, assistance and rehabilitation, we need further research in the following areas:

- Human factor research in UWME.
- Usability of devices for underwater usage (displays, interaction etc.) that take into account diving equipment and also people with disabilities.
- Fast and accurate underwater tracking.
- Reducing latency in underwater wireless communication.
- Robust underwater equipment to set up UWME.
- Systematic approaches for design, test and operation of UWME.
- Reusable building blocks for fast implementation of UWME.

In order to develop solutions that work in practice, it is absolutely necessary to form interdisciplinary teams that combine the expertise of visual computing, the specific application area and underwater technology.

Acknowledgments. The authors wish to thank all the participants in the session on Unconventional Mixed Environments of the Dagstuhl seminar 2013 on Virtual Realities [11] for their valuable contributions to the topic. Furthermore, the authors would like to thank the anonymous reviewers for their suggestions and comments.

References

1. Abramson, C.I., Buckbee, D.A., Edwards, S., Bowe, K.: A demonstration of virtual reality in free-flying honeybees: Apis mellifera. Physiol. Behav. **59**(1), 39–43 (1996)
2. Alankus, G., Lazar, A., May, M., Kelleher, C.: Towards customizable games for stroke rehabilitation. In: CHI, pp. 2113–2122. ACM (2010)
3. Anguita, D., Brizzolara, D., Parodi, G.: Building an underwater wireless sensor network based on optical: communication: research challenges and current results. In: Third International Conference on Sensor Technologies and Applications, 2009. SENSORCOMM 2009, pp. 476–479, June 2009
4. Armutlu, K., Karabudak, R., Nurlu, G.: Physiotherapy approaches in the treatment of ataxic multiple sclerosis: a pilot study. Neurorehabilitation Neural Repair **15**(3), 203 (2001)
5. Baram, Y., Miller, A.: Virtual reality cues for improvement of gait in patients with multiple sclerosis. Neurology **66**(2), 178 (2006)
6. Barnes, H.E., Gennari, J.J.: A review of pressure-tolerant electronics (pte) (1976)

7. Bartlett, A.A.: Note on a common virtual image. Am. J. Phys. **52**(7), 640 (1984)
8. Beckhaus, S., Kruijff, E.: Unconventional human computer interfaces. In: ACM SIGGRAPH 2004 Course Notes, p. 18. ACM, Los Angeles (2004)
9. Bellarbi, A., Domingues, C., Otmane, S., Benbelkacem, S., Dinis, A.: Augmented reality for underwater activities with the use of the dolphyn. In: 2013 10th IEEE International Conference on Networking, Sensing and Control, ICNSC 2013, pp. 409–412 (2013)
10. Betker, A.L., Desai, A., Nett, C., Kapadia, N., Szturm, T.: Game-based exercises for dynamic short-sitting balance rehabilitation of people with chronic spinal cord and traumatic brain injuries. Phys. Ther. **87**(10), 1389 (2007)
11. Brunnett, G., Coquillart, S., van Liere, R., Welch, G.F.: Virtual realities (dagstuhl seminar 13241). Dagstuhl Rep. **3**(6), 38–66 (2013)
12. Butail, S., Chicoli, A., Paley, D.A.: Putting the fish in the fish tank: immersive vr for animal behavior experiments. In: Proceedings - IEEE International Conference on Robotics and Automation, pp. 5018–5023 (2012)
13. Callow, M.E., Callow, J.E.: Marine biofouling: a sticky problem. Biologist (London, England) **49**(1), 10–14 (2002)
14. Chapman, P., Bale, K., Drap, P.: We all live in a virtual submarine. IEEE Comput. Graphics Appl. **30**(1), 85–89 (2010)
15. Chen, T.-P.G., Kinoshita, Y., Takama, Y., Fels, S., Funahashi, K., Gadd, A.: Swimming across the pacific: a virtual swimming interface. In: ACM SIGGRAPH 2004: Emerging Technologies, SIGGRAPH 2004, p. 27 (2004)
16. Chouiten, M., Domingues, C., Didier, J.-Y., Otmane, S., Mallem, M., (eds.) Distributed mixed reality for remote underwater telerobotics exploration: ACM International Conference Proceeding Series (2012)
17. Cobb, S.V.G., Sharkey, P.M.: A decade of research and development in disability, virtual reality and associated technologies: promise or practice? In: International Conference on Disability, Virtual Reality and Associated Technologies, pp. 3–16 (2006)
18. Crosbie, J.H., Lennon, S., McGoldrick, M.C., McNeill, M.D.J., Burke, J.W., McDonough, S.M.: Virtual reality in the rehabilitation of the upper limb after hemiplegic stroke: a randomised pilot study. In: Proceedings of the 7th ICDVRAT with ArtAbilitation, Maia, Portugal, pp. 229–235 (2008)
19. da Silveira Sarmento, G., Pegoraro, A.S.N., Cordeiro, R.C.: Aquatic physical therapy as a treatment modality in healthcare for non-institutionalized elderly persons: a systematic review. Einstein (16794508) **9**(1), 84–89 (2011)
20. Davis, B.C., Patrón, P., Arredondo, M., Lane, D.M.: Augmented reality and data fusion techniques for enhanced situational awareness of the underwater domain. In: OCEANS 2007 - Europe (2007)
21. Dolereit, T., Kuijper, A.: Converting underwater imaging into imaging in air. In: Proceedings of the 9th International Conference on Computer Vision Theory and Applications, vol. 1 (2014)
22. Fletcher, B., Harris, S.: Development of a virtual environment based training system for rov pilots. In: Conference Proceedings of the OCEANS 1996. MTS/IEEE. Prospects for the 21st Century, vol. 1, pp. 65–71 (1996)
23. Flores, E., Tobon, G., Cavallaro, E., Cavallaro, F.I., Perry, J.C., Keller, T.: Improving patient motivation in game development for motor deficit rehabilitation. In: Proceedings of the 2008 International Conference on Advances in Computer Entertainment Technology, ACE 2008, pp. 381–384. ACM, New York (2008)
24. Fröhlich, T.: The virtual oceanarium. Commun. ACM **43**(7), 94–101 (2000)

25. Gehlsen, G.M., Grigsby, S.A., Winant, D.M.: Effects of an aquatic fitness program on the muscular strength and endurance of patients with multiple sclerosis. Phys. Ther. **64**(5), 653–657 (1984)
26. Glotzbach, T., Voigt, A., Pfützenreuter, T., Jacobi, M., Rauschenbach, T.: Cviewvr: a high-performance visualization tool for team-oriented missions of unmanned marine verhicles. In: Bertram, V. (ed.) 8th International Conference on Computer and IT Applications in the Maritime Industries, Compit 2009, pp. 150–164 (2009)
27. Gray, J.R., Pawlowski, V., Willis, M.A.: A method for recording behavior and multineuronal cns activity from tethered insects flying in virtual space. J. Neurosci. Methods **120**(2), 211–223 (2002)
28. Hamilton, F., Rochester, L., Paul, L., Rafferty, D., O'Leary, C.P., Evans, J.J.: Walking and talking: an investigation of cognitive-motor dual tasking in multiple sclerosis. Mult. Scler. **15**(10), 1215 (2009)
29. Haydar, M., Roussel, D., Maïdi, M., Otmane, S., Mallem, M.: Virtual and augmented reality for cultural computing and heritage: a case study of virtual exploration of underwater archaeological sites (preprint). virtual reality **15**(4), 311–327 (2011)
30. Henke, B., Vahl, M., Zhou, Z.: Removing color cast of underwater images through non-constant color constancy hypothesis. In: International Symposium on Image and Signal Processing and Analysis, ISPA, pp. 20–24 (2013)
31. Jaffe, J.S.: Computer modeling and the design of optimal underwater imaging systems. IEEE J. Oceanic Eng. **15**(2), 101–111 (1990)
32. Jaffe, J.S., Laxton, B., Zylinski, S.: The sub sea holodeck: a 14-megapixel immersive virtual environment for studying cephalopod camouflage behavior. In: OCEANS 2011 IEEE - Spain (2011)
33. Jiang, S.: Electromagnetic wave propagation into fresh water. J. Electromagn. Anal. Appl. **03**(07), 261–266 (2011)
34. Jorgensen, R.: Slow steaming: The full story. AP Moller-Maersk Group, Copenhagen (2011)
35. Jung, S., Choi, Y.-S., Choi, J.-S., Koo, B.-K., Lee, W.H.: Immersive virtual aquarium with real-walking navigation. In: Proceedings - VRCAI 2013: 12th ACM SIGGRAPH International Conference on Virtual-Reality Continuum and Its Applications in Industry, pp. 291–294 (2013)
36. Kawamoto Jr., L.T., Slaets, A.F.F.: Software to train scuba dive procedures. Appl. Mech. Mater. **440**, 346–353 (2013)
37. Kuchenbecker, K., Gurari, N., Okamura, A.: Effects of visual and proprioceptive motion feedback on human control of targeted movement. In: Proceedings of the IEEE 10th International Conference on Rehabilitation Robotics (2007)
38. Lee, J.-M., Lee, K.-H., Kim, D.-S., Kim, C.-H.: Active insp ection supporting system based on mixed reality after design and manufacture in an offshore structure. J. Mech. Sci. Technol. **24**(1), 197–202 (2010)
39. Lin, Q., Kuo, C.: Assisting the teleoperation of an unmanned underwater vehicle using a synthetic subsea scenario. Presence Teleoperators Virtual Environ. **8**(5), 520–530 (1999)
40. von Lukas, U.: Virtual and augmented reality for the maritime sector- applications and requirements. In: IFAC Proceedings Volumes (IFAC-PapersOnline), pp. 196–200 (2010)
41. Lynch, D.K., Livingston, W.C.: Color and Light in Nature. Cambridge University Press, Cambridge (2001)

42. Merians, A.S., Poizner, H., Boian, R., Burdea, G., Adamovich, S.: Sensorimotor training in a virtual reality environment: does it improve functional recovery post-stroke? Neurorehabilitation Neural Repair **20**(2), 252 (2006)
43. Milgram, P., Kishino, F.: Taxonomy of mixed reality visual displays. IEICE Trans. Inf. Syst. **E77-d**(12), 1321–1329 (1994)
44. Morales, R., Keitler, P., Maier, P., Klinker, G.: An underwater augmented reality system for commercial diving operations. In: OCEANS 2009, MTS/IEEE Biloxi - Marine Technology for Our Future: Global and Local Challenges (2009)
45. Nassiraei, A.A.F., Sonoda, T., Ishii, K.: Development of ship hull cleaning underwater robot. In: 2012 Fifth International Conference on Emerging Trends in Engineering and Technology (ICETET), pp. 157–162, November 2012
46. Oppermann, L., Blum, L., Lee, J.-Y., Seo, J.-H.: Areef: multi-player underwater augmented reality experience. In: IEEE Consumer Electronics Society's International Games Innovations Conference, IGIC, pp. 199–202 (2013)
47. Riess, T.J.: Augmented reality in parkinson's disease. CyberPsychology Behav. **2**(3), 231–239 (1999)
48. Sendra, S., Lloret, J., Rodrigues, J.J.P.C., Aguiar, J.M.: Underwater wireless communications in freshwater at 2.4 GHz. Ieee Commun. Lett. **17**(9), 1794–1797 (2013)
49. Shen, Y., Ong, S.K., Nee, A.Y.C.: Hand rehabilitation based on augmented reality. In: Proceedings of the 3rd International Convention on Rehabilitation Engineering & Assistive Technology, i-CREATe 2009, pp. 23:1–23:4. ACM, New York (2009)
50. Smyth, M., Wann, J.: Interactive interfaces for movement rehabilitation in virtual environments. In: Proceedings of the Third International Conference Series on Disability, Virtual Reality and Associated Technologies (ICDVRAT), Alghero, Sardinia, Italy, September 2000
51. Snook, E., Motl, R.: Effect of exercise training on walking mobility in multiple sclerosis: a meta-analysis. Neurorehabilitation Neural Repair **23**(2), 108 (2009)
52. National MS Society. Who gets ms?
53. Steffin, M.: Virtual reality therapy of multiple sclerosis and spinal cord injury: design considerations for a haptic-visual interface. In: Riva, G., Wiederhold, B., Molinari, E., Wiederhold, B.K. (eds.) Virtual Reality in Neuro-psycho-physiology: Cognitive, Clinical and Methodological Issues in Assessment and Rehabilitation, p. 185. IOS Press, Amsterdam (1997)
54. Sveistrup, H.: Motor rehabilitation using virtual reality. J. NeuroEngineering Rehabil. **1**(1), 10 (2004)
55. Syed, A.A., Heidemann, J.: Time synchronization for high latency acoustic networks. In: INFOCOM 2006. Proceedings of the 25th IEEE International Conference on Computer Communications, pp. 1–12, April 2006
56. Thiede, C., Buscher, M., Lück, M., Lehr, H., Körner, G., Martin, J., Schlichting, M., Krüger, S., Huth, H.: An overall pressure tolerant underwater vehicle: Dns pegel. In: OCEANS 2009 IEEE Bremen: Balancing Technology with Future Needs (2009)
57. Trivedi, C.A., Bollmann, J.H.: Visually driven chaining of elementary swim patterns into a goal-directed motor sequence: a virtual reality study of zebrafish prey capture. Front. Neural Circuits 86 p. (2013). doi:10.3389/fncir.2013.00086
58. Troy, M.I.: Virtual health and safety could be the answer for infrequent tasks. Virtual Manufacturing for Real Savings column, DELMIA World News, no. 7 (2003)
59. Vasilijević, A., Borović, B., Vukić, Z.: Augmented reality in marine applications: Primjene proširene stvarnosti u pomorstvu. Brodogradnja **62**(2), 136–142 (2011)

60. Wang, J., Ma, Y.: Testing-oriented simulator for autonomous underwater vehicles. In: Sun, Z., Deng, Z. (eds.) Proceedings of 2013 Chinese Intelligent Automation Conference. LNEE, pp. 289–297. Springer, Heidelberg (2013)

61. Wang, J., Zhan, R., Liu, X.: Virtual reality-based forward looking sonar simulation. In: Sun, Z., Deng, Z. (eds.) Proceedings of 2013 Chinese Intelligent Automation Conference. LNEE, pp. 299–308. Springer, Heidelberg (2013)

62. Wang, Y., Chen, Y., Zhang, W., Liu, D., Huang, H.: Study on underwater wet arc welding training with haptic device. In: 2009 IEEE International Conference on Virtual Environments, Human-Computer Interfaces, and Measurements Systems, VECIMS 2009 - Proceedings, pp. 191–195 (2009)

63. Ware, C., Arthur, K., Booth, K.S.: Fish tank virtual reality. In: Proceedings of the Conference on Human Factors in Computing Systems, pp. 37–42 (1993)

64. Wiesmann, A.: Slow steaming-a viable long-term option? Wartsila Tech. J. 2, 49–55 (2010)

65. Zotz, T.G.G., Souza, E.A., Israel, V.L., Loureiro, A.P.C.: Aquatic physical therapy for parkinson disease. Adv. Parkinson's Dis. 2, 102 (2013)

Interaction and User Experience

A Critical Analysis of Human-Subject Experiments in Virtual Reality and 3D User Interfaces

Carlos Andujar[✉] and Pere Brunet

ViRVIG-MOVING Research Group, Universitat Politècnica de Catalunya,
Jordi Girona 1-3, 08034 Barcelona, Spain
andujar@lsi.upc.edu

Abstract. This paper is about the major peculiarities and difficulties we encounter when trying to validate research results in fields such as virtual reality (VR) and 3D user interfaces (3DUI). We review the steps in the empirical method and discuss a number of challenges when conducting human-subject experiments. These challenges include the number of independent variables to control to get useful findings, the within-subjects or between-subjects dilemma, hard-to-collect data, experimenter effects, ethical issues, and the lack of background in the community for proper statistical analysis and interpretation of the results. We show that experiments involving human-subjects hinder the adoption of traditional experimental principles (comparison, repeatability, reproducibility, justification and explanation) and propose some ideas to improve the reliability of findings in VR and 3DUI disciplines.

Keywords: Experimentation · Virtual reality · 3D user interfaces

1 Introduction

A substantial part of the knowledge in science and engineering fields comes in the form of findings supported by experimental research. In contrast to correlational studies, experimentation allows researchers to make strong claims about causality, and is thus one of the key methodologies that sustain the development of science and engineering. Unlike pure observation, experimentation is, in essence, controlled experience, and as such it involves actions to manipulate, in a controlled manner, some of the variables involved in the phenomena under investigation.

Experimentation has been used for years in both science and engineering fields, although addressing different objects and for different purposes. In science, the goal of experimentation is to *understand* a natural phenomenon, whereas in engineering the goal is *test* a man-made artifact. We can thus distinguish multiple types of experiments (Table 1) according to the subjects under investigation (natural objects, man-made artifacts and humans). Notice that we have included

© Springer International Publishing Switzerland 2015
G. Brunnett et al. (Eds.): Virtual Realities, LNCS 8844, pp. 79–90, 2015.
DOI: 10.1007/978-3-319-17043-5_5

Virtual Reality (VR) experiments in a special category, along with Human-Computer Interaction (HCI), 3D user interfaces (3DUI) [5] and disciplines alike. VR has a dual nature in the sense that it shares goals and methodologies from both science and engineering. We are interested both in understanding some aspects of human-related phenomena (e.g. human perception, human performance) as well as to test VR-related artifacts (e.g. software, hardware, interaction techniques), although the relative weights of these two goals vary across subfields. This dual nature implies that experimentation in VR has to deal with the inherent complexities of two worlds: that of the technical artifacts being tested, and that of the humans that test these artifacts. As we shall see, the resulting complexity often limits severely the generalizability of findings from VR experiments.

The key role of human-subject experiments in VR and 3DUI fields is evidenced by the large number of papers thoroughly reporting such experiments in major conferences and journals. It is therefore natural to ask ourselves questions such as: are we doing experimentation in VR the right way? Are the findings of published papers on VR supported by solid evidence? If so, are these findings really useful? How should experiments be documented? In this paper we treat some of these questions by discussing the major peculiarities and challenges of human-subject experiments in VR and 3DUI fields. We show that experiments involving human-subjects hinder the adoption of traditional experimental principles (comparison, repeatability, reproducibility) and propose some ideas to improve the reliability of findings in VR and 3DUI disciplines. We argue that there is a lack of background on experimental research in a large part of our community, and that fundamental ideas of the experimental method should be included in the curricula of computer science students like in all other science curricula. The conclusions are partially based on some discussions of the Dagstuhl Seminar 13241 *Virtual Realities*, June 9th–14th 2013, Dagstuhl.

Table 1. Types of experiments according to the entities under investigation.

Subject	Disciplines
Natural objects (excluding humans)	Natural sciences
Artifacts	Engineering
Humans	Social sciences
Artifacts' use by humans	Human factors, ergonomics, HCI, VR...

2   Experimentation in Related Disciplines

VR teams often bring together professionals from multiple disciplines, including formal sciences (e.g. mathematicians, statisticians), social sciences (e.g. psychologists) and engineering (e.g. computer scientists). However, the concept of experimentation, its methodology, and the aspects that distinguish good experiments from bad experiments vary substantially across these disciplines.

From a scientific point of view, experiments should obey the classical principles of comparison, repeatability, reproducibility, justification and explanation [1]. *Comparison* refers to the possibility of knowing similar research already done in the past, to avoid repeating uninteresting experiments and to get insights on worthy ones. *Repeatability* is the property of an experiment that yields consistent results when repeated in the experimenter's own setup at different times and in different places. *Reproducibility* is the possibility for independent researchers to verify the results of a given experiment by repeating it with similar conditions. Achieving reproducibility is much harder than repeatability because it requires researchers to document thoroughly the experimental setup and to expose all variables that might bias the experiment. *Justification* and *explanation* refer to the possibility of drawing well justified conclusions based on all the collected data.

Experimental research in natural and social sciences most often follow these principles. Psychology experiments, for example, adopt these principles through rigorous protocols. In contrast, experimental methodologies in computer science have not yet reached the level of maturity of other scientific disciplines. Despite its wide-spread use, experimentation is still one of the less well-understood methodologies in computer science, and computer scientists do not seem to agree on the role and relevance of experiments in their field [1]. Whether classic experimentation principles should also apply to computer science experiments is still under discussion [1].

3   Sample Problems from VR

Let us introduce a couple of problems that will help us to illustrate the need for running controlled experiments in VR research. These examples will be used through the text to exemplify major difficulties encountered in VR experiments. The first example is the evaluation of presence in VR systems, that is, to which extent users feel and behave as if physically present in a virtual world. Users of immersive systems might forget about the real environment and the virtual environment can become the dominant reality. The evaluation of presence is very important in many VR applications, from phobia therapies to psychological experiments through pain relief for patients with serious injuries. Many presence evaluation studies report surprising findings when analyzing the human behavior when presented a stress situation in a virtual environment [10,11]. Nowadays, the common practice is to evaluate presence by observing users' behavior and measuring their physiological response (as captured by specialized devices such as heart rate monitors and galvanic skin sensors) in a controlled experiment. The use of unconventional measurement devices might hinder participant recruitment and data collection.

The second example is about the comparison of 3D UIs in terms of their usability. Figure 1 shows three different user interfaces to solve a 3D puzzle [14], using either a physical puzzle, a classic keyboard-and-mouse interface, or a Wii controller. For this task, users must be able to select pieces, manipulate them, and explore the puzzle from different viewpoints. The key problem thus is to

Fig. 1. Different interfaces for a puzzle-solving problem.

determine which UI is better in terms of usability. The only way to know the answer is through a controlled experiment comparing these techniques. Despite some models have been proposed to predict human performance for some tasks (the well known Fitts' law [9] is the most notable example), typical spatial tasks are just too complex to be predicted by such simple models.

4   Major Challenges in VR Experiments

The typical steps of experimental methods are shown below (the list has been adapted from [12] to refer explicitly to experiments involving human subjects):

1. Formulate a hypothesis and make it testable
2. Design an experiment
3. Get approval by ethics committee
4. Recruit participants
5. Conduct the experiment and collect data
6. Pay participants
7. Analyze the data
8. Accept or refute the hypothesis
9. Explain the results
10. If worthy, communicate your findings

The list above will serve to guide the discussion about some major challenges in human-subject experiments for VR and 3DUI not found in other types of experiments.

4.1   Hypothesis Formulation

A first step is to formulate a hypothesis and make it testable. Using the 3D puzzle problem as an example, a general hypothesis might be formulated as follows:

Using the Wii controller will make people more effective when doing manipulation tasks.

A possible testable version of it could be formulated as:

We measured the time it takes for users to solve a particular 3D puzzle, using either Wii or mouse; we hypothesize that users will be faster using the Wii.

Here we find a first major problem: to make the hypothesis testable, we had to choose a particular task which we take as representative (besides fixing some other important variables). Unfortunately, many problems have a task space so large and heterogeneous that it can be really difficult to find a small set of representative tasks. Here we wrote *task* for the 3D puzzle example, but we could have written 3D model, image, movie, stimulus and whatever other elements are fixed to make the hypothesis testable. As a result, a large body of findings in VR and 3DUI only apply to very specific conditions, and it is unclear if the results can be generalized to other contexts. As an example, many interaction techniques for 3D selection have been tested with a single scene attempting to mimic a *typical* real-world scene, but no single 3D scene is really representative of the huge variety of scenarios we encounter in real 3D applications. Some other selection techniques have been tested with synthetic, well-controlled scenes (e.g. varying object size, position and density) and thus provide more insights on which factors influence user performance, but even in these cases many other variables need to be fixed arbitrarily to keep the experiment complexity within reasonable limits.

4.2 Experiment Design

A key aspect of experiment design is to decide which variables will be varied systematically (independent variables or factors) and which variables will be measured (dependent variables). Consider for example the 3D puzzle task. The completion time for a 3D puzzle (dependent variable) might be influenced by a number of variables including the interaction device (Wii, mouse), the viewing conditions (stereoscopic, mono), the mapping between user actions and application tasks, the size of the pieces, and the quality of the graphics [4]. Complex VR setups are incredibly hard to specify, and it is hard to define a set of 'normal conditions' for the ceteris paribus assumption. In an ideal world, VR systems would have zero end-to-end latency, ghosting-free stereo separation, no accommodation-convergence mismatch, accurate, encumbrance-free full-body tracking, natural locomotion and many other features beyond the state-of-the-art. Current VR systems are thus suboptimal to a certain degree, and the best hardware configuration is unclear, making the prediction of user behavior even more difficult.

These facts would suggest trying to control a large number of variables, but as the number of independent variables (and the corresponding levels at which they occur) increases, the number of conditions for a complete factorial design increases rapidly. Therefore, despite the large number of variables that might bias the outcome of a VR experiment, considering more than five or six independent variables is often unpractical, prompting investigators to seek alternative designs that require fewer conditions [6].

Experiment reproducibility is certainly a hard task in VR. The use of non-conventional, rapidly evolving displays, tracking, haptics, props and other specialized devices hinders experiment reproducibility. In some extreme cases, the VR hardware being tested is so sophisticated that, in practice, the experiment cannot be reproduced by independent researchers. Furthermore, VR hardware platforms are hardly ever selected according to an analysis of requirements; instead, hardware selection is influenced by already purchased hardware, prior expertise, available resources and compatibility factors, leaving little opportunities to run the experiment on multiple hardware configurations [16]. From the point of view of software development, VR systems are often 'complex, chaotic and difficult' [16], and VR developer communities are separated by tools that hinder code reuse and shared implementations.

Another important aspect of experiment design concerns the assignment of independent variables. Independent variables can vary in two ways: within-subjects (each participant sees all levels) and between-subjects (each participant sees only one level). The decision on which design is better to confirm or refute a given hypothesis is often controversial. Within-subject designs are more time consuming for the participants, and require the experimenter to counterbalance for carry-over effects (the order of presentation might influence the participant behavior) such as fatigue and learning effects. Between-subject designs, on the other hand, are not free from limitations, as more participants need to be recruited and we are likely to loose statistical power during Null Hypothesis Significance Testing (NHST), and thus have less chances to proof our hypothesis. Within-subject designs are usually preferred in HCI experiments because having fewer participants overall simplify recruiting, scheduling, briefing, demonstrating and practicing [8], and because it is easier to detect differences across levels because each subject's behavior under one condition is compared to that subject's behavior under the other condition.

4.3 Ethics

Many usability guides address in depth all the ethical issues related with user studies [2,7]. Most organizations require experimenters to get the approval by an ethics committee before running the experiment. After the approval, it is often a hard task to recruit participants and get their informed consent, in particular when participants should be chosen from a specific target user group (such as physicians for VR medical application).

Experiments involving immersive VR systems often need a detailed informed consent. Researchers should never deceive participants about aspects that would affect their willingness to participate, such as risks (VR users might bump into walls, trip over cables), discomfort (many 3D interaction techniques for spatial tasks are physically demanding) and unpleasant experiences (some VR systems cause motion sickness). Frustration handling is also important when measuring user performance. In case of failure to complete a task, experimenters should make it clear that the responsible is the technology. Usability tests should not be perceived as tests of the participant's abilities [7].

4.4 Running the Experiment and Collecting Data

Wingrave and LaViola summarize multiple VR issues that can impact scheduled appointments and impact experiment repeatability [16]. VR systems are still not robust; some specialized VR hardware such as data gloves are fragile and might stop working, some projectors might go out of alignment, cables tangle, and cluster rendering is less robust than single-machine rendering.

Data collection is a further issue in typical VR applications. At the lowest level, a classic WIMP interface requires tracking a single pointing device whose position can be described by a stream of (x,y) values. In contrast, VR interfaces often requires 6-DoF tracking of multiple body parts. Although some dependent variables can be measured easily (e.g. task completion times, error counts, scores), some VR experiments need to measure hard-to-collect data such as user heart rate variability and galvanic skin response.

Pilot experiments are often required prior to running the main VR experiment because many issues cannot be identified until participants experience the VR system. Besides software and hardware affordances, the multisensory nature of VR experiences hinders the prediction of human factors such as fatigue, stress, and nausea, that should be detected in pilot experiments [16].

Experimenters should be careful to avoid manipulating the experiment. In addition to the well known placebo effect, there are other experimenter issues that often hinder data collection. The Hawthorne effect occurs when increased attention from superiors or colleagues increases user performance. The performance of a participant might change if somebody else, e.g. the previous participant, is observing. Observer-expectancy effect occurs when the researcher unconsciously manipulates the experiment, using e.g. body language. Experiments should be double-blind, but researchers in non-life critical fields often disregard these issues.

4.5 Data Analysis and Explanation

Proper data analysis is absolutely required to accept or refute the hypothesis and to provide statistical evidence of the findings. The usual statistical procedure is to run Null-Hypothesis Significance Testing (NHST) to compute a p-value that expresses the conditional probability of getting an outcome as extreme as or even more extreme than what we observed, assuming the null hypothesis holds. The p-value p is compared against a previously-defined significance level α (often 0.05). If $p < \alpha$, we reject the null hypothesis H_0 and embrace H_1 (thus we get a result). Otherwise, we fail to reject H_0 and conclude that there is no evidence in the data to confirm H_1. Since NHST is well-known to be biased by sample size (i.e. with a sufficiently large sample we can detect statistically significant differences even when such differences are really tiny), a measure of the effect size should be included in the experiment report.

Unfortunately, a part of the VR community seems to lack enough background on experimental design and statistical analysis to conduct the user studies required to evaluate their own research. This is evidenced by the large number of submitted and even published papers with serious evaluation errors related with the statistical analysis of the results (see next section). Unlike other disciplines like medicine, where journal editors often send manuscripts to expert statistical reviewers to check the statistical analysis, this is no common practice in major VR journals.

Experimenters are expected to provide a plausible explanation of the observed data and to draw well justified conclusions based on the experiment findings. The explanation should rely on widely accepted guidelines and theories. Due to the multidisciplinary nature of VR experiments, plausible explanations might require acquaintance with theories from a variety of fields (e.g. perceptual, cognitive, social and cultural psychology, control theory, ergonomics, biomechanics, proxemics...) beyond the experimenter expertise. These experiments would greatly benefit from feedback provided by other members of the VR community, but papers with poorly explained outcomes have little options to be accepted for publication and this reduces the opportunities to get such a feedback.

4.6   Reporting the Experiment

Documenting an experiment is a substantial task within experimental research, and one of the issues most frequently criticized by reviewers. A typical report would include detailed information about the hypotheses being tested, the experiment design, the procedure, apparatus, participants, and statistical analysis.

The way data analyses are reported in VR should not differ much from other disciplines, but in practice the VR community does not seem to demand the same level of rigor found in other disciplines. The American Psychological Association provides well-established protocols and guidelines for reporting experiments on social and behavioral sciences [3]. Unfortunately, no such protocol exists for VR papers and alike; although some authors do follow to some extent some of these guidelines, a large body of VR literature still reports data analysis in a nonstandard, often incomplete manner.

Besides data analysis, the description of the experiment setup itself is another widely criticized aspect. We have already argued about the extraordinary complexity of VR experiments, which have to deal with (complex, immature, imperfect, fragile, heterogeneous) technical artifacts, as well as with many aspects of human phenomena (perception, cognition, human factors...). As a consequence, the number and variety of variables potentially influencing the outcome of a VR experiment is often beyond reasonable complexity limits. Experimenters are thus faced with a hard dilemma: if too few details about the experiment setup are reported, the experiment will be far from being reproducible; if too many details are included, this might result in an overly long paper, a large portion of it would be of interest only for those researchers aiming to reproduce the experiment. In such cases, experiment reproducibility must be seen as a goal rather than a strict requirement to be enforced during reviewing.

Concerning the information about the participants, it has been shown that humans vary widely in their ability to perform tasks in VR environments [16]. Besides age, gender and education, demographics and cognitive aptitudes can also account for variance [15]. For example, a new interaction technique might prove to outperform competing techniques on young gamers but not on older adults. Unfortunately, there is no de-facto standard for reporting such information about participants, making results difficult to generalize.

5   Common Errors in Submitted Papers

Precise criteria for deciding which VR papers should include results from a human-subject experiment and which should not is out of the scope of this paper, although obviously we can find examples of papers where such a validation does not apply or it is unnecessary (e.g. rendering papers with strongly convincing visual results), as well as examples where validation through a controlled experiment should be enforced (most papers on new interaction techniques fall into this category). We now summarize some common experimentation-related errors found in submitted (and sometimes published) VR papers.

A first error is the lack of inferential analysis; some manuscripts include graphs and descriptive statistics but draw conclusions directly from the raw comparison of summary statistics (e.g. simple mean comparison). Although in some fields hypothesis testing is culturally unnecessary provided that plots convincingly show enough power [13], most experiments have outcomes with subtle effect sizes and do require proper statistical analysis.

A second common error is improper hypothesis formulation. Before describing an experiment, it is important to state clearly its purpose in terms of one or more hypotheses. Continuing with the 3D puzzle example, consider the following hypothesis:

We measure the time it takes for subjects to solve a particular 3D puzzle under Wii and mouse conditions. We hypothesize that users will be slower with the Wii controller due to the lack of a physical support for free space interaction.

What is wrong with the hypothesis above is that it includes both a testable hypothesis (Wii slower) and one of the many plausible explanations for it; NHST could confirm the first part, but not the second (unless we manage to vary systematically the physical support condition).

Now consider this hypothesis:

The stereo condition (mono/stereo) has no influence on user performance.

The problem here is that NHST can be used to detect significant differences between conditions (i.e. confirm the alternative hypothesis) but not to prove the truth of the null hypothesis. We could, however, test if the difference between means is below some effect size threshold [13].

Another common error is to choose the wrong statistical test to analyze the data. It is not uncommon to find manuscripts analyzing within-subjects data with a classic (independent-samples) t-test or ANOVA instead of using the repeated-measures version of these tests. Even when the right test is chosen, the ANOVA table is often miss-constructed. For example, consider a between-subjects version of the 3D puzzle example. With n subjects and m trials per subject we get $n \times m$ measures. These m trials, however, need to be aggregated per participant before running the ANOVA. Running the ANOVA with $n \times m$ rows violates the assumption of independence and ruins the analysis. Experimenters should always report the parameters of the sampling distribution so that reviewers could double-check for these errors. For example, when running an ANOVA test, the two parameters of the F-distribution must be reported [12].

Many manuscripts also forget to check the assumptions underlying the chosen statistical test, or at least forget to report it. A last and more serious mistake concerns the interpretation of p-values. Failure to reject the null hypothesis does not imply the null hypothesis is true, although this fundamental mistake can be found in many manuscripts containing no power analysis at all. For example, the following outcome report is misleading:

We found no significant effect of interaction technique on completion time. Therefore we conclude both techniques perform equally well.

6   Conclusions

In the last decades some computer science disciplines such as VR are experiencing a shift of focus from *implementing the technology* to *using the technology*, and validation through experimentation is becoming critical. In this paper we have discussed some major issues of such validation experiments: lack of background on experimentation, psychology and psychophysics, time-consuming and resource-consuming nature of human-subject experiments, and the difficulties to fulfill all requirements (double-blind experiments, informed consent, representative users, representative datasets/models/tasks, reproducibility).

The user performance during a typical computer-related task depends on a number of domain-specific factors as well as hardware-related factors. Considering all these factors simultaneously as independent variables in controlled experiments is clearly not practical. This fact limits the validity of the findings reported in the VR literature to a specific domain and a particular setup. The lack of protocols and de-facto standard datasets for testing purposes (more common in other scientific communities) along with the plethora of VR hardware configurations makes it difficult to make fair comparisons. Furthermore, many techniques are still proposed and evaluated in isolation, whereas in the real world user tasks are mixed with other tasks. These are issues that must still be addressed.

Although guaranteeing reproducibility of VR experiments is often unfeasible or impractical, researchers should take some steps to facilitate fair comparisons. One way of doing this is by sharing code and data so that other researchers can verify the results by repeating the experiment with the same or similar conditions. In this sense the concepts of reproducible research and executable papers (which are being promoted by some publishers) is quite promising. Reproducible research refers to the idea that academic papers should include not only text, tables and figures, but also a complete environment including code, models and data, that can be used to reproduce the results and to create new work based on the research. Nevertheless, non-standard VR hardware configurations still limit reproducibility under identical conditions. Experimenters should also be careful to avoid manipulating experiments, although sophisticated VR equipment make double-blind experiments hard to implement.

Researchers, and in particular journal editors and reviewers, should enforce correct data analysis and experiment reporting. Papers with serious experimental flaws should not be accepted for publication, as they contain unreliable findings and can mislead novice researchers who might follow mistaken experimental procedures.

Finally, our recommendation for VR professionals, researchers and students is to ensure a strong education on the principles of sound experimentation with human subjects. In research projects, at least one of the research team members should be an expert on experiment design and statistical data analysis.

Acknowledgments. This work was greatly influenced by the contributions to the Workshop on the *Role and Relevance of Experimentation in Informatics*, held prior to the 8th European Computer Science Summit (ECSS 2012) of *Informatics Europe*, November 19th 2012, Barcelona, and the discussions of the Dagstuhl Seminar 13241 *Virtual Realities*, June 9th–14th 2013, Dagstuhl. This work has been partially funded by the Spanish Ministry of Science and Innovation under Grant TIN2010-20590-C02-01.

References

1. Andujar, C., Schiaffonati, V., Schreiber, F.A., Tanca, L., Tedre, M., van Hee, K., van Leeuwen, J.: The role and relevance of experimentation in informatics. In: Workshop on the Role and Relevance of Experimentation in Informatics, 8th European Computer Science Summit (ECSS 2012) of Informatics Europe (2012)
2. American Psychological Association: Ethical principles of psychologist and code of conduct (2010)
3. American Psychological Association: Publication Manual of the American Psychological Association, 6th edn. American Psychological Association, New York (2013)
4. Bowman, D.A., Gabbard, J.L., Hix, D.: A survey of usability evaluation in virtual environments: classification and comparison of methods. Presence Teleoper. Virtual Environ. **11**(4), 404–424 (2002)
5. Bowman, D.A., Kruijff, E., LaViola, J.J., Poupyrev, I.: 3D User Interfaces: Theory and Practice. Addison Wesley, Boston (2004)
6. Collins, L.M., Dziak, J.J., Li, R.: Design of experiments with multiple independent variables: a resource management perspective on complete and reduced factorial designs. Psychol. Methods **14**(3), 202 (2009)
7. European Telecommunications Standards Institute (ETSI): Usability evaluation for the design of telecommunication systems, services and terminals. ETSI Guide EG 201472. Sophia Antipolis (2000)
8. MacKenzie, I.S.: Human-Computer Interaction: An Empirical Research Perspective. Morgan Kaufmann, San Francisco (2013)
9. MacKenzie, I.S., Kauppinen, T., Silfverberg, M.: Accuracy measures for evaluating computer pointing devices. In: Proceedings of the SIGCHI Conference on Human Factors in Computing Systems, CHI 2001, pp. 9–16. ACM, New York (2001)
10. Meehan, M., Insko, B., Whitton, M., Brooks, F.P.: Physiological measures of presence in virtual environments. In: Proceedings of 4th International Workshop on Presence, pp. 21–23 (2001)

11. Slater, M., Antley, A., Davison, A., Swapp, D., Guger, C., Barker, C., Pistrang, N., Sanchez-Vives, M.V.: A virtual reprise of the Stanley Milgram obedience experiments. PLoS ONE **1**(1), e39 (2006)

12. Swan, J.E., Ellis, S.R., Adelstein, B.D.: Conducting human-subject experiments with virtual and augmented reality. In: 2006 Virtual Reality Conference. IEEE (2006)

13. Swan, J.E., Gabbard, J.L.: Quantitative and qualitative methods for human-subject experiments in augmented reality. In: Tutorial Presented at the International Symposium on Mixed and Augmented Reality (ISMAR 2012). IEEE (2012)

14. Takala, T.M., Pugliese, R., Rauhamaa, P., Takala, T.: Reality-based user interface system (RUIS). In: 2011 IEEE Symposium on 3D User Interfaces (3DUI), pp. 141–142. IEEE (2011)

15. Wingrave, C.A., Bowman, D.A.: Baseline factors for raycasting selection. In: Proceedings of Virtual Reality International (2005)

16. Wingrave, C.A., LaViola, J.J.: Reflecting on the design and implementation issues of virtual environments. Presence Teleoper. Virtual Environ. **19**(2), 179–195 (2010)

Mobile Devices for Virtual Reality Interaction. A Survey of Techniques and Metaphors

Jens Bauer[✉] and Achim Ebert

Computer Graphics and HCI Lab, University of Kaiserslautern,
Kaiserslautern, Germany
{j_bauer,ebert}@cs.uni-kl.de

Abstract. Virtual Reality applications run in a lot of different environments using several different input devices. This can lead to incoherent input metaphors across different environments, even using the same application. Mobile smart devices, such as smart phones and tablets can be used as alternative input devices. They can provide an uniform way of interaction, independent of the actual setting of the VR environment. Additionally, their use does scale well to the number of users in multi-user environments. This chapter presents the current State-of-the-Art in using smart devices as input devices and assesses their applicability in the field of Virtual Reality.

Keywords: Human computer interaction · Input devices · Mobile devices · VR environments

1 Introduction

Virtual Reality applications run in a multitude of environments, such as CAVEs, Powerwalls, etc. or even on simple personal computers. Some applications are targeted at one special environment, others are more general (maybe through the use of VR libraries). Due to the cost involved in creating a virtual reality environment, it is often not possible to create the ideal environment for a specific application. In most cases, one or two general-purpose environments are created and the applications have to be created for (one of) these environments or existing applications have to be adapted. Another important challenge for virtual reality applications and environments is the trend towards collaboration. Traditional VR environments are tailored to single-user experiences. This simplifies the setup and simultaneously allows for a better immersive experience (e.g., due to 3D screens only allowing for a single "sweet spot" that is usually centered on the single user). In all cases however, input devices are tailored towards their specific usage scenario. While a feasible approach, this causes a number of problems as well. Application developers might need to implement the same functionality for multiple input devices, causing a higher workload. Users on the other hand need to adapt to different devices even for the same application if they use it in different environments. The emerging collaboration

© Springer International Publishing Switzerland 2015
G. Brunnett et al. (Eds.): Virtual Realities, LNCS 8844, pp. 91–107, 2015.
DOI: 10.1007/978-3-319-17043-5_6

aspect in VR poses a new requirement to input devices. Many of the traditional devices generally scale not well to the number of users. Reasons for this include the availability and pricing per device, spacial requirements for input devices (e.g., a computer mouse needs a stable surface to be operated on), etc. Thus many collaboration meetings become a kind of presentation, where one user has the only input device available and is therefore the only one able to interact [9]. One approach to counteract the generally low number of input devices, is to have users bring their own devices (referred to as BYOD in some literature). Since smart phones and tablets are in wide-spread use and their popularity is growing, they might be a good alternative to more traditional devices. They are also becoming more and more powerful. Current consumer-level products are featuring multi-core CPUs and dedicated GPUs. They incorporate multi-touch screens, GPS receivers, compasses and accelerometers, furthermore connectivity through WiFi, bluetooth, Near Field Communication (NFC) and 3G technologies. They offer several benefits, due to their added functionality compared to typical input devices. For example, they can be used as output devices, even on a per-user basis to provide individualized views. With their growing memory capacity they can also serve as a portable data storage. They can provide uniform means of interaction across different VR environments.

While research in Virtual Reality interaction is generally aiming more at specialized input devices, there is ongoing research about the possible application of smart phones and tablets as input devices in the field of Human-Computer-Interaction (HCI). This paper presents the most current and important results of this research and rate their applicability in Virtual Reality. While it is impossible to present all results in this field, we aim to present a selection of different approaches. It is unlikely that a more specialised overview will generally help designers of VR environments or applications, since there is a wide field of requirements in VR. In order to classify the results, we will first present taxonomies of input devices and metaphors in Sect. 2. In the later sections notable research results in this regard will be presented: techniques that base on trackpad-like interaction (Sect. 3), methods using the camera of the mobile device (Sect. 4), menu-based approaches (Sect. 5), gestures (Sect. 6) and application-tailored methods (Sect. 7) before concluding in the last section.

2   Taxonomy and Classification

There are some possibilities to classify the research results presented in the later sections. Quality dimensions of different input device approaches include the actual capability to effectively execute tasks in applications, the volume of control or number of different input vectors (e.g., degrees-of-freedom) and other small factors. In this section we introduce the taxonomy of tasks by Foley, Buxton's input device taxonomy and a few additional criteria. With Foley's taxonomy we can show the capabilities of input devices (and techniques) to execute different tasks. Buxton's taxonomy can be used to measure the amount of control vectors. A few special properties of input methods in the area of virtual reality interaction are not covered by these two taxonomies, which is why we added four additional factors.

2.1   Foley's Taxonomy of Tasks

An old, but still useful taxonomy is from Foley et al. [13] (as for example confirmed by [4,5]). It identifies six different tasks, that cover all uses of input devices. Complex interactions can be decomposed into these six basic tasks.

1. **Position:**
   Set the absolute or relative position of an object in 2D or 3D space.
2. **Orient:**
   Set the absolute or relative orientation of an object in 2D or 3D space.
3. **Select:**
   Select an item out of a list of several items.
4. **Ink:**
   Define a path consisting of one or more positions and orientations. The name Ink refers to the visual line represented by a path.
5. **Quantify:**
   Select a number from a continuous or discrete set.
6. **Text:**
   Enter arbitrary sequences of characters.

2.2   Buxton's Taxonomy of Input Devices

Another taxonomy of devices by Buxton [10] might seem appropriate at first. It classifies input devices by their physical properties, like the control agent (e.g., the hand), what is sensed by the input device and in how many dimensions (i.e., this is related to the number of Degrees-of-Freedom (DOF) provided by the device). This is also affected by the number of buttons or similar triggers and modifiers on a device.

This approach does not work well to classify different metaphors and techniques on similar input devices. But it still can be used in some circumstances, when a technique is deviating from the default multi-touch screen interaction schema. Additionally, as smart phones and tablets are not only input devices, but also feature output facilities (i.e., the screen, speakers, vibration, etc.), this taxonomy can be extended to the kind of output used (if any) by a certain method.

2.3   Other Traits

The taxonomies explained above do not cover all important characteristics. More interesting traits are:

- **Eyes-free interaction:**
  This is a characteristic, that is not very important for traditional input devices. Most of them are eyes-free by design. For example, a simple computer mouse can be operated without any trouble while looking at the screen instead of the mouse. This goes for almost all input devices in common use, with the notable exception of keyboard, at least for inexperienced users. But with the screen on smart phones and tablets and the resulting possibility of displaying content to the user via the input device, the discrimination between eyes-free techniques and those requiring the screen of the hand-held device is important.
- **Tracking:**
  While technically part of Buxton's taxonomy (as the number of dimensions provided), it is especially interesting for collaborative setups to know, if a certain method needs some form of tracking. This is due to the fact, that tracking does not scale really well to the number of users, as most tracking systems have a fixed maximum number of markers to track.
- **Secondary Device/Method:**
  Some methods and techniques might be usable only for a subset of features provided for the main input device. This can either help to provide at least a minimum number of interactivity to users who would otherwise be only spectators, or to have a specialised device, that is only used for a certain interaction and will do this in a better way than a standard input device.
- **Scalability:**
  It is important to measure for each technique, if it is actually applicable to more than one user and if there is a point, where it will perform worse when additional users are employing this technique concurrently. For example, all methods needing a mouse pointer will suffer from this, since it is becoming more and more difficult for the users to distinguish their mouse cursor from the others.

3   Trackpad-Based Techniques

The most straight-forward method of using a (small) touchscreen is probably to have it emulate a trackpad. This has the advantage of most users already knowing the trackpad metaphor and being able to easily handle it. Of course with this technique none of the advanced capabilities of smart phones and tablets are actually used. Several commercial apps doing this are already available, like *Remote Mouse*[1]. Such apps usually allow to send text to the connected computer. Extending from this, the *ArcPad* [20] can be used as a trackpad, but additionally tapping on any point of the pad will move the mouse cursor to the position on the screen according to the point tapped on the pad. E.g., a tap on the lower left corner will put the mouse cursor to the lower left corner of the screen. Respectively tapping the center of the pad will put the mouse cursor to the center of the screen. This method was created for large display environments, where movement of a mouse cursor might be cumbersome. Unfortunately, users

---

[1] http://www.remotemouse.net/.

can run into trouble with losing track of the cursor when tapping on the pad. This is especially an issue for users of computers with trackpads, where a tap normally is interpreted as a click instead of a cursor-relocation.

Since these methods are used to control a mouse cursor, they are basically able to complete all 6 of Foley's taxonomy (including text since text can be entered through the keyboard on the mobile device) through a level of indirection. Directly only position, select and text can be supported. Trackpads (including the *ArcPad*) provide 2DOF and one or two buttons. Output facilities of the smart phone or tablet are not used in this approach. It works eyes-free, as there is nothing to be displayed at the screen at all and does not need any tracker to be used. But it will not scale well to many users, as multiple mouse cursors will puzzle the users. Depending on the setup and the experience of the users this might work for a small group of users, with coloured mouse cursors or a similar technique to help differentiating the cursors.

For VR environments the use is actually limited due to the fact that it is only 2D-cursor-based. This creates a big problem when interacting in a 3D space, when requiring multiple DOF. Still this might be a viable solution for special setups, where 2D interaction is sufficient (e.g., selection of objects in a 2.5D scene on a powerwall).

4   Camera-Based Techniques

Some interaction methods rely on the camera of the mobile device. While all of the papers in this section use phones as devices, they also apply to tablets with cameras. They rely of markers that are available for the device to scan as a base.

Prior to the smart phone era, Madhavapeddy et al. [19] created a system where users can use a phone with a camera and bluetooth to interact with a world map application (Fig. 1). The application displayed a map of the world, augmented with Spot Codes, a circular bar code. The user(s) can take pictures of the application, containing a Spot Code. The phone will then query the application via the bluetooth connection using the Spot Code's content as an id, to get further information about the special spot on the map.

Thelen et al. [27] took this idea further by customizing the information transferred to the user's phone. This leverages on the idea of having a separate device for each user. The *3D Human Brain Atlas* (Fig. 2) [27] is basically a quiz about the human brain, featuring different levels of difficulty. By scanning a barcode prior to the beginning of the quiz, users select their own difficulty level. The phone remembers this throughout the game and the combination of a code scanned on the main screen together with the difficulty is sent to a server, which in turn sends the quiz question. Also the phone is used as a identification mechanism, where certain phones can be registered as instructor phones and will get the answers together with the question.

Point and Shoot by Ballagas et al. [6] uses the visual marker approach, but displays them only for short periods of time. The phone will send a notification to the main application to display the markers, then the picture is taken including

Fig. 1. Selection on the world map with spot codes [19].

Fig. 2. A marker being selected on the *3D Human Brain Atlas* [27]

the markers, after which the markers disappear. The position where the phone was pointed to is then calculated based on the markers.

In the same paper another technique, called *Sweep* [6], was introduced. By optical flow calculations done directly on the phone, it is possible to detect the phones movement and use it similar to an optical mouse, even in mid-air. Unfortunately, due to technical limitations, this method incurred a high latency (about 200 ms) making its usage cumbersome. To our knowledge, there is no current study if the technical advances till today could lift this restriction, but it is very likely.

Rhos [25] proposed to use markers on physical objects to create Augmented Reality (AR) games. While this is not directly related, this can still be used with the approaches above, to create additional content and seamlessly add it into the basic content provided by the application to all users.

The following classification will exclude *Sweep*, since it is different from the other methods. It will be classified separately. The methods are basically only used to perform selection tasks (according to the Foley taxonomy). It can be noted that some of the techniques follow up with text input after the selection by using the phone's native keyboard. Combining several selections allows for the other tasks to be completed, too, but this might be cumbersome for the users.

All of these techniques feature input in 2 dimensions (as restricted by the camera). It is notable, too, that the input device is also used as an output device for most of the methods, making collaboration easier on a larger scale, since interaction is possible without interrupting the workflow of other users.

None of the methods are actually eyes-free, as it is necessary to point with the device at some position on the screen, which is of course only possible by looking at it. This might interrupt the user's workflow, but assuming this is used to present further information on the screen of the mobile device, this is not a problem. Tracking systems are also not needed for any of those methods, all of them are actually designed to do their own kind of tracking their position. Depending on the application, external tracking might be used to improve the accuracy of the chosen method. Transferring content to the smart phone or tablet makes it also a valuable secondary device. A program might provide the standard means of interaction (depending on the program and setup) and additionally can allow for mobile devices to be used for further information, or for additional users to get information. Regarding scalability, all the methods work well with many users, actual restrictions are posed by available screen space where the users can interact. *Point and Shoot* might also have some scalability issues because of the bar codes flashing up on the screen, whenever a user interacts. This might distract other users looking at the screen. The problem increases with more people using the system at the same time.

Depending on the actual setup of a VR environment, these method might work very well (e.g., a powerwall) or might not be a good choice at all (e.g., fully immersive environment).

Sweep can only be used for position tasks, adding a button functionality will also allow for selection and, through composition, all other tasks as defined by Foley. It tracks input in 2D, but it could be augmentable to actually support 3D. It is eyes-free, as it does not use any of the output facilities of smart phones and tablets and is used similar to a mouse. It is also not dependant on external tracking, since doing its own tracking is the core of *Sweep*. The technique in itself is highly scalable. The real problem is similar to trackpads: the number of mouse cursors that need to be displayed on the screen. The cursor is also the problem why this might not be a good choice of input method for VR applications. Similar to the trackpad solutions already described, this is only useful if a 2D pointer can be effectively used with the application.

5   Menus

Another approach of using smart phones and tablets as input devices is an external menu structure on the mobile device. This can be as simple as presenting all required functionality in the device's native UI and transferring all user input to the actual application. But this most likely causes a break in user interface design between main application and mobile device and is additionally not eyes-free in most cases, interrupting the workflow when used. For this reason several advanced menu versions have been proposed, most of them featuring an eyes-free interaction mode.

Many of those menus base on the idea of Marking Menus [18]. Marking Menus are basically a structure of radial menus. The user can use them eyes-free after learning the menu structure, by just remembering the path to draw (with finger or pen) to a certain menu item. When applied to mobile devices, the device can present the menu to the user who can then either progress to move to the desired menu item blindly, or look at the structure to find the menu item and thus help to remember the path next time. The strokes of the path can be drawn continuously or stroke-after-stroke, depending on the actual implementation.

As current smart phones and tablets allow for multi-touch interaction, standard Marking Menu interaction can be improved by utilizing this. Kin et al. [17]

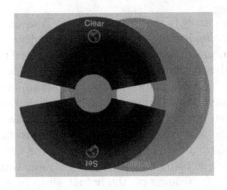

Fig. 3. Two-handed Marking Menus [17] employ multi-touch to draw parts of the Marking Menu strokes using alternating fingers.

Fig. 4. Marking Menus with continuous strokes are the base for the multi-touch extensions by [7].

used multi-touch to enable faster input of the strokes, using two fingers at the same time (Fig. 3). They use the stroke-after-stroke version of Marking Menus, allowing to either draw the strokes simultaneously one with each finger, or one after another, alternating between fingers, a bit slower, but offering double the number of menu items, by changing the menu depending on the starting finger.

Another possibility of multi-touch extensions are proposed by Bauer et al. [7]. Using the continuous version of Marking Menus (Fig. 4), multi-touch can be used to continue strokes even when the user hits the edge of the screen by just using another finger to continue the strokes. Using the same technique, it is possible to have one finger on the screen, only to have the menu stick to the current state and have another finger select menu items from the same point. If a menu item *next* is accessible through a up-left-stroke sequence, one finger can do the "up" stroke, another one then can do the left stroke over and over again, without needing to add "up" in front of each stroke, as long as the first finger is on the touch screen. Also the number of items in the menu structure is increased by presenting different menus, depending on how many fingers are used to initiate the stroke-sequence. By including the idea of *Control Menus* [24], it is possible to not only select an item, but also to add value control as an item. Combined with multi-touch this can be used for higher dimensional value control and 3D interaction. Additonally, the accelerometer sensors on the smart phone or tablet can be used for further input variations.

Flower Menus by Bailly et al. [2] improve the number of items in a Marking Menu structure by not only allowing straight strokes, but instead take the curvature of a stroke into account. Using the stroke-after-stroke variant of Marking Menus, they have 12 items on each level. Each basic direction (i.e., Up, Down, Left, Right) can be combined with either a straight stroke, or a curved stroke to either the left or right side to get up to 12 items per level. Of course multiple levels of menu structure can be chained one after another (Fig. 5).

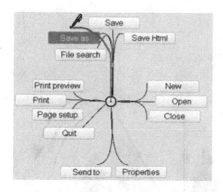

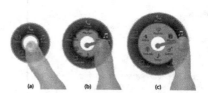

Fig. 5. The design of *Flower Menus* [2]. Each basic stroke direction (Up, Down, Left, Right) has 3 variations (straight, curved left/right).

Fig. 6. *Wavelet Menus* [14,15] are a sequence of radial menus, that are conceptually hidden under each other and revealed as the user strokes from the center towards an menu item.

Basing on the idea of novice and expert mode interaction as used by Marking Menus, Francone et al. [14,15] proposed the *Wavelet Menu* (Fig. 6). It is derived from the Wave Menu by Bailly et al. [3], but better suited to the small screen estate on mobile devices. The first time the user touches the screen, the root level of the menu is revealed around the touch point. Then when the user starts moving the finger towards one menu item, the submenu is appearing from below the current menu, with the current menu expanding outwards. When the user releases the finger at the menu, the next level of menu (or actual functionality) gets selected. If the touch is released prior to this, the last menu stays on top instead. Like with Marking Menus, the user can remember the sequence of strokes needed to access a certain item and can then do the strokes without actually looking at the device.

Gebhardt et al. [16] use a HTML-based menu displayed on a mobile device to interact with VR spaces. It is targeted for use with configuration tasks of the system, but can also be used for other tasks. They created a custom set of widgets to be presented on the mobile device. An example of this can be seen in Fig. 7. The strong point of this method is the device-independence, since the only requirement for the mobile device used is HTML5-support. Also there are basically no requirements for the server-VR-system; it does not even need to be a VR system.

Menu selection only offers support for selection tasks. By including the Control Menu mechanic, quantify tasks can also be accomplished, and by composition everything else, even text (if paired by a technique like QuikWrite [23]). The input dimension of menus is defined by the number of items it contains, which can be a large number. With the Control Menu mechanic and common multi-touch gestures, like rotation and pinch-to-zoom, four dimensions of input can be achieved, enough to allow for 3D interaction, important for VR applications.

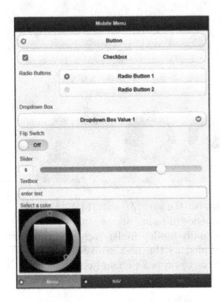

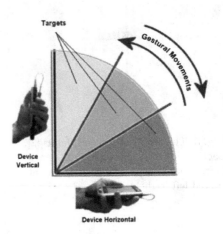

Fig. 7. A *HMTL5 Menu* [16] composed of several standard and custom widgets.

Fig. 8. The principle of *Motion Marking Menus* [22] is to divide the possible angle range into different parts, each corresponding to a menu item. By alternating the movement or adding small stops in between, a menu structure can be traversed.

All of the presented menus, with the exception of the HTML-based menu, can be used eyes-free after a training period. They do not need external tracking, but it could be used to provide a means of positioning and/or rotational input to the presented method. This will, of course, negatively affect the scalability of that method. Still any of the menu methods can be used as a secondary input method, especially to avoid menu structures in immersive environments, where navigating menus can be very cumbersome. Without tracking, menu interaction scales very well to the number of users, due to the minor communication overhead per device, the fact that users can practically interact from any position they can see the application screen/area and individual mobile devices do not interfere with each other during interaction.

For these reasons, all presented menu approaches are very well suited to be used in a VR environment, with the actual implementation being dependent on the parameters of the VR application.

6   Gestures

Using the built-in sensors of smart phones and tablets, especially accelerometers, gestures with the device itself can be recognised. Since these gestures do not use the touch screen or only for activation of the gesture sensing, it is easy to implement the same gesture recognition for other devices as well, as long as they feature the necessary sensors.

Device gestures can also be added to other input methods, such as the menus presented in the previous section. One has to keep in mind, that the gestures are more difficult to execute with larger and heavier devices, so large tablets are not a good input device to use the following methods with.

Motion Marking Menus (Fig. 8) as presented by Oakley and Park [22], base on the concept of Marking Menus, as shown in the last section. But instead of using swipes for the selection of menu items, selection is done via the angle it is held in. They use a button or a touch on the screen as an activation mechanic. The angle the device can be held is divided into a number of menu items. Two menu items, for example, each get a 45° angle, meaning that holding the device horizontally or up to a 45° deviation from the horizontal plane will invoke the first menu item, any other posture will activate the second item. By tilting the device up and down from the current posture while still holding the activation button, a menu sequence can be invoked, similar to touch menus.

Building from this general idea, *Jerk-Tilts* (Fig. 9) is a method by Baglioni et al. [1] for selection by gesture. Instead of having the user remembering a special posture or sequence of postures, they use a single tilt-and-back gesture in different directions to invoke functionality. For example, holding the device and executing a quick tilt to the right and then back to the original posture will invoke a selection of a certain kind. The same can be done in all four basic direction and combining two directions allow for a total of eight different possibilities. A big advantage of this method is, that it works without any activation button, allowing to use this together with other input methods using the touch screen.

Dachselt and Buchholz [11] suggest to use a throw gesture alongside tilt gestures (forming *Throw and Tilt* (Fig. 10)). Tilt can be used for selections, similar to the methods presented above in this section or to move a mouse cursor, while the throw gesture can be used to transfer data to the main application. Care has to be taken when the throw gesture is executed to have a firm grip on the input device, but it is intuitive to throw content towards the application.

All the techniques above provide means to accomplish selections tasks. Using tilt, *Throw and Tilt* can additionally provide means for position and/or rotation tasks. This can again be composed into all other possible tasks. The number of input dimensions is different for all methods. *Motion Marking Menus* have a dimensionality dependent on the number of menu items. *Jerk-Tilts* have a fixed dimensionality of eight, the number of possible gestures. With only three dimensions (two tilt dimensions and throw) *Tilt and Throw* has the least number of dimensions. All methods work eyes-free and need no external tracking and are also scalable to the number of users. Due to the greater motion of the throw gesture, *Tilt and Throw* might scale a little bit less than the other approaches, but this can be somewhat mitigated by providing an alternative to the throw gesture.

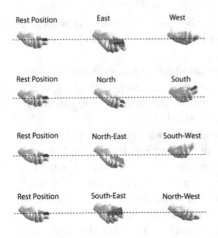

Fig. 9. *Jerk-Tilt* [1] are a tilt-and-back kind of gesture, that can be done in eight different directions, allowing for eight different functions to be invoked.

Fig. 10. The characteristic throw gesture from *Tilt and Throw* [11].

All these methods can well be used as a secondary input method to provide a subset of the application's main functionality to additional users. The methods can also be used with tracked input devices, that might already be present in a given VR setup, such as flysticks. This allows for a common input metaphor over multiple input devices.

7   Application-Tailored Techniques

This section contains several techniques, that are specifically tailored towards a certain application. While this limits their general applicability, it is still possible to use them in similar usage scenarios. Because these techniques do not have much in common, their classification will be written individually instead of grouping them together as in the previous sections.

The *Mod Control* (Fig. 11) system by Deller and Ebert [12] was designed for interaction with a map application. The system itself is modular and not directly tailored towards the application. But the reference implementation features several interaction modules to improve control of the map application through a smart phone. Among them is a combined touch/accelerometer interface for 3D navigation. The user can modify the current view as flying, controlling the forward and sideward speed using the touchpad while the devices rotation control yaw and heading of the view. This is a common problem, especially in VR environments. This module can be classified to accomplish position and orientation tasks, in 5 DOF, it can be used eyes-free and does not need external tracking, it is usable as a secondary device to other input devices which do have less DOF. Also it scales well to the number of users.

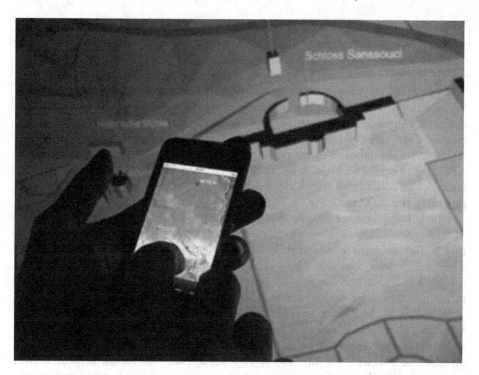

Fig. 11. *ModControl* [12] can be used to present an overview of the content to a mobile device and allows independent interaction.

Another interesting module is the image module, featuring a small version of the map shown by the main application. This allows users to explore the map independently from other users and send their current view back to the application if needed. It fulfils a position and select task, in two dimensions. Though it cannot be operated eyes-free, it scales very well since every user can interact totally independent of the others. For the same reason it also makes for a good secondary device for additional users. The applicability in the VR domain is dependent on the VR application. For terrain simulations, for example, it will work very well, while it is not useful for architectural applications.

Seewonauth et al. [26] propose two techniques, *Touch & Connect* and *Touch & Select* to initiate data transfer between a phone and a computer. Since today's smart phones and tablets have quite large memory capacity, they can be used as a mobile data storage. To avoid complicated file management, one of those two method can be used to easily copy a data set. *Touch & Connect* bases on NFC. The users select a file on the source device and simply touch a NFC tag on the target computer to copy the file. Note that the same approach can be used to get the current data set from the display or to initiate a connection (as input device) to the currently running application, avoiding the need to enter IP-Addresses or Host names.

Touch & Select uses several NFC tags to track the position of the mobile device. The user again selects a file on the smart phone or tablets and touches a point directly on the screen. This initiates the file transfer. The same principle can be used to interact with the screen directly for other effects.

Both methods allow to accomplish selection tasks, with *Touch & Select* having additional two dimensions of input. Since the user has to point with the device, it cannot be used eyes-free, but especially if used for data transfer, both methods are valid secondary input means. It does not scale as well as other methods to the number of users, since it is also dependent on the number of NFC tags provided and also it requires the users to stand near the tagged spots, limiting the concurrent use. External Tracking is only needed by the means of providing the NFC tags.

For VR applications, *Touch & Connect* is probably more useful than *Touch & Select*, since the latter selects a 2D screen position, which is only situational useful. But to initiate connections between a mobile device and a stationary computer system, *Touch & Connect* is very convenient. Please also note, that a similar behaviour is achievable by providing a visual tag, that can be scanned by a smart phone or tablet camera if NFC is unavailable.

Bauer et al. [8] provide another specialised approach for four different usage scenarios. Beside two scenarios where the content of the main screen is transferred to mobile devices, similar to the image view from *ModControl*, they also present two scenarios for interaction with 3D scenes. One design is using a joystick metaphor. The smart phone or tablet is used to control forward movement by tilting in the appropriate direction. Turning is done by tilting the device sidewards, not unlike a steering wheel.

In another scenario, users control 3D objects by using combined input from the touchscreen and accelerometers. Tilting the device causes the object to move in the X-Y-plane and using the touchscreen movement in the X-Z-plane is available. This makes it a 3DOF input method.

Both methods provide means to accomplish position tasks and with an added button or gesture it can also select. Through composition then all six tasks are possible. The first method provides only two dimensions of input, while the other one provides 3 dimensions (actually four, but since the X direction is mapped in two ways this reduces to three different dimensions). Both techniques can be used eyes-free, without external tracking and scale well to the number of users. They are useful for additional users to provide a reduced set of controls to interact with an application. And as both methods are designed for 3D interaction, they are in general useful for VR applications.

Semantic Snarfing describes a technique by Myers et al. [21] using a laser pointer to mark a spot on a large display. The semantic area (e.g., a dialog) this spot belongs to is then transferred to a mobile device's screen. Due to technical progress since the time the paper was published, the method can be used today without a laser pointer by utilizing the camera of a smart phone or tablet. This makes *Semantic Snarfing* a method similar to the camera methods described in their own section. What makes *Semantic Snarfing* special from the camera techniques is the semantics that needs to be provided in order to make the system work. The method has in general the same properties as the camera methods, as it allows selection (and then more tasks on the mobile device's screen), scales generally well to the amount of users, but does not support eyes-free interaction. Tracking is not required. Its usability in VR environments is dependent on the application and setup, quite similar to the camera methods. But as a secondary device, *Semantic Snarfing* is applicable to even more VR environments, as the primary device can be used to select the "snarfing point" for the mobile device.

Table 1. Overview of all presented methods. (★: methods using output capabilities.; c: achievable through composition; parenthesis depict simple improvements to the method.)

Method	Position	Orient	Select	Ink	Quantify	Text	Dimensions	Eyes-free	Tracking	Secondary	Scalability
Trackpad - Methods											
ArcPad	✓	(c)	(✓)	(c)	(c)	(✓)	2(4)	✓	✗	✗	-
Camera - Methods											
World Map			✓			✓	2★	✗	✗	✓	o
3D Humand Brain Atlas			✓			✓	2★	✗	✗	✓	o
Point and Shoot			✓			✓	2★	✗	✗	✓	o
Sweep	✓		(✓)				2 (3)	✓	✗		-
AR			✓			✓	2★	✗	✗	✓	o
Menu - Methods											
Marking Menus			✓				any	✓	✗	✓	+
Multi-touch Marking Menus			✓				any	✓	✗	✓	+
Improved Marking Menus	(c)	(c)	✓	(c)	✓	(c)	any+any	✓	✓	✓	+
Flower Menus			✓				any	✓	✗	✓	+
Wavelet Menus			✓				any	✓	✗	✓	+
HTML Menus	(c)	(c)	✓	(c)	✓	✓	any	✓	✗	✓	+
Gesture - Methods											
Motion Marking Menus			✓				any	✓	✓	✓	+
Jerk Tilts			✓				any	✓	✗	✓	+
Throw and Tilt	✓	✓	✓				any	✓	✗	✓	+
Application-Tailored - Methods											
Mod Control - Navigation	✓	✓					5	✓	✗	✗	+
Mod Control - Image	✓		✓				2	✗	✗	✗	+
Touch & Connect			✓				-	✗	✓	✓	o
Touch & Select			✓				2	✗	✓	✓	o
Joystick	✓						2	✓	✗	✓	+
Touch + Tilt	✓						3	✓	✗	✓	+
Semantic Snarfing	(✓)	(✓)	(✓)	✓		✓	2★	✗	✗	✓	+

8   Conclusion

Several interaction techniques are possible with smart phones and tablets. For applications where collaboration is expected, supporting interaction via mobile devices will add benefit to users and their collaboration. Even if not the full set of functionality can be accessed by smart phone or tablet interaction, it will still help users to be active users of an application instead of being only passive spectators.

However, it is important to choose the right form of interaction for the application in question in order to reach a high usability of the resulting system. The overview given by this paper should help in considering which methods are feasible for certain settings. Table 1 contains an overview of the properties reviewed in the previous chapter for easier comparison.Moreover, it can form a starting point for implementation of an own interaction metaphor. If possible, a metaphor for the mobile device should not deviate from the metaphor of the main device to avoid the necessity of learning to use two devices. In some application areas it is possible to avoid the usage of other devices completely, and using smart phones or tablets as the only input device.

References

1. Baglioni, M., Lecolinet, E., Guiard, Y.: JerkTilts: using accelerometers for eight-choice selection on mobile devices. In: Proceedings of the 13th International Conference on Multimodal Interfaces, ICMI 2011, pp. 121–128. ACM, New York (2011)
2. Bailly, G., Lecolinet, E.: Flower menus: a new type of marking menu with large menu breadth, within groups and efficient expert mode memorization. In: AVI 2008 Proceedings of the Working Conference on Advanced Visual Interfaces, pp. 15–22 (2008)
3. Bailly, G., Lecolinet, E., Nigay, L.: Wave menus: improving the novice mode of hierarchical marking menus. In: Baranauskas, C., Abascal, J., Barbosa, S.D.J. (eds.) INTERACT 2007. LNCS, vol. 4662, pp. 475–488. Springer, Heidelberg (2007)
4. Ballagas, R., Borchers, J., Rohs, M., Sheridan, J.G.: The smart phone: a ubiquitous input device. IEEE Pervasive Comput. 5(1), 70–77 (2006)
5. Ballagas, R., Borchers, J., Rohs, M., Sheridan, J.G., Foley, J., Wallace, V., Chan, P.: The smart phone: a the input design space. Shoot (2006)
6. Ballagas, R., Rohs, M., Sheridan, J.: Sweep and point and shoot: phonecam-based interactions for large public displays. In: CHI 2005 Extended Abstracts on Human Factors in Computing Systems, pp. 1200–1203. ACM (2005)
7. Bauer, J., Ebert, A., Kreylos, O., Hamann, B.: Marking menus for eyes-free interaction using smart phones and tablets. In: Cuzzocrea, A., Kittl, C., Simos, D.E., Weippl, E., Xu, L. (eds.) CD-ARES 2013. LNCS, vol. 8127, pp. 481–494. Springer, Heidelberg (2013)
8. Bauer, J., Thelen, S., Ebert, A.: Using smart phones for large-display interaction. In: 2nd International Conference on User Science and Engineering (I-USEr) (2011)
9. Birnholtz, J.P., Grossman, T., Mak, C., Balakrishnan, R.: An exploratory study of input configuration and group process in a negotiation task using a large display. In: Proceedings of the SIGCHI Conference on Human Factors in Computing Systems - CHI 2007, p. 91 (2007)

10. Buxton, W.: Lexical and pragmatic considerations of input structures. SIGGRAPH Comput. Graph. **17**(1), 31–37 (1983)
11. Dachselt, R., Buchholz, R.: Throw and tilt seamless interaction across devices using mobile phone gestures. In: Proceedings of the MEIS 2008, pp. 272–278 (2008)
12. Deller, M., Ebert, A.: Modcontrol – mobile phones as a versatile interaction device for large screen applications. In: Campos, P., Graham, N., Jorge, J., Nunes, N., Palanque, P., Winckler, M. (eds.) INTERACT 2011, Part II. LNCS, vol. 6947, pp. 289–296. Springer, Heidelberg (2011)
13. Foley, J., Wallace, V., Chan, P.: Human factors of computer graphics interaction techniques. IEEE Comput. Graph. Appl. **4**(11), 13–48 (1984)
14. Francone, J., Bailly, G., Lecolinet, E., Mandran, N., Nigay, L.: Wavelet menus on handheld devices: stacking metaphor for novice mode and eyes-free selection for expert mode. In: Proceedings of the International Conference on Advanced Visual Interfaces, AVI 2010, pp. 173–180. ACM, New York (2010)
15. Francone, J., Bailly, G., Nigay, L., Lecolinet, E.: Wavelet menus: a stacking metaphor for adapting marking menus to mobile devices. In: Proceedings of the 11th International Conference on Human-Computer Interaction with Mobile Devices and Services, pp. 2–5 (2009)
16. Gebhardt, S., Pick, S., Oster, T., Hentschel, B., Kuhlen, T.: An evaluation of a smart-phone-based menu system for immersive virtual environments. In: 2014 IEEE Symposium on 3D User Interfaces (3DUI), pp. 31–34, March 2014
17. Kin, K., Hartmann, B.: Two-handed marking menus for multitouch devices. ACM Trans. Comput. Hum. Interact. (TOCHI) TOCHI Homepage Archive **18**(2), 16:1–16:23 (2011)
18. Kurtenbach, G.P.: The design and evaluation of marking menus. Ph.D. thesis, University of Toronto (1993)
19. Madhavapeddy, A., Scott, D., Sharp, R.: Using camera-phones to enhance human-computer interaction. In: Proceedings of Ubiquitous (2004)
20. McCallum, D., Irani, P.: Arc-pad: absolute + relative cursor positioning for large displays with a mobile touchscreen. In: Proceedings of the 22nd Annual ACM Symposium on User Interface Software and Technology, pp. 153–156. ACM (2009)
21. Myers, B.A., Peck, C.H., Nichols, J., Kong, D., Miller, R.: Interacting at a distance using semantic snarfing. In: Abowd, G.D., Brumitt, B., Shafer, S. (eds.) UbiComp 2001. LNCS, vol. 2201, pp. 305–314. Springer, Heidelberg (2001)
22. Oakley, I., Park, J.: Motion marking menus: an eyes-free approach to motion input for handheld devices. Int. J. Hum. Comput. Stud. **67**(6), 515–532 (2009)
23. Perlin, K.: Quikwriting: continuous stylus-based text entry. In: Proceedings of the 11th Annual ACM Symposium on User Interface Software and Technology, UIST 1998, pp. 215–216. ACM, New York (1998)
24. Pook, S., Lecolinet, E., Vaysseix, G., Ura, E.C., Bp, M.: Control menus: execution and control in a single interactor. In: CHI 2000 Extended Abstracts on Human Factors in Computing Systems, pp. 263–264, April 2000
25. Rohs, M.: Marker-based embodied interaction for handheld augmented reality games. Virtual Reality **4**(5), 1–12 (2007)
26. Seewoonauth, K., Rukzio, E., Hardy, R., Holleis, P.: Touch & connect and touch & select: interacting with a computer by touching it with a mobile phone. In: Proceedings of the 11th International Conference on Human-Computer Interaction with Mobile Devices and Services, p. 36. ACM (2009)
27. Thelen, S., Meyer, J., Ebert, A., Hagen, H.: A 3D human brain atlas. In: Magnenat-Thalmann, N. (ed.) 3DPH 2009. LNCS, vol. 5903, pp. 173–186. Springer, Heidelberg (2009)

Hand Pose Recognition — Overview and Current Research

Daniel Mohr and Gabriel Zachmann[✉]

University of Bremen, Bremen, Germany
{mohr,zach}@cs.uni-bremen.de

Abstract. Vision-based markerless hand tracking has many applications, for instance in virtual prototyping, navigation in virtual environments, tele- and robot-surgery and video games. It is a very challenging task, due to the real-time requirements, 26 degrees-of-freedom, high appearance variability, and frequent self-occlusions. Because of that, and because of the many desirable applications, it has received increasing attention in the computer vision community of the past years. A lot of approaches have been proposed to (partially) solve the problem, but no system has been presented yet that can solve the full-DOF hand pose estimation problem robustly in real-time.

The purpose of this article is to present an overview of the approaches that have been presented so far and where future research of hand tracking probably will go.

First, we will explain the challenges in more detail. Second, we will classify the approaches; third, we will describe the most important approaches, and finally we will show the future directions and give a short overview of our current work.

1 Motivation and Applications

The task of vision-based hand tracking is to estimate the human hand pose based on one or multiple cameras. The scientific interest in this task is very high, and the importance of hand tracking is larger than ever due to the increasing interest in natural user interfaces.

The applications for hand tracking are manifold. On the one hand, there are a lot of professional applications such as assembly simulation, motion capture, virtual prototyping, navigation in virtual environments, and rehabilitation. Hand tracking also has a high potential in medical applications, e.g. for sterile interaction with patient related data or tele-surgery. On the other hand, the interest in hand gesture driven game control is increasing strongly. For example, human motion tracking found its way to the consumer market through Nintendo Wii, Sony Move, and Microsoft Kinect. The goal of all three products is to track the human body. The Kinect is the first markerless vision-based consumer product. It is able to track the whole body with fairly high accuracy. The next consequent step is the precise tracking of the human hand, which can significantly improve the interaction with many game genres and desktop applications. The most recent

© Springer International Publishing Switzerland 2015
G. Brunnett et al. (Eds.): Virtual Realities, LNCS 8844, pp. 108–129, 2015.
DOI: 10.1007/978-3-319-17043-5_7

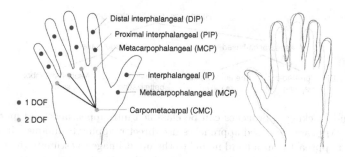

Fig. 1. (a) The left figure illustrates the degrees of freedom (DOF) of the human hand. The valid hand poses form a manifold in the 20-dim space. **(b)** The right figure illustrates five different hand shapes we captured from our group and some students. Any hand pose recognition approach has to take into account this shape variability.

application with strongly increasing interest in hand tracking are mobile devices to improve the natural interaction with them.

These are only a few of the numerous applications for hand tracking. Obviously, most of them need the hand to be tracked precisely and in real-time. Thus, algorithms to achieve this are an enabling technology. But robust hand detection and recognition in uncontrolled environments is still a challenging task in computer vision, especially on mobile devices due to their limited hardware resources.

1.1   Challenges of Hand Tracking

The main challenges of camera-based hand tracking are the high-dimensional hand configuration space, the high appearance variation, the limitations of cameras, and the potentially disturbing environment. In the following, the challenges are described in detail.

High-dimensional Configuration Space: The problem dimension to estimate the full-DOF hand pose is very high. Figure 1a illustrates the articulations. Each finger has 4 degrees of freedom (DOF) which yield in 20 local DOF for the hand pose. Often, an additional DOF for axial rotation is modeled the thumb. With the 6 DOF for the global position and orientation the problem space has 26 dimensions.

Hand Motion and Appearance Variation: The human hand to be tracked varies strongly from person to person. The skin color for example depends on the ethnic origins and the skin browning. The geometry of the hands are also very different, e.g. thickness and length of the fingers, and width of the hand to mention only some of the varying parameters. Even the kinematic can vary slightly between human beings.

Additionally, the appearance variability of the hand is very high, and thus, it is challenging to detect the hand in an input image because neither its appearance nor its position are known in advance.

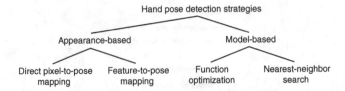

Fig. 2. Hand tracking approaches can be classified into appearance and model-based approaches. Appearance-based approaches use direct mapping techniques. In contrast, model-based approaches fit a hand model to the input image to estimate the pose. Pose estimation can be formulated as function optimization (the hand pose is the parameter set to be optimized) or nearest-neighbor search (find the hand pose most similar to the observed hand).

Unconstrained Background: To be able to detect the hand in an input image, one first has to identify the image region corresponding to the hand by applying a segmentation algorithm (e.g. skin color segmentation or background subtraction) or extract features whose distribution on the hand and the background are sufficiently different (e.g. edges). The more complex the background the less likely those features can be used to discriminate between hand and background. For example skin colored regions in the background will heavily disturb a skin color segmentation. Moving object in the background are an error source for background subtraction and textured regions (consider for example a keyboard) will produce a lot of edges in the background that heavily disturbs any edge-based matching.

Camera Limitations: Current camera technology is limited in its capturing capability. In most real setups there are over- and/or underexposed regions due to the low dynamic range of the cameras. Even HDR-cameras have a by some orders of magnitude lower dynamic range than the human eye has. Furthermore, most cameras capture only the usual three color channels and not the whole spectrum of light.

Real-time Tracking Condition: Most hand tracking applications need the hand to be tracked in real-time i.e. at least 25 full pose estimations per second. This is a very strong condition in particular due to the high dimensional search space. This condition is particularly challenging for tracking on mobile devices.

2   Classification and Overview of Approaches up to Now

Due to the aforementioned challenges, hand tracking is a very interesting and active research area. A lot of approaches have been presented in the past, using different algorithms, ranging from neural networks over hashing to hand pose hierarchies. The motivation of this article is to give an overview and classification of the various approaches. We hope to help both new researchers in this area, who want to get familiar with hand tracking, and advanced researchers, who want to get a different point of view on the research area.

In the following, we will first classify the approaches and then explain many approaches in more detail.

There are several ways to categorize hand tracking approaches [1, 2] e.g. gesture of full-DOF pose recognition, approaches that need automatic or manual initialization and so forth. The most popular categorization is: appearance-based vs model-based (Fig. 2). The term model-based means that a 3D hand model is fitted somehow against the input image. Model-based approaches can either be formulated as optimization or nearest neighbor search. The idea behind the optimization is simple: based on a initial match, the model is adapted and fitted again until convergence. The nearest neighbor formulation considers a database with all possible hand poses, which have to be tracked. Then, the goal is to find the most similar hand pose and the corresponding position in the input image.

By contrast, appearance-based approaches try to learn a direct mapping from the input image to the hand pose space. Most of them use fairly low-level features (e.g. edges or color blobs) or even no features at all (e.g. artificial neural networks). Thus, such approaches do not need to search the whole configuration space because the information of the hand poses is encoded in the learned mapping. This typically makes them computationally less expensive. On the other hand, they suffer from accuracy and stability due to poor handling of noise and partial occlusion in the input image. Of course, appearance-based approaches need to contain the information about the hand model in some way, too. For example, in a neural network-based approach, which maps the image pixels to the pose, a hand model is implicitly stored in the neural network itself. Figure 3 visually compares the idea of model- and appearance-based approaches.

Appearance-Based Approaches. A typical appearance-based approach is used in [3, 4] to detect the hand position in a gray-scale image. In a training step, multiple hand poses are trained. During tracking, "attention images" are used for segmentation. Basically, the image pixels are directly used as input vector and a principal component analysis (PCA) is applied for dimension reduction. A hand pose is successfully segmented by validating a training image to be close enough in the low-dimensional space. Nearest neighbor search is performed using a Voronoi diagram. The hand segmentation probability is evaluated using kernel density estimation.

A set of specialized mappings is trained based on data obtained by a Cyberglove in [5]. After a skin segmentation, moment-based features are computed and used as weak mapping functions. This mapping functions are combined to get a strong classification function.

Another classical appearance-based approach for hand tracking is used in [6]. They used a so-called Eigentracker to be able to detect a maximum of two hands. Color and motion cues are used for initialization. The eigenspace is updated online to incorporate new viewpoints. Illumination variations are handled by a neural network.

In [7] skin-colored blobs are detected to localize the hand position. Next, the hand pose is estimated by detecting the finger tips. The blobs are detected

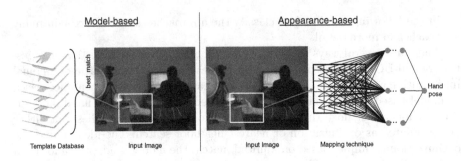

Fig. 3. Model-based approaches (left) use an object model (here the human hand) and match the templates, each representing a hand pose, to the input image. In contrast, appearance-based approaches (right) try to learn a direct mapping from the image space to the pose space.

using a Bayesian classifier. Color changes during time are handled by an iterative training algorithm.

Wang et al. [8] detect the hand position in the image using Camshift. A contour in Fourier space is computed to obtain a scale and rotation invariant hand descriptor. After locating the hand position, the finger tips are determined by a semicircle detector. Particle filtering is used to find finger tip location candidates. A k-means clustering is applied to the candidates. The cluster centers (prototypes) are used as the final finger positions.

One of the main disadvantages of appearance-based approaches is their high sensitiveness to noise, feature extraction errors, and partial occlusion. For example, if a finger tip is occluded, but not necessarily the remainder of the finger, the above approaches will fail to detect the finger. It is not even easy to determine which fingers are occluded. A promising alternative are model-based approaches.

Model-Based Approaches. Model-based approaches search in the large configuration space to find the best matching hypothesis. Basically, a descriptor, optimized for fast and accurate matching, is defined first. Then for all hand poses to be tracked, the corresponding *template* is generated. During tracking, the hand poses are compared to the input image by computing the similarity between the corresponding templates and the (preprocessed) input image. Depending on the needs of the approach the templates are precomputed or generated online during tracking. The main differences between the approaches is the method to compute the similarity between hypothesis and input image, how to compute each similarity evaluation as fast as possible, and acceleration data structures to avoid as many similarity measure evaluations as possible.

The advantage of model-based approaches compared to appearance-based approaches is that arbitrary hand poses can be modeled including self occlusion. Partial occlusion by other objects can be handled robustly as well because the similarity measure between a hypothesis and an input image is only affected by a limited amount.

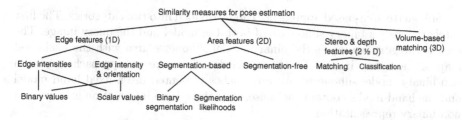

Fig. 4. Similarity measures for hand pose estimation can be categorized into four different types. The categorization is based on the input modality used for matching. Most often used are edges, color (segmentation) and depth images. Edge and color segmentation likelihood can either be used directly for matching or binarized before matching. Area-based features also allows to use the shape hypothesis directly without applying a segmentation. Depth images can be used for segmentation or direct matching.

In the next section, we will first provide an overview of the different categories of similarity measures. In the section following that we will categorize and describe the acceleration data structures.

2.1 Similarity Measures

In the area of hand tracking the most often used features in the past are skin color and edges. Edges and silhouette area (e.g. extracted using skin color) are complementary features and often combined into a single measure using weighting functions. In the recent years, depth cameras (e.g. Kinect, Mesa SR 4000) became available and popular. The hand (and other objects) can more easily be distinguished from other objects. Depth images, in some way, provide area information (continuously changing depth values) and edge information (strongly changing depth values). Thus, depth images became very popular in the area of hand tracking in the most recent years. Volume reconstruction-based approaches [9–12] directly work on a 3D volume, but these approaches need a lot of cameras and get a very coarse volumetric representation of the hand. Only a few approaches exist using volume reconstruction. Due to space limitations, we will not present any such approaches in detail. Figure 4 gives an overview of the different similarity measure classes.

We will first present approaches using classical area based similarity measures based on color images, then approaches using depth images, and finally, depth image based approaches.

Silhouette Area-Based Similarity Measures. Silhouette-area based similarity measures are very effective and fast for articulated object tracking. The measure is continuous with respect to changes in pose space and robust to noise. Basically, the segmented silhouette of the input image is compared to a hypothesis (also represented by its silhouette area). The more similar both silhouettes are, the higher the matching probability is.

Silhouette area-based approaches can be divided into two categories. The first category needs a binary silhouette of both the model and the query image. The second category compares the binary model silhouette area with the likelihood map of the query image. To our knowledge there are no approaches using a non-binary model silhouette. All approaches presented use a fixed hand model and the hand model contains no noise, thus there is no information gain using a non-binary representation.

A simple method belonging to the first class is proposed in [13]. They assume that the hand is in front of a homogeneous, uniformly colored background. First, they apply skin segmentation to extract the foreground. Based on the segmented region, hand size, center, and differences between particular pixels on the boundary are used to detect the hand position. This information is used to recognize some simple gestures, e.g. an open hand or a fist.

A more robust approach is proposed in [14,15]. First, the difference d between the model silhouette and the segmented foreground area in the query image is computed. Then, the exponential of the negative squared difference is used as silhouette matching probability P i.e. $P = \exp(-d^2)$. A slightly different measure is used by Kato et al. [16]. First, they define the model silhouette area A_M, the segmented area A_I and the intersecting area $A_O = A_I \cap A_M$. The differences $A_I - A_O$ and $A_M - A_O$ are integrated into the overall measure in the same way as described above.

In [17], the non-overlapping area of the model and the segmented silhouettes are integrated into classical optimization methods, e.g. Levenberg-Marquardt or downhill simplex. Nirei et al. [18] first compute the distance transform of both the input image and the model silhouettes. Regarding the distance transformed images as vectors, they compute the normalized scalar product of these vectors. Additionally, the model is divided into meaningful parts. Next, for each part, the area overlap between the part and the segmented input image is computed. Then, a weighted sum of the quotient between this overlap and the area of the corresponding model part is computed. The final similarity is the sum of the scalar product and the weighted sum.

All the aforementioned approaches have the same drawback: to ensure that the algorithms work, a binary segmentation of the input image of high quality is a pre-requisite. Binarization thresholds are often difficult to determine, and even an optimal threshold often yields a loss of important information about pixel-belonging-to-hand probabilities. To overcome this problem, approaches have been presented that work directly on the segmentation likelihood map. In [19] the skin color likelihood is used. For further matching, new features, called likelihood edges, are generated by applying an edge operator to the likelihood ratio image. However, in many cases, this leads to a very noisy edge image.

In [20–22], the skin color likelihood map is directly compared to the hand silhouette. Given a hypothesis, the silhouette foreground area of the corresponding hand pose and the neighboring rectangular background of a given size are used to compute the similarity measure. In the skin likelihood map, the joint matching probability for foreground and background are computed and combined into one similarity measure. Stenger et al. [20,21] proposed a method to compute the joint probability in linear time w.r.t. the contour length.

Mohr et al. [23] further reduced the computational complexity to compute the joint probability as similarity measure proposed by [20,21] from linear to near-constant time. Consequently the computation of a similarity is resolution-independent. For this purpose they used the integral image and a novel representation of silhouette-areas based on axis-aligned rectangles.

Segmentation-based approaches have two main drawbacks. The first one is the segmentation itself: it is an error-prone step because the segmentation is based on an assumption about the color distribution of the foreground. The second drawback of segmentation-based approaches is the silhouette area, which is a projection of the 3D hand to 2D and, thus, a lot of important information about the hand shape is lost.

Mohr et al. [24] proposed a novel similarity measure that does not need any kind of segmentation at all. The idea is to compute the color distributions in the input image that correspond to the shape of the hand and the corresponding background described by the template. They used the rectangle-based template representation from [23] to be able to compute the similarity measure efficiently. A further advantage of this similarity measure is that it trivially can be extended from color images to other input modalities such as range images.

The most important disadvantage of area-based approaches in general, and using a monocular camera in particular, is that several hand poses can be hardly distinguished. The reason is that the silhouettes are too similar from a specific point of view, i.e., a silhouette-based representation introduces a lot of ambiguities. Such cases are, for example, fingers in front of the palm with a moderate flexion, as shown in Fig. 5.

Edge-Based Similarity Measures. Edge gradient features are complementary to silhouette area-based features. While the silhouettes information utilizes the hand foreground and background, the idea of edge features is the border

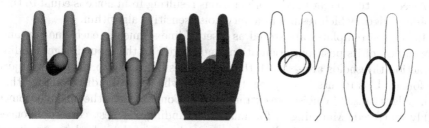

Fig. 5. Silhouette area-based similarity measures cannot resolve all ambiguities. Two example hand poses (left) illustrate the problem. Using the silhouette-area as feature does not allow to distinguish between both poses because the difference area (middle image, light blue area) is by far to small. In contrast, edge features allows us to distinguish both poses because the edges significantly change (right, highlighted by a red ellipsoid) between the two poses(Color figure online).

between fore- and background and even more important the separation of the fingers from the palm. The idea is to disambiguate hand poses that are unable to be distinguished using the silhouette. A further advantage of edge features is that they are fairly robust against illumination changes and varying object color. However, edges are not completely independent of illumination, color, texture, and camera parameters. Therefore, smart algorithms are still essential.

Most of the edge-based approaches need binary edges, i.e. an edge extraction is applied to both a projection of the hand model and the input image. Next, a distance measure between the edges is defined to compute the similarity between a hypothesis and the input image. As distance measures, for example the Hausdorff distance can be used. But much more popular is the Chamfer distance [25, 26] $\mathcal{C}$, which is a modification of the Hausdorff distance. Chamfer matching for tracking of articulated objects is, for example, used by [16, 20, 22, 27–31]. A disadvantage of the chamfer distance is its sensitivity to outliers.

Both, chamfer and Hausdorff distance can be modified to take edge orientation into account, albeit with limited accuracy. One way to do this is to split the template and query images into several separate images, each containing only edge pixels within a predefined orientation interval [20, 32]. To achieve some robustness against outliers, [20] additionally limited the nearest neighbor distance from template to image edges to a predefined upper bound. A disadvantage of these approaches is, of course, the discretization of the edge orientations, which can cause wrong edge distance estimations.

Olson et al. [33] integrated edge orientation into the Hausdorff distance. They modeled each pixel as a 3D-vector. The first two components contain the pixel coordinates, the third component the edge orientation. The maximum norm is used to calculate the pixel-to-pixel distance. Sudderth et al. [22] presented a similar approach to incorporate edge position and orientation into chamfer distances.

Edge orientation information is also used by [34] as a distance measure between templates. They discretized the orientation into four intervals and then generated an orientation histogram. Because they do not take the edge intensity into account, the weight of edge orientations resulting from noise is equal to that of object edges, which results in a very noise sensitive algorithm.

In [35] the templates are stored as a set of line segments, each line contains information of its position, orientation, and length. In the input image, the line extraction thresholds are set such that most lines belonging to the target object are found. This results in very low thresholds, which has the disadvantage that many edges caused by noise are extracted, too. Consequently, the image becomes highly cluttered. Matching is formulated as finding the best correspondences between template and input lines. Because a large number of edges, produced by noise, are processed in the line matching step, the probability of false matching is highly dependent on the input image quality and background.

Mohr et al. [36] avoided thesholding or discretization of the edge gradient. For this purpose they first mapped the edge gradients such that they can directly be compared using scalar product by keeping invariance with respect to the sign of the gradient. The similarity measure can be formulated as convolution and its computation time further reduced using Fourier transform. The similarity measure is designed to behave robust in noisy regions by integrating the edge gradient of the neighborhood of the template edges. But, as most other approaches, they still have to cope with varying edge intensities of important object edges.

The general problem with edge-based approaches is that they depend on the edge detection operators quality. There always is a trade-off between high clutter and missing object edges, i.e. often, the hand pose cannot be uniquely identified or not detected at all. Thus, if the input images have a cluttered background, edges is not the best choice. An additional problem are edge responses of wrinkles on the hand itself. They are hard to be modeled correctly by the artificial hand model, typically used for matching. Thus, they have to be treated as noise, and disturb edge-based similarity measures.

Depth images do not have the problems of false positive edges due to hand wrinkles or texture. Additionally, they do not need any color segmentation, which often is error prone. In the following, we will present approaches using depth images.

Depth Images Based Similarity Measures. Gudmundsson et al. [37] used projective geometry to match the hand template to the depth image. First, a part of the 26-dimensional configuration space was sampled and a dimension reduction using PCA performed. A particle filter in the low-dimensional space was used to find the hand pose in the next frame. Their distance measure between the hand hypothesis and the input image uses both image coordinates and depth information.

In [38], the hand pose is estimated using a ToF camera. The depth information was primarily used to segment the hand from the background. Features like finger tips, finger-likeness and palm candidates are extracted. A graph is built based on the features and the candidates/nodes best meeting some specific conditions are considered as finger tips and palm. Additionally, the knowledge of the palm pose in the previous frame is taken into account. The approach is able to detect two hands simultaneously.

Oikonomidis et al. [39] integrated the Kinect into their hand tracking algorithm. The hand is localized conventionally through skin segmentation. Hand pose estimation is formulated as an optimization problem. The difference-of-the-depth-values between the hypotheses and the Kinect data are added to the objective function. They use Particle Swarm Optimization (PSO) as optimization function. In [40] they extended the approach to track two interacting hands.

A tracking by classification approach is proposed by [41]. They adapt the method of human body tracking [42] to hand tracking. In [42], the body is partitioned into 31 parts. Then, they train a decision forest to be able to classify each part. They use a simple but effective difference-of-two-depth-values classifier for each node in the trees. The feature is inspired by [43]. After classification of each position in the depth image, they compute the body part positions by the mean shift algorithm. Keskin et al. [41] argue that for hand poses the random forests will become too large. To overcome this problem, they subdivided the hand pose estimation into two sub-problems. First, random forests for several hand poses are trained. Second, for each hand pose individual random forests for the finger parts are learned. Matching is performed by first classifying the hand pose and then detecting the finger poses for the most probable hand pose.

With the great advances in range cameras over the past years, depth images based matching seems to facilitate the most promising avenues for future research. One advantage is that the depth can be used to compute the size of the hand in image space. Additionally, a partial volume representation of the hand can be computed, which is a very useful information a color image does not provide. Furthermore, current depth cameras have their own NIR light source, and thus, are less dependent from the environmental lighting conditions. This yields a much more stable image, except in direct sunlight where depth cameras always fail due to the high amount of NIR light the sun emits. One drawback of depth images is that they cannot differentiate between a real hand (skin colored) and an artificial hand (e.g. made of plastic). But for practical use this is rarely relevant.

Similarity measures, in general, are often expensive and have to be computed very often for each frame due to the large hand shape variability (which yields a large number of templates). Thus, acceleration strategies are essential to achieve real-time hand pose estimation.

2.2   Fast Template Search Strategies

So far, we have discussed similarity measures for efficient hypothesis testing using template matching. The similarity measure, basically, is responsible for the quality of the pose estimation. For full-DOF hand tracking application, a huge number of templates have to be matched. To be able to perform hand pose estimation and tracking in real-time, one has to avoid as many similarity measure computations as possible to save computation time. For this purpose, several acceleration data structures for template matching have been proposed, which will be described in the following section.

Many approaches avoid the problem of simultaneous object detection and pose estimation by a manual initialization, or they assume a perfect image segmentation. Manual initialization, however, means that the approach needs to know the object location and pose from the previous frame.

In [44], an approach is proposed that needs both, manual initialization and a perfect segmentation. They convert the hand silhouette into a descriptor, which is used to compare the query silhouette against the database. Local PCA is applied to further reduce the dimension of the descriptor. To avoid an exhaustive search, they assume an initial guess and search for the best match in the low-dimensional neighborhood.

Manual initialization is also needed in [22]. They use nonparametric belief propagation, which is able to reduce the dimension of the posterior distribution over hand configurations. They integrate edge and color likelihood features into the similarity measure, and consequently, they do not need the hand to be perfectly segmented.

Similar preconditions are needed in [45, 46]. The similarity measure is integrated into an objective function, which is then optimized by gradient descent methods. Hand texture and shading informations are used in [46] and skin color in [45].

Lin et al. [14] uses a two-stage Nelder-Mead (NM) simplex search to optimize the hand position. They sample the hand pose space using a CyberGlove. The first NM search is constrained to the samples to avoid getting invalid hand poses. The second NM stage is a refinement and performs an unconstrained search in the continuous configuration space. They employ edge and silhouette features to measure the likelihood of the hypothesis.

Oikonomidis et al. [47] proposed a hand tracking approach that is designed to handle interactions with simple objects like cylinders and spheres. They manually initialize the hand pose and then optimize the objective function using the particle swarm optimization (PSO) algorithm. The objective function consists of two parts. The first part contains the incremental fitting of the hand model to the input image. This is done using the chamfer distance between binary edges, and the overlapping area between the hand silhouette and the binary segmentation. The second part penalizes self-penetration of the hand and penetration of the hand with the object the hand is interacting with.

Often, in real applications, neither a perfect segmentation nor an initial pose is given. A manual initialization is always tedious or not possible at all. Thus, several approaches are developed to search in the whole configuration space to be able to estimate the object pose in (near) real-time. This is even more challenging if the position of the object has to be detected as well. Particularly for objects with a high shape variability such as the human hand, localization and detection cannot be done separately because neither the appearance nor the location is known in advance.

Hashing [48, 49] is also used by [50] for hand pose classification. Binary hash functions are built from pairs of training examples, each pair building a line in the pose space. The hash values are in $\{0, 1\}$ depending on whether the projection of the input to the line is between two predefined thresholds or not. The projection is computed using only distances between objects (e.g. hand pose images). The binary hash functions are used to construct multiple multibit hash tables.

The idea to convert the evaluation of similarity measures to vector distances is used in [29, 51]. They used a Euclidean embedding technique to accelerate the template database indexing. A large number of 1D embedding is generated. An 1D embedding is characterized by a template pair. AdaBoost is used to combine many 1D embeddings into a multidimensional embedding. A database retrieval is performed by embedding the query image, and then, comparing the vector in the embedded Euclidean space to all database elements. Each embedding needs the similarity computation between the input image and all pairs of templates characterizing the high-dimensional embedding.

Thayananthan et al. [32] used a relevance vector machine (RVM). They used skin segmentation to localize the hand. The RVM's are trained using an EM type algorithm to learn the one-to-many mapping from binary image edges to pose space. From a training set of 10.000 hand templates, 455 are retained.

Tomasi et al. [52] used a hierarchical approach for hand gesture tracking with application to finger spelling. They use a small database consisting of real hand

Table 1. Hand pose estimation approaches can be categorized in the above six families. Some families are able to initially detect the hand pose and position themselves, others are not. The reliability means how often the estimated pose of the approach is (close to) the true hand position. For all approaches, any similarity measure could be used.

Family of approach	Initialization method	Reliability of results
Function optimization [14,45,47]	manual	high
Dim reduction and NNS [22,44]	manual	medium–high
Hashing [50]	automatic	medium
Hierarchies: pose [20] and image space [23,52]	automatic/manual	med
Machine learning [29,32,51]	automatic	med–high
Cascading [28]	automatic	med–high

images. The hand silhouette is extracted utilizing skin segmentation. Applying a Fourier Transform to the silhouette, they obtain a high-dimensional feature vector. They build a hierarchy by recursively applying PCA-based vector quantization to the vectors.

Stenger et al. [20] proposed an approach that hierarchically partitions the hand pose space. "The state space is partitioned using a multi-resolution grid". The nodes at each level are associated with non-overlapping sets of hand poses in the state space. "Tracking is formulated as a Bayesian inference problem". During tracking, they process only the sub-trees yielding a high posterior probability.

In contrast to the pose space hierarchy of [20,23] used a feature space hierarchy to be able to build a deeper template tree, which allows for faster matching. Their hierarchy is based on the silhouette area of the templates. Inner nodes represent the intersection area of their child nodes. Leaves represent hand poses and inner nodes represent the hand poses of all leaves in the sub-tree. Matching is performed through traversal. During the traversal of the tree from the root node to a leaf, the hand silhouettes are getting closer to a hand pose.

In [28], cascading [53] is used for hand shape classification. Four different classifiers are employed, based on edge locations, edge orientations, finger locations, and geometric moments. "Database retrieval is done hierarchically by quickly rejecting the vast majority of all database views" using finger and moment-based features. They reported that they could reject 99 % of the database in this step. Then, the remaining candidates are ranked by a combination of all four classifiers.

Table 1 shows another way to categorize the many approaches to hand pose estimation; for each category, it lists a few references that pursued the respective approach, which are, in our view, exemplary for that approach.

2.3 Conclusions

In this section, we provided an overview on the area of hand pose estimation. A detailed description about the main challenges of vision-based hand pose estimation is given. Clearly, in the past decade a lot of approaches have been presented that tried to solve the problem. Many approaches make an important contribution to robust real-time hand tracking. Several similarity measures and input modalities can, of course, be combined to increase the robustness, e.g. edge features, color-based features, and depth information.

In the following section, a new direction for tackling the problem of hand tracking is proposed. We believe it to be very promising, and our preliminary results prove its great potential. The new approach uses depth images for similarity measure computation and machine learning to learn the hand poses as well as invariance to hand geometry e.g. finger length. The approach explained in the following is our current research in progress. Similar methods for human pose estimation exist but its application to hand pose estimation is challenging due to the high self-similarity of the fingers and much more unconstrained hand movement. We will start with the motivation for choosing machine learning for hand pose recognition.

3 Our RF–Based Hand Pose Recognition

The survey given in the previous section shows that the most often used and promising approaches are model-based. Almost all model-based approaches use similarity measures defined by experts to compare a pose hypothesis with the observation, i.e., an expert manually designs the kinds of features such as hand silhouette or edges to be used and how exactly the hypothesis is compared against the observation (e.g., non-overlapping area or chamfer distance). This has two drawbacks: first, manually defined kinds of features and similarity measures between features may not necessarily be optimal. They cannot be learned from examples. Second, similarity measures from experts use a fixed (mostly artificial) hand model. But, the more the real hand to be tracked differs in shape from the artificial hand model, the more inaccurate the pose estimation will be. Coping with the variability of hand geometry is often hard or impossible with such similarity measures. Of course, one could add them as additional hand poses to the template database, but they would all have to be matched to the input image, which would dramatically increase the execution time of the recognition system, and they would dramatically increase the memory needed for storing the template data base.

The approach introduced in this section uses a machine learning approach based on random forests[1] (RF) that can learn to be invariant to different hand geometries as well as achieve a high pose recognition rate. Hand pose estimation, which is a regression problem, is mapped to a classification problem in a natural way. This enables to use the well-proven random forest techniques for classification.

---

[1] Random forests (sometimes also called decision forests, were first introduced by Leo Breiman [54]. Precursors were introduced, e.g., by [55, 56].

3.1   Random Forests

This section gives a quick recap of the general idea of random forests. A random forest is a set of decision trees. Decision trees are a common technique to make any kind of decision based on a set of individual test functions called weak classifier. Each weak classifier yields a small amount of information gain. One of the main problems of decision trees is that they tend to overfit to the training data, and consequently, do not generalize well. To get rid of this problem, Leo Breiman [54] proposed to use a set of decision trees. Each individual tree is trained using for each tree a random subset of both, the training data and weak classifiers. The idea behind random forest is that some individual decision trees can make a wrong decision but the majority of the trees will make the right decision. Random forests have been widely used and proved to outperform many other machine learning approaches and generalize very well. Note that RF's can also be used to solve other tasks e.g. regression or density function estimation.

3.2   Learning Random Forests for Hand Pose Recognition

The RF–based approach is used for hand pose recognition in terms of estimating the hand orientation (3 degrees of freedom) and joint angles (20 degrees of freedom) with a high accuracy. This yields a 23 dimensional search space. The remaining 3 DOFs are the location in the image. The approach most similar to our method is [41]. Their approach depends on a clustering algorithm that assigns each hand pose to a gesture, and the number of gestures they use. The RF–based approach proposed in this section uses a more natural way, that directly maps the hand pose estimation to classification without the needs of additional error prone methods.

Description of the Kind of Input Dataset: The input data for our hand pose recognition method are depth images obtained using a time-of-flight camera. Depth images provide the distance from the camera for each pixel. Depth images are superior over color images because they are independent of color distortions, lighting conditions and the depth information itself can solve a lot of ambiguities a color image is not able to.

Our Features Set: Crucial for the performance of any RF is the automatic choice of good features and the per-node weak classifiers, respectively. The choice of the features is specific to the task, which, here, is hand pose recognition from depth images.

Choice of the Features: Given an input image I and a candidate position $\mathbf{x}$ the hand is supposed to be located at, [41,42] proposed differences between depth values of randomly selected pixels as features. This approach can be generalized to arbitrary rectangles R_i. Rectangles are a good choice because the sum of a rectangular area can be computed in constant time utilizing the integral image [53]:
$f(I, \mathbf{x}) = d_I\left(\mathbf{x} + \frac{\mathbf{R}_i}{d_I(\mathbf{x})}\right) - d_I\left(\mathbf{x} + \frac{\mathbf{R}_j}{d_I(\mathbf{x})}\right)$. The notation $\frac{\mathbf{R}_i}{d}$ denotes a scaling of

rectangle $\mathbf{R}_i$'s position and size relative to the hand distance, and $d_I(\mathbf{R}_i)$ denotes the mean of all distance values in $\mathbf{R}_i$. The choice of the features have two main advantages. First, range images from state-of-the-art hardware are very noisy. Using rectangles trivially allows for an averaging of the depth values. It could be much more robust than single pixel. Second, using a rectangle can provide more information to a weak classifier than a single pixel. The integral image as acceleration data structure allows constant time complexity for the computation time of the feature response.

Background Handling: Similar to [42], we use a large value ω for $d_I(\mathbf{y})$ if $\mathbf{y}$ belongs to the background. To determine whether a pixel $\mathbf{y}$ belongs to the background, we apply the threshold test $d_I(\mathbf{y}) - d_I(\mathbf{x}) \notin [\tau_m(\mathbf{x}), \tau_M(\mathbf{x})]$. The RF–based scheme uses more sophisticated, adaptive thresholds. During RF training, in each decision node depth images are used for training. $\tau_m(\mathbf{x}), \tau_M(\mathbf{x})$ is computed by recording the minimum/maximum distances of all pixels inside all hands relative to the average hand distance. Additionally, a small offset ε is added to the thresholds to increase the background detection robustness during tracking.

To ensure that our features are independent with respect to the overall depth of the hand i.e. $d_I(\mathbf{x})$, in the case where $\mathbf{y}$ is a background pixel, the constant ω $d_I(\mathbf{x})$ is added to the background.

Infinite Training Dataset Generation: An artificial hand model is used to train the RF. This is very advantageous because we are able to draw samples from an *arbitrarily large* ground truth database of hand poses for any pose and shape variability. This yields a very flexible and virtually inexhaustible source of ground truth data for RF training.

Of course, any approach should be highly robust against different hand geometries. In order to achieve that, the length and thickness of each bone has to be explicitly be parametrized in the hand model. Additionally, Perlin gradient noise is added to the hand geometry to model "curvy" hand silhouettes produced by skin, tissue, phalanx "imperfections", and camera noise. This allows to generate images with various shapes for our training set. In this way, the RF learns various hand geometries for each and every pose.

We denote a hand pose in pose space by $\theta \in \Theta$ and a specific hand geometry by $\gamma \in \Gamma$. The hand geometry space consists of parameters for the finger, palm, and forearm length and thickness, as well as the Perlin noise parameters to modify the bending of the hand. Overall, the rendered depth image $I_k(\theta, \gamma)$ depends on those two properties. In the following, we will explain how we use our artificial hand model to train the decision trees.

Mapping Hand Pose Recognition to RF Learning: The RF–based scheme uses an elegant mapping of hand pose recognition, which is a regression problem, to a random forest classification problem. This has the advantage that the well proven Shannon entropy-based information gain measure can be used. For a robust estimation, it is crucial to recognize different hand poses independently of the hand geometry (e.g., finger length and thickness) to some amount. Therefore, the mapping to a classification problem is as follows: random samples of uniform distribution are taken from the hand pose space Θ; each sample $\theta_i \in \Theta$ represents a class c_i our RF should recognize. Each hand pose sample θ_i is rendered at a different geometry $\gamma_j \in \Gamma$ taken randomly from uniform distribution, too; all of them are put in to the same class.

That way, a random forest for classification with the Shannon Entropy based information gain is trained. Consequently, the RF–based scheme learns to classify depth images of hand poses robustly against hand shapes.

Recognizing Hand Poses with RFs: Arriving at a leaf node of a decision tree, the predicted class labeled with a hand pose is obtained In case of discrete classes, typically a voting over all trees is done and the class with the most votes wins. However, the set of poses estimated by the decision trees in our RF can be considered as density function because the hand pose space is a continuous space. For this reason, the mode of the density function is used as the final estimated pose. Due to the high-dimensional pose space, the mode finding is applied to each degree of freedom separately. For maximum finding, the well known mean shift algorithm [57] is used.

Fig. 6. The figure shows first results of the proposed RF–based method scheme using a random forest for classification for full-DOF hand pose recognition. The above images show just 6 frames taken from a larger dataset consisting of flexing and abducting the index, middle, ring and little finger in arbitrary combination. Each of the 6 frames consists of two panels. The left panel shows the depth image mapped such that you can clearly see the hand pose. On the right panel the image is mapped such that you can see the whole scene, superimposed with an artificial hand at the pose estimated by our proposed approach.

For qualitative evaluation, a real hand with flexing and abducting 4 fingers (index, middle, ring, and pinky) is captured. For the real dataset no ground truth is available thus, we provide screenshots of a few selected frames that shows the power of our approach in Fig. 6.

4   Conclusions

In the near future it might be a good idea to use multi-modal sensors and features, such as depth and conventional camera images, most often denoted by RGB-D image. The depth image can be used to increase the robustness of the hand localization and rough pose estimation, and the color image could heavily improve the accuracy of the pose estimation. First approaches using depth images have been presented by [37–39].

In the long-term future, when the sensor resolution of depth cameras will have been improved substantially, hand tracking can significantly benefit from depth information and the color image could become unnecessary in many situations. However, one can always find cases with many objects, one of them being the hand, that have similar distance from the camera, which make it hard to detect the hand using depth information only. In such cases, conventional color images could help a lot to detect and estimate the hand pose. Thus, the approaches using color images should be useful for the future, independent of the quality of upcoming depth cameras.

Hand tracking is a challenging task due to the high-dimensional pose space but also due to the highly non-linearity of the pose space and the high variability of the hand geometry of different persons. We took images of 5 people (Fig. 1b) and found that the palm and finger length and thickness differ a lot. Simple model-based approaches cannot handle this geometry variability appropriately because they have to use a particular hand-model. But machine learning-based approaches can cope with them. Hands with different geometry can be fed into machine learning algorithms much in the same way as different hand poses such that the learning algorithm (e.g. AdaBoosting, support vector machine or random forests) can learn them. For this reason our current work (Sect. 3) focuses on one of the most popular machine-learning approaches, the random forest. Thayananthan et al. [32,41] also proposed to use machine learning for hand pose recognition.

Finally, we want to mention that in the past many approaches used local optimization for hand pose estimation and tracking. They need the hand pose and position to be known in the previous frame. Consequently, they need a *manual* initialization which is tedious and sometimes not practicable at all. Another consequence it that the hand motion speed is strongly limited by the computational power. Both limitations make such approaches unusable for any real applications. The future of hand tracking, thus, will focus tracking by detection approaches which estimate hand pose and position for each frame independently.

References

1. Moeslund, T.B., Hilton, A., Krüger, V.: A survey of advances in vision-based human motion capture and analysis. Comput. Vis. Image Underst. **104**, 90–126 (2006)
2. Erol, A., Bebis, G., Nicolescu, M., Boyle, R.D., Twombly, X.: Vision-based hand pose estimation: a review. Comput. Vis. Image Underst. **108**(1–2), 52–73 (2007)
3. Cui, Y., Weng, J.J.: Hand segmentation using learning-based prediction and verification for hand sign recognition. In: Proceeding IEEE Conference Computer Vision Pattern Recognition. pp. 88–93 (1996)
4. Cui, Y., Weng, J.: Appearance-based hand sign recognition from intensity image sequences. Comput. Vis. Image Underst. **78**(2), 157–176 (2000)
5. Rosales, R., Athitsos, V., Sigal, L., Sclaroff, S.: 3D hand pose reconstruction using specialized mappings. In: International Conference on Computer Vision, pp. 378–385 (2001)
6. Barhate, K.A., Patwardhan, K.S., Roy, S.D., Chaudhuri, S., Chaudhury, S.: Robust shape based two hand tracker. In: IEEE International Conference on Image Processing, pp. 1017–1020 (2004)
7. Argyros, A., Lourakis, M.: Tracking multiple colored blobs with a moving camera. In: IEEE Conference on Computer Vision and Pattern Recognition, p. 1178 (2005)
8. Wang, X., Zhang, X., Dai, G.: Tracking of deformable human hand in real time as continuous input for gesture-based interaction. In: International Conference on Intelligent User Interfaces, pp. 235–242 (2007)
9. John, C.: Volumetric hand reconstruction and tracking to support non-verbal communication in collaborative virtual environments. Dissertation Submitted to the University of Otago, Dunedin, New Zealand (2011)
10. Ueda, E., Matsumoto, Y., Imai, M., Ogasawara, T.: A hand-pose estimation for vision-based human interfaces. IEEE Trans. Industr. Electron. **50**, 676–684 (2003)
11. Schlattmann, M., Klein, R.: Simultaneous 4 gestures 6 DOF real-time two-hand tracking without any markers. In: ACM Symposium on Virtual Reality Software and Technology (VRST 2007), November 2007
12. Schlattmann, M., Kahlesz, F., Sarlette, R., Klein, R.: Markerless 4 gestures 6 DOF real-time visual tracking of the human hand with automatic initialization. Comput. Graph. Forum **26**(3), 467–476 (2007)
13. Dhawale, P., Masoodian, M., Rogers, B.: Bare-hand 3D gesture input to interactive systems. In: 7th International Conference on Computer-Human Interaction: Design Centered HCI, pp. 25–32 (2006)
14. Lin, J.Y., Wu, Y., Huang, T.S.: 3D model-based hand tracking using stochastic direct search method. In: International Conference on Automatic Face and Gesture Recognition, p. 693 (2004)
15. Wu, Y., Lin, J.Y., Huang, T.S.: Capturing natural hand articulation. In: International Conference on Computer Vision, vol. 2, pp. 426–432 (2001)
16. Kato, M., Chen, Y.W., Xu, G.: Articulated hand tracking by PCA-ICA approach. In: International Conference on Automatic Face and Gesture Recognition, pp. 329–334 (2006)
17. Ouhaddi, H., Horain, P.: 3D hand gesture tracking by model registration. In: Workshop on Synthetic-Natural Hybrid Coding and Three Dimensional Imaging, pp. 70–73 (1999)
18. Nirei, K., Saito, H., Mochimaru, M., Ozawa, S.: Human hand tracking from binocular image sequences. In: 22th International Conference on Industrial Electronics, Control, and Instrumentation, pp. 297–302 (1996)

19. Zhou, H., Huang, T.: Tracking articulated hand motion with eigen dynamics analysis. IEEE International Conference on Computer Vision, vol. 2, pp. 1102–1109 (2003)
20. Stenger, B., Thayananthan, A., Torr, P.H.S., Cipolla, R.: Model-based hand tracking using a hierarchical bayesian filter. IEEE Trans. Pattern Anal. Mach. Intell. **28**, 1372–1384 (2006)
21. Stenger, B.D.R.: Model-based hand tracking using a hierarchical bayesian filter. Dissertation Submitted to the University of Cambridge (2004)
22. Sudderth, E.B., Mandel, M.I., Freeman, W.T., Willsky, A.S.: Visual hand tracking using nonparametric belief propagation. In: IEEE CVPR Workshop on Generative Model Based Vision, vol. 12, pp. 189 (2004)
23. Mohr, D., Zachmann, G.: Fast: fast adaptive silhouette area based template matching. In: Proceedings of the British Machine Vision Conference, pp. 39.1-39.12. BMVA Press (2010). doi:10.5244/C.24.39
24. Mohr, D., Zachmann, G.: Segmentation-free, area-based articulated object tracking. In: Bebis, G., Boyle, R., Parvin, B., Koracin, D., Wang, S., Kyungnam, K., Benes, B., Moreland, K., Borst, C., Di Verdi, S., Yi-Jen, C., Ming, J. (eds.) ISVC 2011, Part I. LNCS, vol. 6938, pp. 112–123. Springer, Heidelberg (2011)
25. Barrow, H.G., Tenenbaum, J.M., Bolles, R.C., Wolf, H.C.: Parametric correspondence and chamfer matching: two new techniques for image matching. In: International Joint Conference on Artificial Intelligence (1977)
26. Borgefors, G.: Hierarchical chamfer matching: a parametric edge matching algorithm. IEEE Trans. Pattern Anal. Mach. Intell. **10**, 849–865 (1988)
27. Athitsos, V., Sclaroff, S.: 3D hand pose estimation by finding appearance-based matches in a large database of training views. In: IEEE Workshop on Cues in Communication (2001)
28. Athitsos, V., Sclaroff, S.: An appearance-based framework for 3D hand shape classification and camera viewpoint estimation. In: IEEE Conference on Automatic Face and Gesture Recognition (2002)
29. Athitsos, V., Alon, J., Sclaroff, S., Kollios, G.: Boostmap: a method for efficient approximate similarity rankings. In: IEEE Conference on Computer Vision and Pattern Recognition (2004)
30. Gavrila, D., Philomin, V.: Real-time object detection for "smart" vehicles. In: Proceedings of the Seventh IEEE International Conference on Computer Vision, vol. 1, pp. 87. IEEE Computer Society, Los Alamitos (1999)
31. Lin, Z., Davis, L.S., Doermann, D., DeMenthon, D.: Hierarchical part-template matching for human detection and segmentation. In: IEEE International Conference on Computer Vision (2007)
32. Thayananthan, A., Navaratnam, R., Stenger, B., Torr, P., Cipolla, R.: Multivariate relevance vector machines for tracking. In: Leonardis, A., Bischof, H., Pinz, A. (eds.) ECCV 2006. LNCS, vol. 3953, pp. 124–138. Springer, Heidelberg (2006)
33. Olson, C.F., Huttenlocher, D.P.: Automatic target recognition by matching oriented edge pixels. IEEE Trans. Image Process. **6**, 103–113 (1997)
34. Shaknarovich, G., Viola, P., Darrell, T.: Fast pose estimation with parameter-sensitive hashing. In: IEEE International Conference on Computer Vision (2003)
35. Athitsos, V., Sclaroff, S.: Estimating 3D hand pose from a cluttered image. In: IEEE Conference on Computer Vision and Pattern Recognition (2003)
36. Mohr, D., Zachmann, G.: Continuous edge gradient-based template matching for articulated objects. In: International Joint Conference on Computer Vision and Computer Graphics Theory and Applications (2009)

37. Gudmundsson, S.Á., Sveinsson, J.R., Pardàs, M., Aanæs, H., Larsen, R.: Model-based hand gesture tracking in ToF image sequences. In: Perales, F.J., Fisher, R.B. (eds.) AMDO 2010. LNCS, vol. 6169, pp. 118–127. Springer, Heidelberg (2010)
38. Hackenberg, G., McCall, R., Broll, W.: Lightweight palm and finger tracking for real-time 3D gesture control. In: IEEE Virtual Reality Conference, pp. 19–26 (2011)
39. Oikonomidis, I., Kyriazis, N., Argyros, A.: Efficient model-based 3D tracking of hand articulations using kinect. In: BMVC 2011, BMVA (2011)
40. Oikonomidis, I., Kyriazis, N., Argyros, A.: Tracking the articulated motion of two strongly interacting hands. In: CVPR. IEEE, June 2012
41. Keskin, C., Kıraç, F., Kara, Y.E., Akarun, L.: Hand pose estimation and hand shape classification using multi-layered randomized decision forests. In: Fitzgibbon, A., Lazebnik, S., Perona, P., Sato, Y., Schmid, C. (eds.) ECCV 2012, Part VI. LNCS, vol. 7577, pp. 852–863. Springer, Heidelberg (2012)
42. Shotton, J., Fitzgibbon, A., Cook, M., Sharp, T., Finocchio, M., Moore, R., Kipman, A., Blake, A.: Real-time human pose recognition in parts from single depth images. In: Cipolla, R., Battiato, S., Farinella, G.M. (eds.) Machine Learning for Computer Vision, pp. 119–135. Springer, Heidelberg (2011)
43. Lepetit, V., Lagger, P., Fua, P.: Randomized trees for real-time keypoint recognition. In: Computer Vision and Pattern Recognition, pp. 775–781 (2005)
44. Shimada, N., Kimura, K., Shirai, Y.: Real-time 3-D hand posture estimation based on 2-D appearance retrieval using monocular camera. In: IEEE International Conference on Computer Vision, pp. 23 (2001)
45. de La Gorce, M., Paragios, N.: A variational approach to monocular hand-pose estimation. Comput. Vis. Image Underst. **114**(3), 363–372 (2010)
46. de La Gorce, M., Paragios, N., Fleet, D.J.: Model-based hand tracking with texture, shading and self-occlusions. In: IEEE Conference on Computer Vision and Pattern Recognition (2008)
47. Oikonomidis, I., Kyriazis, N., Argyros, A.: Full dof tracking of a hand interacting with an object by modeling occlusions and physical constraints. In: ICCV 2011. IEEE (2011)
48. Kulis, B., Darrell, T.: Learning to hash with binary reconstructive embeddings. In: Proceeding NIPS, pp. 1042–1050 (2009)
49. Kulis, B., Grauman, K.: Kernelized locality-sensitive hashing for scalable image search. In: IEEE International Conference on Computer Vision (ICCV) (2009)
50. Athitsos, V., Potamias, M., Papapetrou, P., Kollios, G.: Nearest neighbor retrieval using distance-based hashing. In: Proceedings of the 2008 IEEE 24th International Conference on Data Engineering. ICDE 2008, pp. 327–336. IEEE Computer Society, Washington, DC (2008)
51. Athitsos, V., Alon, J., Sclaroff, S., Kollios, G.: Boostmap: an embedding method for efficient nearest neighbor retrieval. IEEE Trans. Pattern Anal. Mach. Intell. **30**(1), 89–104 (2008)
52. Tomasi, C., Petrov, S., Sastry, A.: 3D tracking = classification + interpolation. In: International Conference on Computer Vision, pp. 1441–1448 (2003)
53. Viola, P., Jones, M.: Rapid object detection using a boosted cascade of simple features. In: IEEE Conference on Computer Vision and Pattern Recognition, vol. 1, pp. I-511–I-518 (2001)
54. Breiman, L.: Random forests. Mach. Learn. **45**(1), 5–32 (2001)
55. Quinlan, J.R.: C4.5: Programs for Machine Learning. Morgan Kaufmann Publishers Inc., San Francisco (1993)

56. Ho, T.K.: Random decision forests. In: Proceedings of the Third International Conference on Document Analysis and Recognition (Volume 1), ICDAR 1995, vol. 1, pp. 278-282. IEEE Computer Society, Washington, DC (1995)
57. Fukunaga, K., Hostetler, L.: The estimation of the gradient of a density function, with applications in pattern recognition. IEEE Trans. Inf. Theor. **21**(1), 32–40 (2006)

Virtual Humans

Applications of Avatar Mediated Interaction to Teaching, Training, Job Skills and Wellness

Charles E. Hughes[✉], Arjun Nagendran, Lisa A. Dieker,
Michael C. Hynes, and Gregory F. Welch

University of Central Florida, Orlando 32826, USA
{ceh,arjun}@cs.ucf.edu, {lisa.dieker,michael.hynes,
welch}@ucf.edu

Abstract. The focus of this chapter is on the application of a framework for remotely delivering role-playing experiences that afford users the opportunity to practice real-world skills in a safe virtual setting. The framework, AMITIES, provides a single individual the capabilities to remotely orchestrate the performances of multiple virtual characters. We illustrate this by introducing avatar–enabled scenarios that range from teacher preparation to effectively dealing with complex interpersonal situations such as resistance to peer pressure and participation in job interviews (either as the interviewer or the interviewee).

1 Introduction

The education of school teachers usually involves a capstone experience, called an internship, where each has the opportunity to deliver instruction to real children either as the sole instructor or in an apprentice role. This puts children (and prospective teachers) at risk while skills, especially soft skills associated with human-to-human interaction, are still being learned. Virtual environments provide an opportunity for teachers to practice without interfering with the education of children and without placing themselves at the mercy of these same children while their classroom management, pedagogy and even content skills are still developing. Unfortunately, purely virtual worlds (ones driven by programmed behaviors) are not yet adaptive enough to provide realistic responses to verbal and non-verbal interactions, and are not capable of handling the almost random directions that the conversations may or should take. Similarly, the demands imposed by virtual worlds that deal with protective strategies, e.g., for college freshmen or pre-teens facing enormous peer pressure, and other applications that need to reflect the subtleties of human interaction, are not presently met through programmed behaviors, even those encompassing evolutionary changes in those behaviors.

This chapter focuses on how a human-in-the-loop paradigm can provide the realism needed to address the areas mentioned above, as well as other applications involving intense human-to-human verbal and non-verbal interaction. Specifically, we focus first on TeachLivE (Teaching and Learning in a Virtual Environment), a system in current use at 55 universities and four school districts in the U.S. The TeachLivE system provides in-service and pre-service teachers the opportunity to practice skills and reflect

G. Brunnett et al. (Eds.): Virtual Realities, LNCS 8844, pp. 133–146, 2015.
DOI: 10.1007/978-3-319-17043-5_8

on their own performances. The reflection component is achieved through an integrated after-action review system that supports automated and semi-automated tagging of events, along with the use of these tags to select video sequences that demonstrate the teacher's performance in different contexts. The system's scalability is enhanced by a micropose-based network protocol and the use of just one human inhabitor, called an interactor, to orchestrate the performances of multiple avatars (human surrogates) and agents (software controlled characters).

In addition to teacher rehearsal, this chapter discusses the uses of avatar-mediated interaction for development of protective strategies for the wellness of self and others, and the employment of the underlying virtual settings for other complex interpersonal interactions such as interviewing prospective employees or being interviewed by prospective employers. Finally, we discuss how the system can prepare people for the complex task of leading debriefing sessions; in effect, showing how the paradigm can be used to train people on how to effectively use reflection, one of the most useful features of our system called AMITIES (Sect. 2).

2   The AMITIES Framework

AMITIES™ is an acronym for Avatar-Mediated Interactive Training and Individualized Experience System. This is the technical framework on which all our avatar-based systems are built. AMITIES supports a blend of agent-based and avatar-based behaviors. AMITIES encapsulates all the software components, including device interaction, needed to remotely deliver, receive and observe avatar-based role-playing experiences. This infrastructure permits the creation of a broad range of detailed realistic and compelling interactive scenarios for training, education, wellness, and similar areas. AMITIES also includes components to help its users reflect on their performance (e.g. for after action review), with or without a coach providing guidance during such reflection.

All experiences presented in this chapter are built on the AMITIES framework. Each involves scenarios that include virtual characters whose personalities are set, but whose actions are heavily influenced by the behaviors of users who take part in the experience. For example, a virtual character may proactively make a personalized comment (such as requesting details about a user's profession) to increase engagement of the seemingly less-involved user during conversation. A key to the AMITIES paradigm is the use of an interactor who orchestrates the interaction of a troupe of avatars and agents in their communications with one or more human users. Technical details of the AMITIES framework are presented in Nagendran, et al. (2014). For our purposes, the brief description above is sufficient.

3   Teacher Education: Experiences in TeachLivE

TeachLivE™ stands for Teaching and Learning in a virtual Environment. This refers to the virtual classroom environment that we use for preparing teachers for the challenges of working in K-12 classrooms. TeachLivE is supported by the underlying infrastructure of AMITIES (described above). Its primary use is to provide teachers the opportunity to rehearse their classroom management, pedagogical and content delivery skills in an environment that neither harms real children nor causes the teacher to be seen as weak or insecure by an actual classroom full of students. TeachLivE also uses the AMITIES framework to support reflective learning following an experience in the virtual classroom.

3.1 TeachLivE Overview

Consider the situation of walking into a classroom setting where the students are virtual and yet exhibit personalities that are appropriate for members of their age group (Dieker et al., 2014). This is what a TeachLivE experience provides, currently supporting classes of middle (Fig. 1) and high school students, with elementary students coming in fall 2015.

Fig. 1. TeachLivE middle school classroom

The members of these classes have personalities that are diverse enough to represent the population of a typical classroom, even though there are only have five students in each such setting. The basis for the selection of personalities comes from the research of Long 1988. Essentially, we have two major pairs of factors: aggressiveness and passiveness, and independence and dependency. This provides four personality types. When we address the middle school classroom students (Fig. 2), we find that Ed (first row, left side) is a passive dependent, who wants your approval but is far too polite to push for it. Sean (first row, right side) is an aggressive dependent whose need for approval by the teacher leads to his wanting to answer nearly every question, whether posed to him or not. Maria (second row, left side) is a passive independent who is an aspiring engineer with no self-perceived need for your assistance or attention. CJ (second row, middle) is an aggressive independent who is the class leader and tends to not care about school or rules. Kevin (second row, right side) is CJ's most loyal follower who wants her approval for everything he does. The dynamics between Sean and CJ are a bit tense as he openly disapproves of her inappropriate behaviors (e.g., texting during class) and she blatantly views him as being the ultimate uncool kid. Sean's need for attention leads some teachers to spend all their time with him and others to angrily try to shut him up. Maria rarely opens her mouth, and so many teachers never engage her in conversation, missing out on discovering and encouraging her wonderful intellect. Ed is very easy going and has clear goals but needs some assistance especially in mathematics. Kevin also gets ignored sometimes as his focus on creating YouTube videos does not culturally connect him to some teachers.

Fig. 2. TeachLivE middle school kids – Ed, Sean, Maria, CJ and Kevin

The most important thing about these characters and, in fact, all characters that exist within the AMITIES framework is that they always remain true to their personalities, backstories and needs. Thus, if you are a teacher in their classroom, your only hope for change is in your own way of approaching them, not in their essential ways of dealing with you. As one might expect, the high school versions of these characters are much less rigid, and the elementary school versions are more compliant. Thus, as in real life, the middle school classroom is the most challenging but potentially the most rewarding.

3.2   The Roles of the Interactor and User

The key to achieving consistency in the personalities of characters in TeachLivE and other AMITIES-based experiences is the use of interactors. Our interactors are like talented orchestra leaders. While the orchestra members have their own skill sets, it is this orchestration that brings harmony or, if desired, discordance to the performance. What makes interactors different from traditional orchestra leaders is that the performances they direct are interactive and unscripted. The direction of the dialogue and non-verbal behaviors (facial and body) depends on the actions, verbal and non-verbal, of the audience members (generally, but not necessarily, an audience of one). The interactors achieve this level of control in any scenario via a highly customized user-interface that is designed in accordance with their cognitive comfort during the development phase. The process itself is a very iterative one with programmers, artists and interactors all working together to achieve the best blend of control for faithful reproduction of selected behaviors.

The user (trainee teacher) has free movement in a TeachLivE experience. As he or she walks towards or away from a large flat screen display of the classroom, the virtual camera moves in ways that match the user's actions. Thus, if the user moves towards Maria, the camera position moves towards her as well, thereby compressing space and allowing the user to move as if in the same space as the virtual characters. Bending down provides the user an eye-to-eye view of Maria. This ability to achieve proximity and intimacy provides a sense of place illusion (I'm in the same space as these students) which can also be reflective of the degree of immersiveness of the system. This is critical to the effectiveness of the experience (Slater, 2009). The mapping of the user motion to smooth camera motion is achieved via standard data filtering techniques implemented on the depth stream and skeletal data from a Kinect.

3.3 Reflection

Learning through any experience is greatly aided if the learner has an opportunity to reflect on his or her performance. Such reflection can occur alone, sometimes just mentally replaying the details of the experience, or with a coach who provides a guided replay of one's actions, offering alternative choices that may lead to more desirable outcomes. This latter coach-assisted reflection is often called after-action review (AAR) or debriefing. One approach, called Debriefing with Good Judgment (Rudolph et al., 2007), is particularly effective when dealing with team performance but also offers excellent guidance for single-user coaching.

Independent of whether reflection is guided or not, the availability of objective data is critical to the process's success. Our observation is that inexperienced (and often experienced) teachers who are asked if they spent an approximately equal amount of time with each student will invariably offer the subjective answer of yes and the objective answer is invariably no.

A transcript of a sample dialogue during a Math Lesson between a trainee teacher and students in the classroom is provided below:

Context: Pick a number that does *not* satisfy the equation $4*x + 1 = 3$
Relevance: Explain the concept of equations with rational number solutions.

[VC] Sean:
Ok, Can we just pick any..umm..we get to pick any number we want?
[Trainee] Teacher:
Well, if you want to take that technique, yeah, give it a try. Pick any number you want.
[VC] Cindy:
[giggles …] I'm picking zero, 'cause I think that zero, that's the best.
[Trainee] Teacher:
Zero is a good one. Actually, I like zero. Why did you pick zero?
[VC] Cindy:
Just 'cause I like multiplying by zero 'cause it's super-easy
[Trainee] Teacher:
Me too … very easy. Umm..Ok, so let's go ahead and do those calculations. What calculations do you have then, Cindy? Stick a zero in there.
[VC] Cindy:
Well zero works, right ? 'cause zero times zero is just zero and then plus one is just one and then that doesn't equal three.
[Trainee] Teacher:
Exactly, excellent! Ok, so let's play …
[VC] Sean:
[interrupts teacher …] I used, I used ten.
[Trainee] Teacher:
You used ten? Alright …
[VC] Sean:
[continues to explain answer ….]

AMITIES provides support for reflection in the form of automated and manually entered tagging of events. Automated data can include time spent in front of the class, time spent in proximity of each character, percentage of time spent in each zone of the classroom and time spent talking by the user versus that spent by the virtual characters (Fig. 3). Data that presently requires human judgment includes (i) number of high-level questions asked, (ii) number of low-level questions asked, (iii) specific praise offered to students, (iv) general praise offered to students and (v) time from asking a question to giving an answer. As we progress in our research, we are finding that we are gathering enormous amounts of data that we can now mine for other actions that correlate with success. A recent study has shown positive correlation between body posture and perceived success, which appears to also correlate to better performance (Barmaki 2014). Other studies are looking at metrics related to perceived social presence (Okita et al. 2008) and its correlation with performance (Hayes et al. 2014).

3.4   TeachLivE Effectiveness

Over the year, the TeachLivE team ran a series of experiments to determine its effectiveness in conveying new strategies to teachers. Our focus was on math instruction in

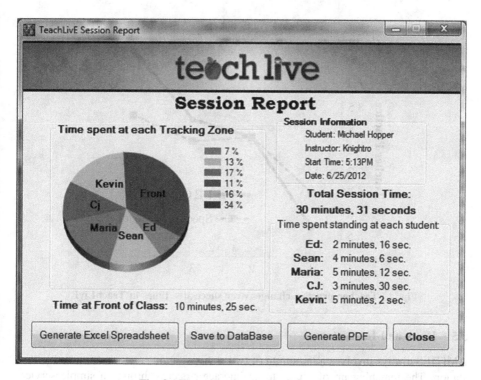

Fig. 3. Example of automated feedback

middle schools in the United States. These students are typically in the age range from 11 to 14 years-old. The experiment started 157 in-service teachers at 10 distinct sites across the country. Due to attrition, 22 dropped out of the experiment resulting in a final total of 135 participants.

Each participating teacher received four levels of professional development, including computer simulation, synchronous online instruction, and lesson resources based on the Common Core standards (2011). We initially observed the teachers in their classrooms, then in the TeachLivE simulation and then back in their classrooms. The goals were to see if improvement occurred in the simulation and if that improvement continued once the teachers returned to their classroom settings. The first specific skill addressed was the use of describe/explain versus short-response versus yes/no questions; here we want high-order questions that involve students in the process of analysis and thinking about their own learning processes. The second was the provision of specific versus general feedback; here, we wanted feedback that relates to the student's actual performance rather than generalities.

Results indicated that four 10-minute professional learning sessions in the Teach-LivE classroom simulator improved targeted teaching behaviors while in the simulator, and those improvements were seen in the real classroom as well. Improvements in frequencies of Describe/Explain questions and Specific Feedback across the four sessions can be seen in Fig. 4. Details of the study can be found in (Straub et al., 2014).

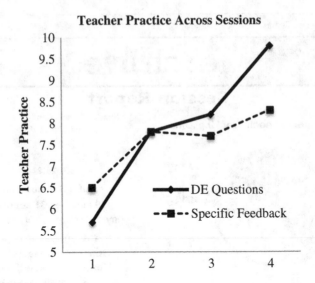

Fig. 4. Teacher practice changes over successive times in TeachLivE

3.5   Users and Interactors

AMITIES always involves a minimum of two stations: an interactor station and a user station. The matching up of a user to an interactor occurs through a simple service architecture in which the user publishes a need for a specific scenario at a particular level of intensity and an interactor chooses to provide those services to this specific user. The matching agent also verifies identities against a database of users and interactors and, where appropriate, a time schedule previously agreed upon. This approach is taken to insure that matching is appropriate – the user has arranged for the service and the interactor has the right skill set and is approved to provide that service.

Once a match is made, the user and interactor are in direct communication, where the interactor can see and hear the user, but not vice versa. There is also a mode, where the interactor sees and hears an anonymized version of the user. That mode is only used in very sensitive training situations or as part of research projects where it is important that the interactor not be aware of the gender and race of the user.

The interactor typically orchestrates actions of all virtual characters in a gross manner, e.g., by setting the moods of groups of individuals or controlling the behavior of a specific character. Actions are mapped to those of the character in a manner where gestures are associated with poses, animations and facial expressions. The specific mapping of gestures to poses is calibrated individually by each interactor to reduce his or her physical and cognitive loads. Data associated with these poses is transmitted as a set of weights that are interpreted at the user and interactor sites to achieve pose and facial gesture displays that are consistently viewed at both sites. This lightweight protocol is a key element in achieving low lag and bandwidth requirements. We refer a reader to Nagendran et al., 2014 for further details.

Although we have discussed only one interactor and one user so far, the AMITIES paradigm actually supports multiple interactors, multiple observers and multiple users, provided one is chosen as the lead for purposes of movement of the virtual camera. This drives the scalability aspects of the system. For example, one can imagine a classroom of 10 students being driven by 2 interactors, displayed on a large projection screen. When more than one interactor is operating, these interactors typically control non-overlapping sets of virtual characters. However, there is nothing in AMITIES that limits more than one interactor from controlling a single character and, in fact, we use this capability when a master interactor is remotely coaching a novice or intermediately skilled interactor. Observers, in contrast to interactors, can only watch an experience take place. In most cases, an observer only sees the virtual scene, but hears voices of both the user and the virtual characters in order to protect the identity of the trainee. However, AMITIES can also support a special class of observers who see the user as well. This is reserved for coaches and coders who are tagging events for after-action review.

4   Other Applications of AMITIES

4.1   CollegeLivE

CollegeLivE is an acronym for College Life in a virtual Environment. It refers to the virtual role-playing environment we have created to help college freshmen develop protective strategies for self and others. These skills can be used to effectively deal with the challenging choices that these young adults face in what is often their first time experiencing independence from home and family. As with TeachLivE, CollegeLivE uses the capabilities of AMITIES, including its tools for reflective learning. Figure 5 depicts a scene from CollegeLivE.

Protective strategies in our context refer to both self-protection and protection of others. Self-protection is the ability to exercise strategies that help an individual protect themselves from dangers that arise from peer pressure. Protection of others refers to strategies where we intervene when a person other than ourselves is being pressured to do something against his or her wishes. This can be an explicit assault, but it can also be a situation where the person is not in complete control, e.g., under the influence of alcohol.

In CollegeLivE, users are placed in situations typical of parties that take place in college settings. Here, as with TeachLivE, each participant is largely in control of the directions that the experience heads. If the participant chooses to drink heavily (in the virtual environment) then opportunities evolve where they might choose to walk or drive home while still intoxicated. Most think that walking is safe, but this is not so in highly travelled areas as those that surround our university. Death and injury to intoxicated pedestrians are unfortunately far too common. Those who choose to drink only moderately or not at all are often put in situations for protecting fellow party-goers, with typical examples including the opportunity to stop others from driving or walking home while intoxicated or intervening when another is being pushed to act in

Fig. 5. CollegeLivE scene

ways that are counter to their best interests. This can involve sexual advances or even pushing someone to drink heavily who chooses not to do so.

4.2   Interviewing and Being Interviewed

TeachLivE has given rise to numerous other applications of the AMITIES framework. These include using the system to prepare teachers for parent-teacher meetings and principals for interviewing prospective teacher candidates (Fig. 6). In both these applications, the user's position is not tracked as we are simulating one-on-one dialogues across an intervening table. We, however, set this so the physical table at which the user sits and the virtual table at which the interviewer or interviewee sits blend into a single physical-virtual scene.

This same paradigm has also been used to help prepare young adults diagnosed with Autism Spectrum Disorders (ASD) for their first job or college interviews. Recent studies (Trepagnier et al., 2011, Alcorn et al. 2011) have shown the effectiveness of the use of Virtual Environments in interventions for those with ASD. Our system builds upon these results and leverages the human-in-the-loop to enhance the natural interactions during such interventions thereby keeping a human subject more immersed and engaged in the conversation. A key component of this use is the presence of a coach with strong experience addressing the needs of this community.

4.3   Debriefing with Good Judgment

Outside of the K-12 school domain, we have also employed AMITIES for helping team trainers rehearse their debriefing skills. This is particularly useful with the efforts of the US Office of Veterans Affairs to keep their trainers current in both hard and soft skills.

Fig. 6. Prospective teacher candidate

One approach that they use is to bring trainers into their SimLEARN facility in Orlando, Florida, where these trainers are put into live simulation of emergency situations, e.g., airway crisis management. Trainers from different clinical professions are assembled as members of teams. It is their job to organize rapidly to take on the roles necessary to carry out the procedures on a patient mannequin that would, if done right, save a human life in similar circumstances. Once the simulation is done, a SimLEARN master trainer carries out a debriefing exercise intended to help each person reflect on his or her performance as an individual and as a team member. The goal is to teach a process known as Debriefing with Good Judgment (Rudolph et al., 2007). After another day or two of simulations, coaching and debriefing, these trainers are expected to return to their home bases and employ the same techniques to strengthen the technical and team skills of their fellow clinical staff members. Experience shows that these individuals are very strong on retaining the learned technical skills but that their debriefing skills deteriorate rapidly.

To meet the needs of these trainers, we have developed experiences that allow rehearsal of debriefing skills in a contextually valid environment. Here, we show the trainers a video of a team performance and then the virtual counterparts of those team members come alive in a TeachLivE-like experience, except now the virtual characters are clinical team members and the context is a conference room, as is typically used for such debriefings. Whatever personalities were observed and whatever conflicts were seen in the video directly influence how the virtual characters interact with each other. Those interactions present challenges to the trainer, e.g., soothing the ego of a nurse who feels abused by the perceived arrogance of an ER physician without disrespecting

Fig. 7. Debriefing members of a clinical team

the strengths that the physician brings to the team. Figure 7 shows a sample scene from such an interactive session. As with interviews, movement of the virtual camera is not considered necessary, in fact, it is probably detrimental for the effectiveness of this type of experience. This movement is not just distracting but can be perceived to break the concept of place illusion since the point of view must be held fairly static when a human subject is seated (and not moving) in the scene.

5 Future AMITIES-Based Experiences

While TeachLivE's primary use is for teaching education, we have found this paradigm potentially useful for helping young students to develop a greater command of material and an increased confidence in their own abilities to communicate by having them become peer tutors for virtual children. While our research in this area is in a nascent state, early indications are that this approach has great promise. In particular, the human peer tutors seem to naturally show a desire to find alternative ways to present material when the virtual child (or children) does not appear to be catching on. We hypothesize that such activities build new pathways in the mentor, thereby strengthening their content knowledge and their ability to retain this knowledge.

The concept of protective strategies seen in CollegeLivE is now being employed in the preparation of people who are first-line advocates for those who are experiencing extreme stress, ranging from academic issues to physical or psychological abuse. These include teachers, counselors, law enforcement and military personnel.

Our strategies for preparing young people for job interviews can be equally effective in preparing foundation personnel for the tricky job of convincing people to become donors. As with many other multi-stage activities, job shadowing, a common approach, can be successful but is very time-consuming and may miss many complex situations that arise only rarely. In contrast, scenarios can easily be developed that cover the rare as well as the common. In fact, our university's Foundation now uses our AMITIES-based role-playing as a regular part of their preparing and evaluating new staff members.

Debriefing exercises as described in our VA example are of use in almost all clinical settings, e.g., nurse and physician training, as well as in non-clinical activities such as project planning and even software walkthroughs.

In essence, we see an almost unlimited set of applications of the AMITIES framework and hope that the diversity discussed in this chapter will convince others of this.

Acknowledgements. The authors wish to recognize the contributions made by members of the SREAL and TeachLivE teams. We also wish to acknowledge the support provided by the Office of Naval Research Code 30 (Program Manager - Dr. Peter Squire) (N00014-12-1-0052 and N00014-12-1-1003), the National Science Foundation (CNS1051067, IIS1116615) and the Bill & Melinda Gates Foundation. This project also received partial support from the Veterans Health Administration (SimLEARN). Any opinions, findings, and conclusions or recommendations expressed in this material are those of the authors and do not necessarily reflect the views of the sponsors.

References

Nagendran, A., Pillat, R., Kavanaugh, A., Welch, G., Hughes, C.: A unified framework for individualized avatar-based interactions. Presence: Teleoperators Virtual Environ. **23**(2), 109–132 (2014)

Dieker, L.A., Rodriguez, J.A., Lignugaris/Kraft, B., Hynes, M.C., Hughes, C.E.: The potential of simulated environments in teacher education: current and future possibilities. Teach. Educ. Spec. Educ.: J. Teach. Educ. Div. Counc. Except. Child. **37**(1), 21–33 (2014)

Long Jr, W.A.: Personality and learning: 1988 john wilson memorial address. Focus Learn. Prob. Math. **11**(4), 1–16 (1988)

Rudolph, J.W., Simon, R., Dufresne, R., Raemer, D.B.: Debriefing with Good Judgment: combining rigorous feedback with genuine inquiry. Anesthesiol. Clin. **25**, 361–376 (2007)

Barmaki, R.: Nonverbal communication and teacher performance. Educational Data Mining 2014 Doctoral Consortium. London England (2014)

Hayes, A.T., Straub, C.L., Dieker, L.A., Hughes, C.E., Hynes, M.C.: Ludic learning: exploration of TLE TeachLivE™ and effective teacher training. Int. J. Gaming Comput.-Mediated Simul. **52**(2), 23–26 (2014)

Okita, S.Y., Bailenson, J., Schwartz, D.L.: Mere belief in social action improves complex learning. In: Proceedings of the 8th International Conference for the Learning Sciences 2, Utrecht, The Netherlands, pp. 132–139 (2008)

CCSI: Common Core Standards Initiative. Preparing America's students for college and career (2011). Retrieved from http://www.corestandards.org

Slater, M.: Place illusion and plausibility can lead to realistic behaviour in immersive virtual environments. Philos. Trans. R. Soc. B: Biol. Sci. **364**(1535), 3549–3557 (2009)

Straub, C.L., Dieker, L.A., Hynes, M.C., Hughes, C.E.: The effects of virtual rehearsal using mixed-reality classroom simulation in TLE TeachLivE™ on the performance of practicing teachers. Unpublished Technical report (2014)

Alcorn, Alyssa, Pain, Helen, Rajendran, Gnanathusharan, Smith, Tim, Lemon, Oliver, Porayska-Pomsta, Kaska, Foster, Mary Ellen, Avramides, Katerina, Frauenberger, Christopher, Bernardini, Sara: Social communication between virtual characters and children with autism. In: Biswas, Gautam, Bull, Susan, Kay, Judy, Mitrovic, Antonija (eds.) AIED 2011. LNCS, vol. 6738, pp. 7–14. Springer, Heidelberg (2011)

Trepagnier, C.Y., Olsen, D.E., Boteler, L., Bell, C.A.: Virtual conversation partner for adults with autism. Cyberpsychology Behav. Soc. Network. **14**(1–2), 21–27 (2011)

VR-Assisted Physical Rehabilitation: Adapting to the Needs of Therapists and Patients

Marcelo Kallmann[1]([✉]), Carlo Camporesi[1], and Jay Han[2]

[1] School of Engineering, University of California Merced, Merced, USA
mkallmann@ucmerced.edu
[2] Department of Physical Medicine and Rehabilitation,
University of California Davis, Davis, USA

Abstract. Virtual Reality technologies are slated to transform the practice of physical rehabilitation and the potential benefits have only started to be explored. We present in this paper a direct motion demonstration approach for allowing therapists to intuitively create and edit customized exercises and therapy programs that are responsive to the needs of their patients. We propose adaptive exercise models, motion processing algorithms, and delivery techniques designed to achieve exercises that effectively respond to physical limitations and recovery rates of individual patients. Remote networked solutions are also presented for allowing therapists and patients to intuitively share their motions during real-time collaborative therapy sessions. Our solutions have been implemented as a low-cost portable system based on a Kinect sensor, and as a high-end virtual reality system providing full-scale immersion. We analyze and discuss our methods and systems in light of feedback received from therapists.

Keywords: Physical therapy · VR interfaces · Motion capture · Character animation

1 Introduction

Physical therapy is a broad field that addresses the recovery and treatment of injuries, physical impairments, disabilities, diseases and disorders related to motor and balance dysfunctions affecting many daily life activities. A rehabilitation process is usually necessary for patients after a specific type of injury involving physical (impingement, surgery, arthritis, etc.) or neurological (strokes, neuropathies, etc.) impairments.

Rehabilitation and physical therapy are optimal when assessment, monitoring, patient engagement, and adherence to the therapy program can be achieved. Different processes are involved: physical examination, evaluation, assessment, therapy intervention, monitoring, and modification of the therapy program according to patient recovery [4]. In traditional physical therapy, after a preliminary step of diagnostic and quantitative measurement a patient is guided

© Springer International Publishing Switzerland 2015
G. Brunnett et al. (Eds.): Virtual Realities, LNCS 8844, pp. 147–168, 2015.
DOI: 10.1007/978-3-319-17043-5_9

by a trained therapist to perform specific therapeutic exercises. The tasks performed are designed according to a recovery plan, which implies repetitions of exercises and constant progress evaluation both qualitatively and quantitatively.

The process is usually intensive, time consuming and dependent on the expertise of the therapist. It also implies the collaboration of the patient who is usually asked to perform the therapy program multiple times at home with no supervision [2, 37]. Patients often perceive the tasks as repetitive and non-engaging, consequently reducing their level of involvement [20, 24]. This fact is related to a number of aspects: lack of customization on how to execute exercises, communication and interaction practices that are unsuitable to a particular patient, no clear perception of improvement, lack of coaching and monitoring while at home, etc. Addressing these many aspects is also important to improve therapy outcomes, and in particular to reduce the risk of injuries due to wrongly executed exercises.

While it is clear that VR-based computer systems for therapy delivery have great potential to well address most of these issues, implementing effective solutions involves multiple challenges. In any case, current practices can be certainly improved. For example, Fig. 1 illustrates how exercises are typically described in paper to patients when they are given a set of exercises to be executed at home. Paper descriptions suffer from perceptual limitations and lack of interactivity, and mostly important they do not provide monitoring and logging capabilities that are crucial for determining patient adherence to the program and the effectiveness of the exercises.

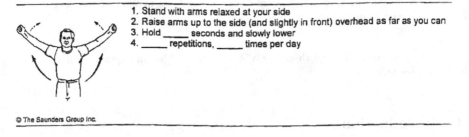

1. Stand with arms relaxed at your side
2. Raise arms up to the side (and slightly in front) overhead as far as you can
3. Hold _____ seconds and slowly lower
4. _____ repetitions, _____ times per day

© The Saunders Group Inc.

Fig. 1. Example of a typical paper description of an exercise given to patients.

Our approach addresses these challenges in an unified way. We first design motion demonstration methodologies that allow therapists to intuitively create, edit and re-use customized exercises that are responsive to the needs of their patients. In this way we integrate in our systems the ability to configure exercises to particular patients, both in terms of creating new exercises as needed and in terms of designing how exercises should adapt to patient preferences, physical limitations, and recovery rates. Several factors can be also considered to adjust a system to the user's preferences: from the language and pace to display messages and instructions, to the appearance of the virtual character demonstrating the exercises, etc. Multiple interaction channels can be customized in order to approach a similar set of communication channels that the patient is used to experience during his or her daily human-human interactions. Cultural background, social and age groups all play important roles in the wide variation of preferences that can be identified and modeled in VR systems.

We describe in this paper our first steps towards such an adaptive and responsive interactive therapy system. We discuss adaptive exercise models, motion processing algorithms, and exercise delivery and monitoring techniques that are able to effectively respond to physical limitations and recovery rates of individual patients. The presented solutions provide a basic framework to experiment and address a first set of adaptation and customization features, and we focus on adaptation of exercises for the shoulder complex. We also present remote networked solutions for allowing therapists and patients to share motion performances in real-time. The transmitted data is lightweight and remote collaboration can well scale to several patients at the same time. The capability of remote sessions is important in order to keep patients motivated and engaged in the therapy when they are supposed to work on their therapy programs at home. Remote sessions also have great potential to reduce costs and to widen health care delivery.

A number of additional features are also presented for achieving a complete framework for therapy modeling, delivery and analysis. Our system provides 3D assessment tools for monitoring range of motion, and for allowing the visualization of a number of therapy parameters during or after execution of exercises. We have implemented our system in two configurations: a low-cost version based on a Kinect sensor and a high-end version based on a full-scale immersive Powerwall (see Fig. 2).

We have collected informal feedback from therapists demonstrating that adaptive and responsive exercise delivery improves their willingness to adopt the proposed solutions in their practice.

2   Related Work

Over the last decade serious games for rehabilitation have become an important research focus with relevant evidence of benefits [15,26]. Different types of applications have been developed targeting both specific and broad types of applications [12,21,41]. Virtual reality has been successfully applied for rehabilitation of stroke patients [5,6], and with a different purpose, fitness applications have also emerged from videogame interfaces [28] and other custom-made light devices [8].

Perry et al. [42] described the typical workflow of applications with respect to neuro-rehabilitation. The workflow in clinics follows a cyclic process of treatment planning (generation), execution (delivery) and performance assessment. The traditional physical therapy protocol follows a similar pattern and the same concept can be extended to develop applications for physical therapy.

Standard commercial physical therapy packages adopted by clinicians rely on regular media to deliver exercises. The information is usually conveyed through

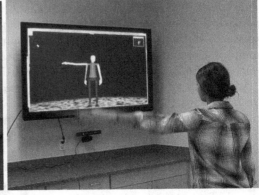

Fig. 2. Our VR-based collaborative system can run in two configurations: a high-end immersive setup provides improved motion capture and visualization results (left), while the Kinect-based setup provides a low-cost solution suitable for patients and therapists using traditional desktop computers (right). The overlapped virtual characters represent the user's avatar and the autonomous character demonstrating exercises, or the user's avatar and the avatar of the remote participant.

simple text information, sequence of images, and/or video recordings. Users are only controlled and assessed while they interact directly with physicians during in-clinic follow-ups. Patients are therefore many times left unsupervised. The use of new technologies to overcome the limitations of standard approaches to physiotherapy is becoming increasingly popular. For example, the prototype product Reflexion Vera [44] tracks and monitors users through a lightweight sensor (Microsoft Kinect or similar) reporting to the therapist each performance.

Due to the high potential, research relying on the Kinect sensor is being performed to estimate the precision and validity of the device for posture assessment [9] or for motion analysis [3,10]. Based on these studies, Kinect can be used to reliably track some types of motions, in particular upper-body exercises [31]. Exoskeletons, robotic arms with force feedback and more precise, marker based, tracking systems have also been employed for assisting and monitoring impaired patients; however, involving cumbersome and costly devices is not suitable for widespread use [18,43,48].

In our approach the creation and delivery of a physical therapy program follows a programming by direct demonstration strategy. The key benefit is to allow users to intuitively define new exercises as needed. The overall approach has been adopted in many areas [7,32,49], and it involves the need to automatically process captured motions according to the goals of the system.

Velloso et al. [50] propose a system that extracts a movement model from a demonstrated motion to then provide high-level feedback during delivery, but without motion adaptation to user performances. The YouMove system [1] trains the user through a series of stages while providing guidance and feedback; however, also without incorporating motion adaptation to user performances.

Our approach incorporates motion adaptation in several ways, allowing greater flexibility to achieve effective exercises to patients of different learning abilities, impairments, and recovery rates.

A typical approach for delivering physical therapy exercises is to track user movements while a virtual character displays the exercises to be executed. The representations of both the user and the virtual trainer are usually displayed side by side or superimposed to display motion differences, improving the learning process and the understanding of the movements [19,51].

Automated systems often allow parameterization capabilities. For instance, Lange et al. [27] describe core elements that a VR-based intervention should address, indicating that clinicians and therapists have critical roles to play and VR systems are tools that must reflect their decisions in terms of taking into account a person's ability to interact with a system, types of tasks, rates of progression, etc. [17,29]. Geurts et al. [12] describe 5 mini-games that can be calibrated and adapted in terms of speed and accuracy. The physical exercises are static and cannot be replaced. In comparison, our approach is much more comprehensive in that it relies on motion capture and on processing entire full-body motions for adaptation. By doing so we propose new motion processing approaches to achieve adaptive motions that are both controllable and realistic.

Significant research on motion capture processing has been performed in the computer animation field. Motion blending techniques with motion capture data [7,23,33,35,45,46] are popular and provide powerful interpolation-based approaches for parameterizing motions; however, they require the definition of several motion examples in order to achieve parameterization. In contrast our proposed techniques are simple and are designed to provide parameterization of a given single exercise motion. We rely both on structural knowledge of exercises and on generic constraint detection techniques, such as detection of fixed points [30,47] and motion processing with Principal Component Analysis (PCA) [13].

Rehabilitation based on tele-consultation between two healthcare services has been studied with different technologies. In physiotherapy, tele-treatment between healthcare and community services using video has been successfully employed in study cases with elderly with stroke [25] and knee pain [52]. Using virtual reality and serious games, Golomb et al. [14] presented a system for remote rehabilitation of hands for in-home use with distributed data sharing. Several studies have also combined live video of the patient integrated with the virtual environment to augment the patients feeling of presence in the interactive space [5,22]. In these applications video was used to provide visual feedback. This choice however does not allow direct interaction in a virtual space. Data collection of a patient performance also becomes a difficult task when users are only captured by regular video.

One development using immersive virtual reality and 3D camera imaging reconstruction has been proposed by Kurillo et al. [24]. This hybrid system allows therapists and patients to share and interact in the same virtual space. The approach however focuses on high-quality rendering and is not suitable as a low-bandwidth solution for physical therapy. An improvement of this work [38] allows the system to additionally detect human poses and assist with balance control. Although remote collaboration has been explored in different ways, a suitable overall solution for interactive sessions has not yet been integrated for remote physical therapy sessions.

We present in this paper our combined approach to achieve exercises that can be modeled by demonstration, that are responsive to the performances of users, and that can be exchanged in real-time in low-bandwidth remote therapy sessions by limiting transmission to joint-angle data.

3   Configurations and Features

We describe in this section the main functionality and configurations that we have developed in our system.

Therapists can design exercises and therapy programs, and then use the system to deliver the exercises in different ways. Created exercises and programs can be stored for further reuse and sharing. When virtual characters autonomously deliver exercises, a number of parameters describing adaptation strategies can be customized, and monitoring and logging tools can be enabled as needed. The provided tools improve patient understanding, motivation and compliance, and also provide data gathering.

Two configurations have been developed, and while the user interface is different the functionality remains the same. Both configurations can work offline, where the patient can only interact with an autonomous virtual (animated) therapist, or online, where remote patients and therapists are tracked simultaneously and their avatars are displayed in the same virtual space. In all cases a number of analysis tools for real-time or post-analysis monitoring, feedback and logging are always available.

The software application has been developed based on the Ogre3D graphics rendering engine [40]. This choice has allowed us to produce and customize a same application across different modalities and platforms. The system can be easily ported to different operating systems or to more complex virtual reality settings like CAVEs.

3.1   Immersive VR Configuration

Our experimental immersive setup consists of a Powerwall system composed of six rendering computers, a main rendering node and an external computer driving input devices and the motion capture system. The interaction with the application is fully immersive; thanks to virtual pointers and a 3D graphical user interface controlled by a Wiimote. See Figs. 2-left and 3.

The high-end configuration allows therapists to immersively model exercises by demonstration and to experience full-scale visualization of patient performances. The patient's motion can be captured and displayed in real-time or it can be loaded from previously logged sessions. The application provides stereo visualization for enhanced comprehension of the motions and data.

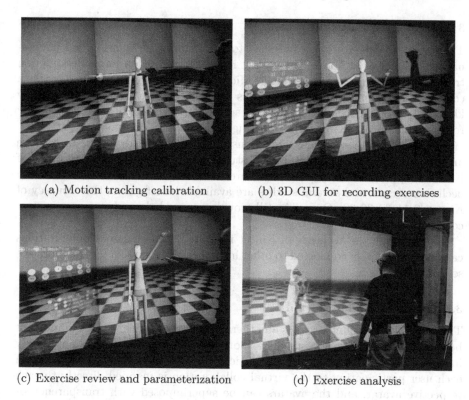

(a) Motion tracking calibration   (b) 3D GUI for recording exercises

(c) Exercise review and parameterization   (d) Exercise analysis

Fig. 3. Example of using the immersive Virtual Reality configuration.

A high-end system configuration also allows the integration of precise tracking capabilities. In our setup the user's upper body motions are tracked using a 10-camera Vicon motion tracking system. For improved usability, our experimental setup is configured to only track markers attached to the hands, torso and head. The motion is calibrated and mapped to the avatar following simple scaling and reconstruction procedures, as described in the work of Camporesi et al. [7]. This solution has been enough to allow us to experiment with the system; however, since we reconstruct the motion from a reduced marker set not all degrees of freedom of the user's motion can be precisely replicated; in particular, the elbow orbit motion around the shoulder-wrist axis is set to be always in a low-energy position. If precise motion replication is needed, in particular for cases where avoiding compensatory movements is important, additional markers have to be placed on the user.

In remote connection mode the immersive system allows to achieve full-scale interactions that are closer to how humans interact to each other. When connected to a remote site, two avatars are displayed for representing the connected patient and therapist. Previously recorded sessions can also be played on any of the avatars. The avatars can be visualized side-by-side or superimposed with transparency.

3.2 Low-Cost Configuration

The low-cost configuration is designed to be of simple installation and maintenance at clinics or at home. The patient is tracked through a markerless motion tracking device, in our case using a Microsoft Kinect sensor or similar. Such configuration is important because it is simple, portable and suitable for any kind of desktop environment. It is also suitable to assist patients in their daily routines in clinical environments. See Figs. 2-right and 7 for examples.

The Kinect imposes some limitations, such as a limited volume of capture and the overall need to maintain a posture facing the sensor. The accuracy of Kinect drops significantly when users are not facing the camera or when body occlusion occurs, and several studies are available investigating the accuracy of Kinect [9,11,34,36,39]. Overall it still provides a good balance between precision, cost and portability.

Even though the accuracy of Kinect is limited, Kinect-based configurations can also be remotely connected to other instances of the system for collaborative sessions.

3.3 Remote Collaboration

The capability of having patients and therapists to remotely interact is important because it can save travel costs, allow more frequent monitoring, and potentially increase access to health care, in particular to remote areas. The motion of each user participating to the virtual collaboration is mapped directly to each respective avatar, and the avatars can be superimposed with transparency or appear side-by-side in the applications. See Fig. 4 for examples.

Fig. 4. Examples of collaborative sessions. Left: one user is being tracked by the high-end system Vicon cameras while the other is being tracked by a Kinect sensor. Right: both users are tracked by Kinect cameras and collaborate with the portable versions of the system running in a desktop and laptop.

The communication between two peers in a collaborative session is based on a client-server UDP communication schema with added packet ordering, guaranteed communication reliability and optional data compression. The server application, after accepting and validating an incoming connection, starts sending information of the avatar of the current user (sender) and waits the update of the client's avatar (receiver). For instance, if the therapist application is started as a server, the therapist's avatar becomes the active character in the communication and the second character, the patient's avatar, becomes a receiving entity. If the patient's application is started as the client, the sender entity becomes the character of the patient's application while the tutor/therapist becomes a receiving entity waiting for further updates.

During a networked session each active character maintains a history containing its previous poses and the streamed information between the peers is limited to the information that has changed between the previous frame and the current frame. This feature has been developed to handle communication between peers with limited bandwidth capabilities.

Feedback and analysis tools (described below) are also available during virtual collaboration. The therapist can demonstrate exercises, analyze the patient motion, load preset exercises from the database, watch the patient's performances, record a patient motion in real time, etc.

3.4   Tools for Real-Time Feedback and Post-analysis

The feedback tools can be activated anytime and they are highly customizable. For example, any joint of the character representation can be tracked and considered for analysis by any tool. Simple commands or text-based configuration files are used for customization. Four types of feedback have been developed in order to provide visual and quantitative information about the user motions in real-time or in post-analysis. The four feedback tools provide information with respect to: trajectories, joint angles, distance to target exercises, and range of motion per exercise. See Fig. 5.

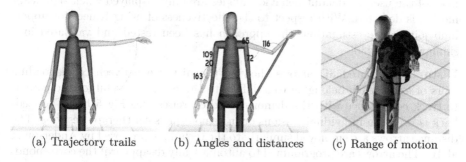

   (a) Trajectory trails   (b) Angles and distances   (c) Range of motion

Fig. 5. Visualization helpers are available for real-time feedback or post-analysis of motions.

Trajectories: Trajectory trails of selected joints can be displayed in real-time, showing the performed trajectory of a joint during a fixed past period of time (see Fig. 5(a)), or after a user's performance, showing the performed trajectory and the trajectory compliance range with the reference exercise. The visualization can be based on fine polygonal segments sampled per frame (for precise analysis for example of tremors), or smoothly generated by B-Spline interpolation.

Angle Estimation (Virtual Goniometer): Joint angles can be visualized (Fig. 5(b)) with a floating label showing the angle value and the local lines used to measure the angle. In practical goniometry for upper-limb physiotherapy [37] angle measurement is important in order to measure progress and intervention effectiveness, via therapy or via surgery. Therapists can therefore instruct specific movements to patients and observe or log the achieved measurements. The provided angle measurements match the angles measured in practical physiotherapy protocols [37]. The proposed angle measurement is simple and yet flexible to accommodate generic needs.

The angle estimation is calculated as follows: let $p_1, \cdots, p_4 \in \mathbb{R}^3$ be the global positions of the extremities of two dependent (bones sharing a joint) or independent bones, and $R_1, R_2 \in \mathbb{SO}^3$ be the user-defined reference frame rotations. The angle estimation between the limbs at the joint in question is obtained with:

$$\phi = \arccos\left((R_1 * \|p_2 - p_1\|) \cdot (R_2 * \|p_4 - p_3\|)\right). \tag{1}$$

The proposed method allows the system to measure any kind of angle by just defining pairs of joints and optional reference frame rotations. The tracked angles are specified in the application's configuration file. It gives to the therapist a flexible and easy mechanism to identify and customize the visualization. To isolate angles for upper-arm flexion (extension or abduction) we track, for instance, the angle generated by the scapula/clavicle and humerus, given the scapula bone aligned to the torso as a consequence of the skeleton hierarchical structure. The measured angle is the angle between the arm and the "body line" of the user. In default behavior, angles are only displayed when significant motion is detected. With respect to the effectiveness of using Kinect for upper-limb joint angle estimation, the approach has been tested and validated in a similar context [36].

Distances: Colored 3D arrows showing the distance between corresponding pairs of joints, each belonging to a different character, are useful for the patient to track compliance with the demonstrated exercises (see Fig. 5(b)). The feedback is useful in individual sessions or in remote physical therapy sessions. The distance arrows are employed similarly to the technique proposed by Anderson et al. [1]. The arrows are programmed to automatically disappear if the corresponding distance is under a given threshold, and different colors can be associated to different ranges of thresholds. This is in particular useful for slow exercises where compliance is important. Figure 6 shows arrow distances enabled together with several angle measurements during execution of one exercise.

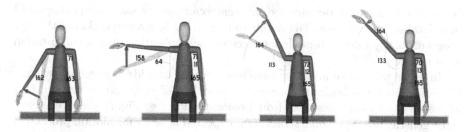

Fig. 6. Example of several feedback tools enabled while a patient executes a given exercise.

Range of Motion: Our range of motion visualization (see Fig. 5(c)) analyzes the rotation of a selected joint overtime. We focus here on the shoulder range of motion evaluation due its importance in rehabilitation of shoulder movements.

The 3 degrees of freedom (DOFs) of the shoulder joint orientation are decomposed into the twist and swing rotation parameterization [16]. The swing motion is then tracked at every frame i, and for each swing orientation s_i measured, the intersection point p_i of the upper-arm skeleton segment at orientation s_i and a sphere centered at the shoulder joint is computed. The history of all traversed p_i points is visualized with colors in the sphere. The sphere is texture-mapped with an image texture initially fully transparent. For every measured point p_i, its position in the texture is determined and the corresponding texture pixel c_i has its color changed. For achieving a clear visualization we employ a relatively high texture resolution and we weight the color increments around c_i with a local Gaussian distribution centered at c_i. The colors are incremented from pure blue to red, providing a colored frequency map of all traversed swing orientations (see Fig. 5(c)).

The boundary of the colored map will represent the range of motion executed in a given exercise. The original points p_i are also recorded and are used for geometrically estimating the polygonal boundary describing the full range of motion during a session. This tool provides an excellent way to log improvement of range of motion during rehabilitation, to observe the patient's ability to execute precise trajectories, and to observe if there are areas that are avoided for instance due pain or discomfort. In summary the representation provides a frequency history of the space traversed by the user, and it offers a comprehensive view of the patient's performance. Frequency maps collected per exercise can clearly represent patient progress across therapy sessions.

4   Adaptive Exercises

The option of providing customized exercises by demonstration enables the therapist to go beyond recovery plans limited to a set of predefined exercises. The therapist can record his or her demonstrations and then trim, save, load, play, and customize them in different ways. After a validation process the motions can be corrected and/or parameterized. Exercises can then be saved and categorized in a database of exercises. The database is used for fast construction of therapy programs using a desktop-mode interface of the application during consultation with patients.

In order to achieve adaptive exercises we need to address exercise parameterization from the beginning, since the modeling of the exercise motion. Our approach of modeling exercises from demonstration (see Fig. 7) allows exercises to be generic; however, some structure is expected in order for motion processing algorithms to be able to parameterize the motions in real-time.

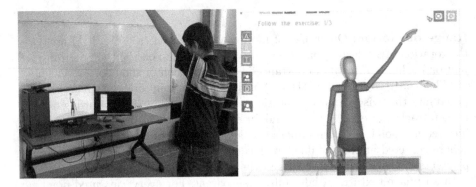

Fig. 7. Illustration of a modeling session by demonstration using the low-cost Kinect configuration.

Given a captured exercise, we propose correction and parameterization techniques that allow (1) detection and fine-tuning of key characteristics of the exercise such as alignments and constraints, (2) parameterization of the exercise by detecting modifiable properties such as speed, wait times and amplitudes, and (3) real-time motion adaptation by monitoring user performances and updating the exercise parameters in order to improve therapy delivery.

The presented techniques facilitate the process of defining exercises by demonstration by providing several modeling and correction mechanisms and at the same time providing parameterization for real-time adaptation. As a result the proposed methods produce realistic continuous motions that can adapt to user responses in order to improve motivation and outcomes.

4.1   Detection of Geometrical Constraints

A constraint detection mechanism is designed for three specific purposes: to inform motion parameterization, to help correcting artifacts and noise in the motions, and to provide metrics for quantifying motion compliance. The metrics are used to provide visual feedback to the user informing the correctness of motion reproduction, to make decisions during the real-time adaptation mechanism, and to achieve an overall user performance score for each session.

Appropriate constraints are not constraints which are to be absolutely followed. Recorded motions may have unintended movements and imperfections introduced by the capture system. Constraints must be detected despite these fluctuations, and should be softly enforced.

We analyze the position in space of a specific joint with respect to a frame of reference F which can be placed at any ancestor joint in the skeleton structure. Since different types of constraints can be recognized with respect to a specific joint (during the overall duration of the motion) a chain of constraints can be also detected and reported to the user during the parameterization process.

The detected constraints are provided to the user and the user then decides (1) if the motion should be modified to better enforce the detected constraint, and (2) if the constraint is to be monitored during real-time execution of the exercise in order to alert the user every time the constraint is significantly violated. For instance, if the elbow joint is detected to be immovable in an exercise, the system will detect that as a point constraint and may alert the user in real-time everytime the user's elbow is too far away from its point constraint.

The detection framework can accommodate any desired type of geometric constraints, such as points, lines, circular trajectories, etc. While we focus here on describing first results with point constraints, plane constraints can be well detected by PCA analysis and the same principles are applicable to several other types of constraints.

A point constraint describes a child joint that is static relative to its parent. Let's $P_i, i \in \{l, \ldots, k\}$ be the cloud of points formed by a joint trajectory with respect to a local frame F generated by re-sampling linearly the motion frames with constant frame rate. The standard deviation of the cloud of points σ is calculated and subsequently checked against a specific threshold α. When the condition is met the current joint is marked as a point constraint and it is represented by the specific point located at the mean μ. When a point constraint is detected the ancestor(s) can be then adjusted to enforce the constraint as an exercise correction filter for customizing the appearance ad correctness of the exercise. It is also useful to not completely correct constraints in order to keep the original humanlike appearance of the recorded motions.

The user is offered a correction percentage to choose. 100 % correction results in motion which always tries to obey constraints, whereas 0 % correction results in no modification the original motion. In a given frame, a point constraint is enforced through spherical linear interpolation between each joint orientation and the computed mean. Figure 8 illustrates results obtained.

4.2   Detection of Exercise Parameterization

Consider a typical shoulder flexion exercise where the arm is raised until it reaches the vertical position or more (initial phase); subsequently the arm is hold for a few seconds (hold phase) and then it relaxes back to a rest position (return phase). This is the type of exercise that we seek to parameterize.

The analysis procedure makes the following assumptions: (a) each motion represents one cycle of a cyclic arm exercise that can be repeated an arbitrary

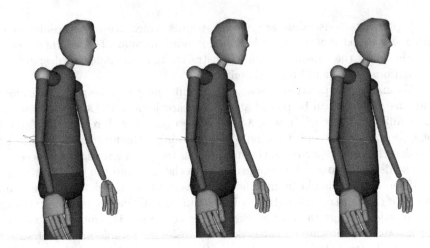

Fig. 8. Point constraint detection example. From left to right: the elbow motion trajectory can be gradually corrected to its mean position while the wrist motion trajectory is gradually corrected to a plane. The elbow and wrist trajectories are shown with different correction factors: 0 %, 50 %, and 95 %. Partial corrections allow to improve alignments while preserving the original naturalness of the exercise motion.

number of times; (b) the first frame of a motion contains a posture that is in a comfortable position representing the starting point of the exercise; (c) the exercise will have two clear distinct phases: the initial phase is when the arm moves from the initial posture towards a posture of maximum exercise amplitude, then the exercise may or not have a hold phase but at some point the exercise must enter the return phase, where the exercise returns to the starting posture at the end of the exercise. This implies that the initial posture is approximately the same as the final one.

The analysis if the exercise can be parameterized starts by detecting the points of maximum amplitude in the motion in order to segment the demonstrated motion. If a mostly static period is detect near the maximum amplitude point, then that period is extracted as the hold phase. If the phase segmentation is successful the input motion is segmented in initial, return and (optionally) hold phases, and the motion can be parameterized.

If the motion can be parameterized it is then prepared for on-line parameterization. We parameterize amplitude in terms of a percentage of the wrist trajectory: 100 % means that the full amplitude observed in the input motion is to be preserved, if 80 % is given then the produced parameterized motion should go into hold or return phase when 80 % of the original amplitude is reached, and so on. Let h be the time duration in seconds of the desired hold duration. When the target amplitude is reached, the posture at the target amplitude is maintained for the given duration h of the desired hold phase. When the hold phase ends, the posture is then blended into the return motion at the current amplitude point towards the final frame. The blending operations ensure that a smooth motion is always produced. Velocity profile adjustment and an idle behavior are also added in order to ensure a realistic final result. See Fig. 9 for an example.

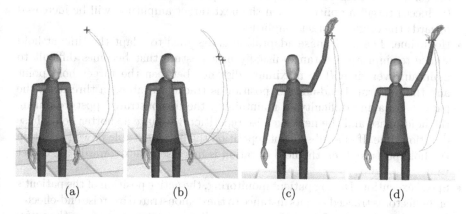

(a)   (b)   (c)   (d)

Fig. 9. The red and blue trajectories show the initial and return phases segmented out of the input motion. (a) The full (100 %) amplitude of the input motion is shown by the trajectories. Two crosses at the end of the trajectories (in almost identical positions) mark the positions of the maximum amplitude points. (b) The two crosses now mark the maximum amplitude points in the initial and return trajectories at 75 % amplitude. (c,d) In this frontal view it is possible to notice that the postures at 75 % amplitude in the initial and return phases are slightly different. The hold phase will start by holding the posture shown in (c) while a breathing behavior is executed, and when the hold phase is over, the posture is blended into the return motion starting at the posture shown in (d), in order to produce a smooth transition into the return phase (Color figure online).

The described procedures allow us to parameterize an input motion with respect to up to four parameters: amplitude a (in percentage), hold time h (in seconds), wait time w (in seconds), and speed s (as a multiplier to the original time parameterization). Given a set of parameters (a, h, w, s), the input motion can be prepared for parameterized blending operations very efficiently and then, during execution of the parameterized motion, only trivial blending operations are performed in real-time.

4.3 Real-Time Adaptation

When the adaptation mechanism is enabled the system collects information about the patients performance in real-time in order to adapt the current exercise in its next repetition. Four types of adaptation mechanisms are provided:

- Amplitude Adaptation: The range can vary from 75 % to 100 % of the target amplitude parameter. The system tracks the distance between the user's end-effector and the point at the target amplitude position. If the minimum distance is larger than the amplitude compliance parameter specified by the therapist, the next exercise execution will have the target amplitude lowered to the position that makes the position reached by the user to become within the compliance range. If in a subsequent repetition the user reaches the current (reduced) target amplitude, then the next target amplitude will be increased towards the original target amplitude.

- Hold time: The hold phase adaptation is designed to adapt the time at hold stance to improve resistance, usually in a posture that becomes difficult to maintain over time. The maximum distance between the target hold point and the performed end-effector position is tracked. If above a threshold, the patient is having difficulty in maintaining the demonstrated posture during the hold phase and the next exercise repetition will have a shorter hold phase duration time. If in a subsequent repetition the patient is able to well maintain the hold posture, then the hold duration is increased back towards the target value.
- Speed execution: During patient monitoring, the active position of the patient's end-effector is tracked and its distance to the demonstrated exercise end-effector is computed for every frame. If the average distance computed across the entire exercise is above a given posture compliance threshold, the next exercise execution speed is decreased. If in a subsequent repetition the difference is under the threshold the play speed will be adjusted back to the previous execution speed.
- Wait-time between exercises: this adaptation mechanism allows the system to update the waiting time between exercise repetitions. If the user is well performing the exercises a shorter wait time is allowed, otherwise a longer wait time is preferred. A target wait time is first specified in the therapy program and then it is decreased or increased according to a performance metric that is used to determine how well the patient is following the exercises overall. The metric can be customized by combining the compliance metrics used for the exercise compliance, speed compliance, and hold phase completion.

The described adaptation mechanisms have been identified as a first set of relevant strategies after many discussions and interactions with therapists. In the next section we present a summary of the main feedback received.

5   Feedback Results and Discussion

Since the beginning of the development of our system we have closely worked with therapists in order to design the described therapy creation, delivery and adaptation functionality. With our first prototype solutions developed, we have then gathered feedback on the provided functionality. The goal was to gather first impressions and to analyze how much the proposed solutions are perceived to be useful.

We gathered feedback in two phases. In the first phase, focus groups were held and open ended questions elicited multiple responses of major factors that should be considered in exercise prescription. In the second phase we demonstrated the current prototype application and then asked the therapists for their feedback.

In the first phase questionnaires were distributed to 40 staff therapists asking about the importance of individualized interactions, the factors used to determine correctness of performed exercises, and the motivational and adaptation strategies commonly used by therapists. For each question, the therapists were asked to rank the factors identified in the first phase between 1 (not important) and 5 (highest importance). The factors that were ranked 4 or 5 by more than 20 therapists are summarized in Fig. 10 for selected questions.

Factors for determining if a patient is performing an exercise correctly		
no compensatory movements		36
ability to maintain a correct posture		34
correctly performed trajectories	32	
pain level	27	

Strategies to improve the patient's ability to perform an exercise correctly		
provide tactile feedback		36
provide visual feedback		35
provide verbal instructions	28	
provide pictures	23	
provide written instructions	23	

Factors that would influence a change in the way the therapy is provided		
patient's ability to learn		37
poor performance on repeated basis		35
patient does not understand		34
increase in pain		34
comorbidities	27	
contractures	26	
patient request	24	

Strategies that help improve the motivation of the patient to correctly perform the exercises		
visible improvement achieved		37
functional outcome improved		37
verbal encouragement	33	
decreased pain	33	
comorbidities	27	
reaching set goals	25	
relational conversations	21	

Factors that influence how to adapt an existing exercise over multiple sessions		
existence of pain		35
increased strength	33	
increased stability	33	
consistency with exercises	30	
patient's athletic ability	29	
range of motion	28	
patient's communication	28	

Fig. 10. Summarized responses. The numbers show how many therapists (out of 40) rated each factor as 4 or 5.

From the collected data summarized in Fig. 10 it is possible to make several observations. Performing exercises in a correct manner is largely related to being close to the prescribed exercises, what is translated in terms of not having compensatory movements and maintaining correct postures and trajectories. The several visual feedback tools that were described well address these issues. In addition, the proposed constraint detection methods for real-time warning if the user performs motions that do not well respect constraints also well address enforcing correct execution of exercises.

One point that cannot be addressed by therapy systems that only give visual output is to provide tactile feedback. However we point out that tactile feedback was considered as important as visual feedback, which is well addressed by our system. The fact that visual and audio feedback were highly ranked is also important because it indicates that they may well compensate for the lack of tactile feedback, which is at the same time a desirable characteristic of the system from a safety perspective.

Several causes were cited as reasons justifying the need for exercise adaptation, for example, the patient's ability to learn, patient improvement, decreased pain, increased strength, etc. The proposed adjustment of wait and hold times, exercise speed and amplitude provide direct ways to adapt the exercise as the patient progresses. In particular, it is also important to adapt in a constant basis given the patient's ability to learn the exercises. At the beginning of an exercise set it is often observed that patients need more time to assimilate an exercise while at the end of a set the patients are well able to perform them quicker and with less wait times. The same can be observed in subsequent sessions, however usually with progressively faster learning rates. The proposed adaptation methods are capable to adjust to patients as needed, thus significantly improving correct exercise execution, improvement observation, engagement, and adherence to the therapy program.

In the second phase we have asked questions to the participants before and after they have seen the capabilities of our system. The questionnaire consisted of generic questions as a follow up of the first phase questionnaire, and it also included open-ended suggestions and preferences to improve the current setup. At first only 45 % of the participants were confident that patients do exercises consistently and correctly at home, but after seeing our system (and if our system was to be employed) that percentage raised to 70 %. When asked about the importance of modifying exercises during the progress of the therapy, 70 % cited as very important and after seeing our system this percentage was even raised to 85 %.

These results indicate that adaptation is an important factor for achieving VR-based therapy systems that have real potential to be adopted. While the presented solutions provide only first results towards addressing adaptation strategies, we believe that the described framework and adaptation techniques provide a significant step towards the right direction. Many variations and adjustments to the described procedures are possible, and our solutions are being fine-tuned in preparation for validation activities with patients.

6 Conclusions

We present innovative solutions based on VR technologies for addressing limitations of traditional upper-limb physical therapy. The proposed solutions simplify the work of therapists and also help patients during their daily exercise routines with adaptive exercise delivery strategies that improve engagement and adherence to the therapy program. As future work, our solutions are being fine-tuned in preparation for validation activities in real practice.

Acknowledgements. This work was partially supported by CITRIS grant number 128, by NSF award CNS-1305196, and by a HSRI San Joaquin Valley eHealth Network seed grant funded by AT&T.

References

1. Anderson, F., Grossman, T., Matejka, J., Fitzmaurice, G.W.: YouMove: enhancing movement training with an augmented reality mirror. In: Proceedings of User Interface Software and Technology (UIST), pp. 311–320. ACM (2013)
2. American Physical Therapy Association: Guide to Physical Therapist Practice. Rev. 2nd edn. American Physical Therapy Association, Alexandria (1999)
3. Bonnechere, B., Jansen, B., Salvia, P., Bouzahouene, H., Omelina, L., Cornelis, J., Rooze, M., Van Sint Jan, S.: What are the current limits of the kinect sensor. In: Proceedings of the 9th International Conference on Disability, Virutal Reality & Associated Technologies, Laval, France, pp. 287–294 (2012)
4. Breeben, O.: Introduction to Physical Therapy for Physical Therapy Assistants. Jones and Barlett, Sudbury (2007)
5. Burke, J.W., McNeill, M., Charles, D., Morrow, P., Crosbie, J., McDonough, S.: Serious games for upper limb rehabilitation following stroke. In: Proceedings of the 2009 Conference in Games and Virtual Worlds for Serious Applications, VS-GAMES 2009, pp. 103–110. IEEE Computer Society, Washington, DC (2009)
6. Cameirao, M., Badia, B., Verschure, P.: Virtual reality based upper extremity rehabilitation following stroke: a review. J. CyberTherapy Rehabil. 1(1), 63–74 (2008)
7. Camporesi, C., Huang, Y., Kallmann, M.: Interactive motion modeling and parameterization by direct demonstration. In: Safonova, A. (ed.) IVA 2010. LNCS, vol. 6356, pp. 77–90. Springer, Heidelberg (2010)
8. Chang, C.M.: The design of a shoulder rehabilitation game system. In: 2010 IET International Conference on Frontier Computing. Theory, Technologies and Applications, pp. 151–156 (2010)
9. Clark, R.A., Pua, Y.H., Fortin, K., Ritchie, C., Webster, K.E., Denehy, L., Bryant, A.L.: Validity of the microsoft kinect for assessment of postural control. Gait Posture 36(3), 372–377 (2012)
10. Gabel, M., Gilad-Bachrach, R., Renshaw, E., Schuster, A.: Full body gait analysis with kinect. In: 2012 Annual International Conference of the IEEE Engineering in Medicine and Biology Society (EMBC), pp. 1964–1967. IEEE (2012)
11. Galna, B., Barry, G., Jackson, D., Mhiripiri, D., Olivier, P., Rochester, L.: Accuracy of the microsoft kinect sensor for measuring movement in people with parkinson's disease. Gait Posture 39(4), 1062–1068 (2014)
12. Geurts, L., Vanden Abeele, V., Husson, J., Windey, F., Van Overveldt, M., Annema, J.H., Desmet, S.: Digital games for physical therapy: fulfilling the need for calibration and adaptation. In: Proceedings of the Fifth International Conference on Tangible, Embedded, and Embodied Interaction, pp. 117–124. ACM (2011)

13. Glardon, P., Boulic, R., Thalmann, D.: A coherent locomotion engine extrapolating beyond experimental data. In: Proceedings of Computer Animation and Social Agent, pp. 73–84 (2004)
14. Golomb, M.R., McDonald, B.C., Warden, S.J., Yonkman, J., Saykin, A.J., Shirley, B., Huber, M., Rabin, B., Abdelbaky, M., Nwosu, M.E., Barkat-Masih, M., Burdea, G.C.: In-home virtual reality videogame telerehabilitation in adolescents with hemiplegic cerebral palsy. Arch. Phys. Med. Rehabil. **91**(1), 1–8 (2010)
15. Golomb, M., Barkat-Masih, M., Rabin, B., Abdelbaky, M., Huber, M., Burdea, G.: Eleven months of home virtual reality telerehabilitation - lessons learned. In: Virtual Rehabilitation International Conference, pp. 23–28 (2009)
16. Grassia, F.S.: Practical parameterization of rotations using the exponential map. J. Graph. Tools **3**(3), 29–48 (1998)
17. Grealy, M., Nasser, B.: The use of virtual reality in assisting rehabilitation. Adv. Clin. Neurosci. Rehabil. **13**(9), 19–20 (2013)
18. Gupta, A., O'Malley, M.: Robotic Exoskeletons for Upper Extremity Rehabilitation, pp. 371–396. I-Tech Education and Publishing, Vienna (2007)
19. Holden, M.K.: Virtual environments for motor rehabilitation: review. Cyberpsychol. Behav. **8**(3), 187–211 (2005)
20. Holden, M.K., Dyar, T.A., Schwamm, L., Bizzi, E.: Virtual-environment-based telerehabilitation in patients with stroke. Presence Teleoper. Virtual Environ. **14**(2), 214–233 (2005)
21. Kizony, R., Weiss, P., Feldman, Y., Shani, M., Elion, O., Kizony, R., Weiss, P., Kizony, R., Harel, S., Baum-Cohen, I.: Evaluation of a tele-health system for upper extremity stroke rehabilitation. In: 2013 International Conference on Virtual Rehabilitation (ICVR), pp. 80–86, August 2013
22. Kizony, R., Katz, N., et al.: Adapting an immersive virtual reality system for rehabilitation. J. Vis. Comput. Anim. **14**(5), 261–268 (2003)
23. Kovar, L., Gleicher, M.: Automated extraction and parameterization of motions in large data sets. ACM Trans. Graph. (Proceedings of SIGGRAPH) **23**(3), 559–568 (2004)
24. Kurillo, G., Koritnik, T., Bajd, T., Bajcsy, R.: Real-time 3d avatars for telerehabilitation in virtual reality. In: MMVR, pp. 290–296 (2011)
25. Lai, J.C., Woo, J., Hui, E., Chan, W.: Telerehabilitationa new model for community-based stroke rehabilitation. J. Telemed. Telecare **10**(4), 199–205 (2004)
26. Lange, B., Flynn, S.M., Rizzo, A.A.: Game-based telerehabilitation. Eur. J. Phys. Rehabil. Med. **45**(1), 143–151 (2009)
27. Lange, B., Koenig, S., Chang, C.Y., McConnell, E., Suma, E., Bolas, M., Rizzo, A.: Designing informed game-based rehabilitation tasks leveraging advances in virtual reality. Disabil. Rehabil. **34**(22), 1863–1870 (2012)
28. Leder, R., Azcarate, G., Savage, R., Savage, S., Sucar, L., Reinkensmeyer, D., Toxtli, C., Roth, E., Molina, A.: Nintendo wii remote for computer simulated arm and wrist therapy in stroke survivors with upper extremity hemipariesis. In: Virtual Rehabilitation, 2008. p. 74 (2008)
29. Levac, D.E., Galvin, J.: When is virtual reality therapy? Arch. Phys. Med. Rehabil. **94**(4), 795–798 (2013)
30. Liu, C.K., Popović, Z.: Synthesis of complex dynamic character motion from simple animations. ACM Trans. Graph. **21**(3), 408–416 (2002)
31. Lowes, L.P., Alfano, L.N., Yetter, B.A., Worthen-Chaudhari, L., Hinchman, W., Savage, J., Samona, P., Flanigan, K.M., Mendell, J.R.: Proof of concept of the ability of the kinect to quantify upper extremity function in dystrophinopathy. PLoS Curr. **5** (2013)

32. Lü, H., Li, Y.: Gesture coder: a tool for programming multi-touch gestures by demonstration. In: Proceedings of the 2012 ACM Annual Conference on Human Factors in Computing Systems, pp. 2875–2884. ACM (2012)
33. Ma, W., Xia, S., Hodgins, J.K., Yang, X., Li, C., Wang, Z.: Modeling style and variation in human motion. In: Proceedings of the ACM SIGGRAPH/Eurographics Symposium on Computer Animation (SCA) (2010)
34. Mobini, A., Behzadipour, S., Saadat Foumani, M.: Accuracy of Kinect's skeleton tracking for upper body rehabilitation applications. Disabil. Rehabil. Assist. Technol. **9**(4), 344–352 (2014)
35. Mukai, T., Kuriyama, S.: Geostatistical motion interpolation. In: ACM SIGGRAPH, pp. 1062–1070. ACM, New York (2005)
36. Nixon, M., Chen, Y., Howard, A.: Quantitative evaluation of the microsoft kinect for use in an upper extremity virtual rehabilitation environment. In: International Conference on Virtual Rehabilitation (ICVR), Philadelphia, PA, USA, May 2013
37. Norkin, C.: Measurement of Joint Motion. A Guide to Goniometry. F.A. Davis Company, Philadelphia (2003)
38. Obdrzalek, S., Kurillo, G., Han, J., Abresch, T., Bajcsy, R.: Real-time human pose detection and tracking for tele-rehabilitation in virtual reality. Stud. Health Technol. Inform. **173**, 320–324 (2012)
39. Obdrzalek, S., Kurillo, G., Ofli, F., Bajcsy, R., Seto, E., Jimison, H., Pavel, M.: Accuracy and robustness of kinect pose estimation in the context of coaching of elderly population. In: 2012 Annual International Conference of the IEEE Engineering in Medicine and Biology Society (EMBC), pp. 1188–1193, August 2012
40. Ogre3D: Object-oriented graphics rendering engine. www.ogre3d.org
41. Omelina, L., Jansen, B., Bonnechre, B., Van Sint Jan, S., Cornelis, J.: Serious games for physical rehabilitation: designing highly configurable and adaptable games. In: Proceedings of the 9th International Conference on Disability, Virutal Reality & Associated Technologies, Laval, France (2012)
42. Perry, J.C., Andreu, J., Cavallaro, F.I., Veneman, J., Carmien, S., Keller, T.: Effective game use in neurorehabilitation: user-centered perspectives. Handbook of Research on Improving Learning and Motivation through Educational Games, IGI Global (2010)
43. Popescu, V.G., Burdea, G.C., Bouzit, M., Hentz, V.R.: A virtual-reality-based telerehabilitation system with force feedback. Trans. Info. Tech. Biomed. **4**(1), 45–51 (2000)
44. Reflexion Health: http://www.reflexionhealth.com
45. Rose, C., Bodenheimer, B., Cohen, M.F.: Verbs and adverbs: multidimensional motion interpolation. IEEE Comput. Graph. Appl. **18**, 32–40 (1998)
46. Rose III, C.F., Sloan, P.P.J., Cohen, M.F.: Artist-directed inverse-kinematics using radial basis function interpolation. Comput. Graph. Forum (Proceedings of Eurographics) **20**(3), 239–250 (2001)
47. Salvati, M., Le Callennec, B., Boulic, R.: A generic method for geometric contraints detection. In: Eurographics (2004)
48. Schönauer, C., Pintaric, T., Kaufmann, H.: Full body interaction for serious games in motor rehabilitation. In: Proceedings of the 2nd Augmented Human International Conference, AH 2011, pp. 4:1–4:8. ACM, New York (2011)
49. Skoglund, A., Iliev, B., Palm, R.: Programming-by-demonstration of reaching motions - a next-state-planner approach. Robot. Auton. Syst. **58**(5), 607–621 (2010)

50. Velloso, E., Bulling, A., Gellersen, H.: Motionma: motion modelling and analysis by demonstration. In: Proceedings of the SIGCHI Conference on Human Factors in Computing Systems, CHI 2013, pp. 1309–1318. ACM, New York (2013)
51. Wollersheim, D., Merkes, M., Shields, N., Liamputtong, P., Wallis, L., Reynolds, F., Koh, L.: Physical and psychosocial effects of wii video game use among older women. Int. J. Emerg. Technol. Soc. 8(2), 85–98 (2010)
52. Wong, Y., Hui, E., Woo, J.: A community-based exercise programme for older persons with knee pain using telemedicine. J. Telemed. Telecare 11(6), 310–315 (2005)

Hierarchical Method for Segmentation by Classification of Motion Capture Data

Samer Salamah[✉], Liang Zhang, and Guido Brunnett

Faculty of Computer Science, GDV Chemnitz University of Technology,
Chemnitz, Germany
samer.salamah@s2008.tu-chemnitz.de, {liang.zhang,
guido.brunnett}@informatik.tu-chemnitz.de

Abstract. In this paper, we present a novel simple and efficient method for segmentation by classification of motion capture data automatically and with high accuracy. Classification of motion capture data demands dealing with high dimensional search space due to the high dimensionality of the motion capture data. The main contribution of this paper is a method for reducing this search space using the divide and conquer principle in a form of a taxonomy-tree which means a multi-level segmentation by classification algorithm, where the highest level classifies motion capture data into dynamic and static segments and the lowest level uses features of single body-parts to recognize wide range of human movements. The first implementation of this algorithm has given very promising results and proved that it is fast enough to be integrated in real-time systems such as robotics and surveillance systems.

Keywords: Human motion · Motion capture · Motion segmentation · Motion classification · Activity recognition

1 Introduction

Motion capture refers to the process of recording motions of a live actor and then using the obtained data to animate a digital actor. The use of motion capture data in animation enables the digital actor to perform very natural motion and to simulate well subtle motion details. Additionally, the reusability of motion capture data can reduce the time and money costs of motion capture data based animation. Therefore it is often used in computer games and movies. In addition, it can find wide applications in industry, for example, in robotics, simulation of production processes and surveillance systems, also in medicine for gait analysis, simulation based training and rehabilitation. For indexing, retrieval and other processing purposes it is useful to have motion capture data in small clips, where each individual clip represents one kind of motion. These clips are called

Electronic supplementary material The online version of this article (doi: 10.1007/978-3-319-17043-5_10) contains supplementary material, which is available to authorized users. Videos can also be accessed at http://www.springerimages.com/videos/978-3-319-17042-8.

G. Brunnett et al. (Eds.): Virtual Realities, LNCS 8844, pp. 169–186, 2015.
DOI: 10.1007/978-3-319-17043-5_10

in this work "segments" and they result from the segmentation process while the process of exploring the kind of motion in a segment is called classification. Usually, long motion sequences are recorded because it is more comfortable for the actors and provide intrinsic natural transitions between different motions. Furthermore for some application fields, such as surveillance systems, we need to analysis long sequences of motion. The manual segmentation and classification of these sequences for the above mentioned purposes is very tedious and time consuming. Therefore we present in this work a method for automatic high-level segmentation and classification of motion capture data, where each of the resulting segments contains one kind of motion or parallel motions (e.g., walking, running, punching, walking and waving).

The contribution of our work is twofold: Firstly, a new method for extraction special meaningful characteristics of joint angles, joints and articulated body-parts or hierarchies of joints; and secondly, a hierarchical method for segmentation by classification of motion capture data into elementary motions or so called motion primitives. The proposed method simulates the human perception of motion segmentation and can be represented as a taxonomy-tree of human movements, which enables a multi-level segmentation and classification of human movement. Additionally, it does not need any training data and it is fast enough to perform in real time.

The main drawback of the proposed method is that each motion primitive, which is required to be recognized, should be defined manually. Motions which are not defined will be segmented into meaningful subsegments but not classified.

The rest of the paper is organized as follows: Sect. 2 provides an overview of the literature. Some terms and concepts used in this work are introduced in the third section. The proposed method is described in the Sect. 4. Next in Sect. 5 some results are depicted and discussed and finally the work is concluded in Sect. 6.

2 Related Work

Generally we can distinguish among three groups of works on segmentation and classification of motion capture data. The first group focuses only on segmenting the motion into distinct movements without giving any information about the classes of these movements, while the second group segments the motion and then classifies the resulted segments. The third group is similar to the second one but here the segmentation is a result of the classification. In the next subsections some examples of these groups are introduced.

2.1 Segmentation

Barbic et al. [1] proposed three methods for segmenting motion capture data streams. The first method is based on the suddenly increase in the intrinsic dimensionality of a local model of the motion, while the second observes the distribution of poses and decide a cut when it changes. The third approach segments the sequence where consecutive frames belong to different elements of a Gaussian mixture model. In contrast to our method, these methods cannot segment periodic motions into single cycles and mostly transitional motions are merged with neighbours segments and cannot be recognized as separated segemts. Kulic et al. [2] represented motion data using Hidden Markov Models (HMM), where the model state represents the probability density estimate over windows of the data. They assumed that data which belongs to the same motion will have the same distribution and thus they segmented the data by finding the optimum state sequence of the model. Yun et al. [3] assumed that high-level motion have many repeated frames within temporal distances. Based on this assumption they constructed a graph, where its vertices represent frames and its edges are weighted by the similarity of the connected frames. The motion stream is then segmented by applying the normalized cuts algorithm on the constructed graph. Zhou et al. [4] extended kernel k- means clustering by using a variable number of features in the cluster means and a dynamic time warping to realize temporal invariance.

2.2   Segmentation then Classification

Lin et al. [5] segmented motion streams at frames with velocity peaks and zero velocity crossings then they used HMM to refine and classify the resulted segments. Gong et al. [6] detected motion transition and motion primitives using kernelized temporal cut (KTC), which is an extension of Hilbert space embedding of distributions for change-point detection based on a spatio-temporal kernel. Nakata [7] observed inter-limb correlations and segmented the data where this correlation changed. Then he used dynamic programming matching to classify the resulted motion segments.

2.3   Segmentation by Classification

Müller et al. [8] introduced the concept of motion template, which captures geometric relational features of a motion class in a matrix, which can be semantically interpreted. Motion templates of different motion classes are learned and then used in segmenting and classifying of motion capture data. Zhao et al. [9] combined unsupervised clustering with active learning to learn Support Vector Machines (SVMs), which can then segment and classify large motion capture datasets using small training and working sets. Cho and Chen [10] utilized the relative positions of joints, temporal differences and normalized trajectories of motion to generate features for each motion frame, which were used in training of deep neural networks. These trained neural networks were used then to classify motion capture data. Lv and Nevatia [11] extracted features from the motion of single and multiple related joints, and then they used HMM and built weak classifiers to learn the dynamics for each motion class of each feature. They combined then all classifiers using the AdaBoost.M2 algorithm and used finally a dynamic programming algorithm to segment and classify the motion capture data at the same time. Li et el. [12] focused on the geometric structures of motion data and used singular value decomposition to extract these structures, then they explored multi-class support vector machine to segment and classify motion capture data streams.

Our proposed method is segmentation by classification method. We have also uti-lized the motion stillness and zero crossings as in [5] but in a way that mimics the human perception of motion segmentation and reduces the search space by classification. Unlike to our proposed method most of the above mentioned methods are unable to separate two consecutive occurrences of one motion, as well as the transitions between two motions are not recognized as transition but merged with the neighbour motions. Additionally, in some methods the learning process by classification is not simple, while our method is simple, easy to implement, efficient and does not need any training phase.

3 Preliminaries

We consider the human body as an open kinematic chain shown in Fig. 1. This kinematic chain consists of rotational joints connected with virtual and real bones respectively forming a tree. Thus, the human body pose can be determined by a set of joint orientations and the global position and orientation of the root joint. In this work, joint angles are used to describe the joint orientations. Each joint has three joint angles where each one of them is related to an axis of the local coordinate system at that joint (Fig. 1). We denote these joint angles together with the joint global positions as *human motion components*. Figure 2 shows the components set C used in this work, where each component is given an ID to be referred to later.

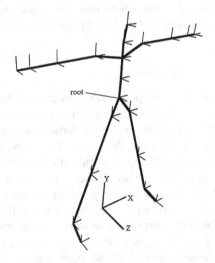

Fig. 1. Neutral pose of the used skeleton. The local coordinate systems are aligned with the world system and shown at each joint.

Generally, any human movement is a result of changes in a sub set of these com-ponents over a time interval. Suppose the function defined in (1) is a discrete function that describes the change of the motion component $c \in C$ over the discrete time interval T, in other words, this function can be considered as a discretization of the motion signal [13].

$$F_c(t) : T \rightarrow \Gamma \tag{1}$$

where $T = [t_1, t_n]$, $\Gamma \subset R$, t_1 and t_n the first and end frame of the motion respectively. We define the derivative of the smoothed function $F_c(t)$ simply as following:

$$F_c'(t) = F_c(t) - F_c(t-1) \text{ where } t \in T = [t_2, t_n]. \tag{2}$$

The proposed approach is based on the assumption that the transition from one motion to another occurs when the functions of some relevant motion components have considerable local minimum or maximum. We utilize the extrema of these functions to derive different types of *component characteristic* which help in reducing search space by classification of motion capture data. These Types of component characteristic are introduced in the next section.

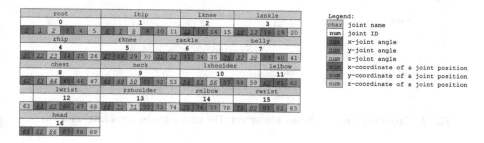

Fig. 2. Motion Components with their assigned IDs.

4 Taxonomy-Tree of Human Movement

The main idea of our method (Fig. 3) is based on the observation that humans tend to segment motion mainly when global body features such as moving, not moving and main body posture change. The features of individual body-parts such as raising an arm or moving one leg have lower attention in this context. Based on this observation, the characteristics mentioned above are arranged in a hierarchical way in order to simulate the human perception of motion segmentation and to reduce the search space by classification of motion capture data. This arrangement is denoted as *Taxonomy-Tree of Human Movement*.

This Taxonomy-Tree consists of 6 levels or layers, which are selected and sorted in a way that simulates the human priorities during motion segmentation. Firstly, static segments are separated from dynamic segments then the dynamic segments are divided into locomotor and non-locomotor segments. After that the main body posture in all segments is recognized and new segments are made where the main body posture is changed. The transitional phase between two main postures is considered as a separated transitional segment. In the next level each main posture is divided into some suitable secondary postures. We take as example the main posture "standing". It can be divided into three secondary postures, which are "standing upright", "standing bent" and "standing not self supported" or "leaned". Not all possible key body postures are listed in these two levels. Main postures are only considered here, so additional secondary postures can be added on demand. In the last level, a set of single body-parts characteristics individually or combined with other characteristics are used to recognize the smallest meaningful motion segments such as walking a step, walking a step and waving with right arm, sitting down, etc.

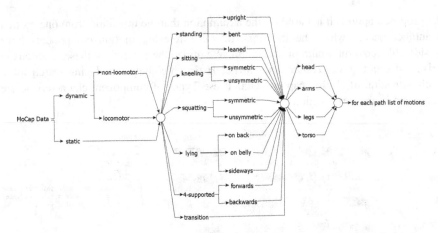

Fig. 3. Taxonomy Tree of Human Movement. The circles can be considered as hubs.

4.1 Characteristic of Human Motion Components

For a given motion sequence we define for each used component $c \in C$ an $n \times 1$ vector called change vector:

$$V_c = (v_0, v_0, \ldots, v_{n-1}), \tag{3}$$

where n is the total number of frames in the given motion sequence, and the value of v_t, where $t = 1,2,..,n-1$, is defined as following:

- $v_t = 0$ means that the component has no considerable change at the tth frame i.e. $F_c(t) = F_c(t-1)$.
- $v_t = +1$ means that the component increases at the frame number t i.e. $F_c(t) > F_c(t-1)$.
- $v_t = -1$ means that the component decreases at the frame number t i.e. $F_c(t) < F_c(t-1)$.
- For v_0 we suppose that $v_0 = v_1$.

A *Component Characteristic* of a component $c \in C$, which has the change vector $V_c = (v_0, v_0, \ldots, v_{n-1})$, is a temporary segment of the motion sequence, that starts at a frame s and ends at a frame e where $v_k = v_{k+1}$ for any $k \in [s, e-1]$. We denote this characteristic as φ_c^τ where c is the component index and $\tau = [s, e]$ is the time interval of the characteristic. Additionally, the difference between the component value at the end frame and start frame of the characteristic is called *characteristic magnitude* and it is defined as following:

$$\overline{\varphi}_c^\tau = F_c(e) - F_c(s), \text{ where } \tau = [s, e].$$ (4)

Figure 4 shows the characteristic of the x- joint angle of the left hip joint during a circular walking motion depicted under the curve that represents the joint angle values.

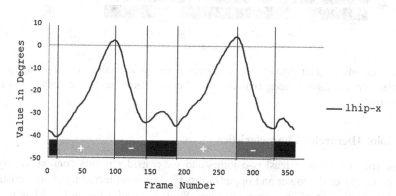

Fig. 4. Example of joint angle (component) characteristics. The Curve represents the values of the joint angle while rectangles represent corresponding characteristics coded as following: black for no considerable change; [+] for increasing value and [−] for decreasing one.

4.2 Joint Characteristics

If a joint has one degree of freedom (for example one joint angle) then the joint characteristics are the characteristics of the component corresponded to this joint angle. In the case of joints with multiple degrees of freedom we find its characteristic ϕ_j^τ that starts at a given frame s as following: Suppose that the considered joint has three joint angles x, y and z, and let the characteristics of these joint angles which include the frame s be, $\varphi_x^{\tau_x}$, $\varphi_y^{\tau_y}$ and $\varphi_z^{\tau_z}$ respectively where $\tau_x = [s_x, e_x]$, $\tau_y = [s_y, e_y]$, $\tau_z = [s_z, e_z]$, $s \in \tau_x$, $s \in \tau_y$ and $s \in \tau_z$ then we define the end frame e of the joint characteristic ϕ_j^τ as:

- the maximum end frame among the three end frames of the joint angle characteristics i.e. $e = max\ (e_x, e_y, e_z)$, if at least one of these characteristics has an considerable change.
- the minimum end frame among the three end frames of the joint angle characteristics i.e. $e = min\ (e_x, e_y, e_z)$, if none of these characteristics has an considerable change.

In Fig. 5 the curves and characteristics of the three joint angles x, y and z of the left hip joint during a circular walking motion are represented. The vertical black lines indicate the boundaries of the joint characteristics.

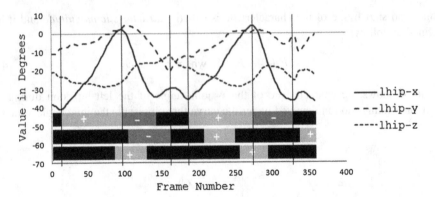

Fig. 5. Example of joint characteristics. Curves represent the values of joint angles while rectangles represent corresponding characteristics. Vertical black lines are the boundaries of joint characteristics.

4.3   Joint Hierarchy Characteristics

A Joint Hierarchy has at least two joints and we consider in this context mainly the joints-hierarchy of the lower and upper limbs. Finding joint hierarchy characteristics is similar to the finding of joint characteristics. Suppose a joint hierarchy B has n joints $J_1, .., J_n$. In order to find the joint hierarchy characteristic Φ_B^τ that starts at a given frame s, for each joint J_i we find the joint characteristic $\phi_i^{\tau_i}$ which includes the given start frame s. Suppose that $\phi_i^{\tau_i}$ ends at the frame e_i, then we set s to e_i and repeat this process for the next joint J_{i+1} until the characteristics of all hierarchy joints are found. Then the end frame of the characteristic of the joint hierarchy is equal to e_n as described in Algorithm 1.

Algorithm 1:

Input: Joint hierarchy $B = \{J_1, .., J_n\}$ with corresponding joint characteristics, start frame s.
Output: Φ_B^τ Characteristic of the joint hierarchy B.
Steps:

1. $\acute{s} = s$
2. for $i = 1$ to n do
   a. find the end frame e_i of the joint characteristic of the joint J_i which includes $\acute{s}$.
   b. $\acute{s} = e_i$
   c. $e = e_i$
3. The characteristic of the joint hierarchy B is Φ_B^τ where $\tau=[s,e]$

Figure 6 shows examples of joint hierarchy characteristics of the joint hierarchy that consists of the left hip joint as parent joint and the left knee joint as child joint during a circular walking movement.

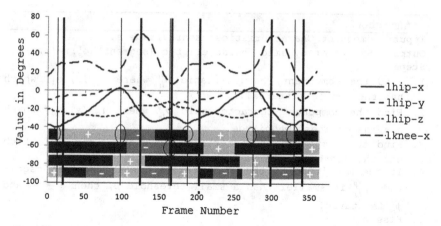

Fig. 6. Examples of Joint Hierarchy Characteristics for hip-knee-hierarchy during a circular walking. Thick black vertical lines are the boundaries of the joint hierarchy characteristics, while thin black vertical ones are the boundaries of the parent joint characteristics. The last characteristics row represents the joint characteristics of the child joint.

4.4 Body Characteristics

Body Characteristics are characteristics that describe the motion or the posture of the whole body and not only body-parts as in component, joint and joint hierarchy characteristics. Three types of body characteristics are defined in this work, two of them depend on the above defined characteristics and the third one is dependent on the size of the spatial spot, in which these characteristics occur, i.e. the horizontal distance that the root joint travel while performing these characteristics. Characteristics of the third type are called locomotor and non-locomotor. The characteristics of the first type are energy characteristics and can be expressed as dynamic and static. The characteristics of the second type are pose characteristics and they are actually the main postures which the human body can take. Each such characteristic consists of a set of subsequent poses which realize certain criteria. Representative poses of each of these characteristics are described below.

Dynamic vs Static. In the first level of the taxonomy tree the motion capture data is classified into dynamic and static segments, where a dynamic segment can contain different types of motion while a static segment is simply a pose repeated for a certain number of frames. The developed approach for extraction of a static or dynamic segment, which starts at a given frame s, is presented below in the Algorithm 2. In order to segment a given stream into static and dynamic segments, this algorithm is executed repeatedly. The first segment starts at the first frame of the stream, and then each next segment is considered to start at the end frame of the previous segment. Then subsequent segments, which are similar with respect to their static and dynamic attributes, are grouped. Figure 7 shows an example result of this algorithm.

Algorithm 2:

Input: Component Characteristics; start frame s.
Output: Static or dynamic characteristic (segment) $\phi_B^\tau : \tau = [s, e]$.
Steps:

1. Find the component characteristic $\varphi_{j_l}^{\tau_l}$ where $\tau_l = [s, e_l]$ which has the longest interval.

2. Find the component characteristic $\varphi_{j_g}^{\tau_g}$ where $\tau_g = [s, e_g]$ which has the greatest magnitude.

3. Find the component characteristic $\varphi_{j_s}^{\tau_s}$ where $\tau_s = [s, e_s]$ which has the shortest interval.

4. If the magnitude of the characteristic with greatest magnitude $\varphi_{j_g}^{\tau_g}$ is smaller than a small threshold μ, then $e = e_s$ and ϕ_B^τ is static.

5. Else $e = e_l$

    5.1.   If the magnitude of the characteristic with the longest interval $\bar{\varphi}_{j_l}^{\tau_l}$ is smaller than μ, then ϕ_B^τ is static.

    5.2.   Otherwise ϕ_B^τ is dynamic

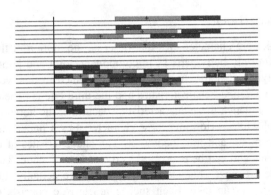

Fig. 7. Characteristics of set of components. Vertical black line is end frame of a static segment while the rest is a dynamic segment. White segments represent no considerable change; [+] for increasing value and [−] for decreasing one.

The threshold μ is used to filter movements caused by noisy data and also to ignore unimportant motions. The value of this threshold is selected as a percent of the smallest motion range among the motion ranges of the following joints: lower back, upper back, shoulders, elbows, wrist, hips, knees, and ankles. It can be also determined experimentally by finding the greatest change of joint angles over a segment which is manually classified as static.

Locomotor vs Non-locomotor. The second level of the taxonomy tree treats only dynamic segments. They are classified in locomotor and non-locomotor segments. A non-locomotor segment consists of non-locomotor movements i.e. movements that occur on the same spot without moving to any another place, while locomotor segment contains locomotor movements that change the global position of the root joint significantly such as walking and running. Examples for non-locomotor movements are bending, waving, sitting down, etc. Algorithm 3 shows how these characteristics are extracted.

Algorithm 3:

Input: set of dynamic segments; vertical positions of both feet; positions of the center of gravity of the body
Output: locomotor and non-locomotor segments
Steps:
1. Split each dynamic segment into sub segments of the three following types where it's possible:
   a. Both feet touch the ground for at least δms (definitely non-locomotor)
   b. At least one foot or the center of gravity is fixed for at least δms,
   c. Neither feet north center of gravity is fixed (definitely locomotor).
2. Check segments which resulted from step 1.b for non-locomotor and locomotor
3. Group subsequent segments which are similar according to their locomotor and non-locomotor attributes.

The threshold δ can be estimated experimentally by measuring the duration in milliseconds which the support foot stays touching the ground during a running movement.

Standing. Generally, "standing" is a main human body posture, in which the body maintains an upright position supported by the feet. The proposed method restricts the upright constraint on the lower body. Therefore a segment is recognized as "standing" if the body maintains at least one leg extended and perpendicular to the ground over the entire segment. "standing" segments can be further classified according to the position of the torso in the following three secondary postures:

1. If the torso stays upright then the segment is classified as "standing upright",
2. Otherwise as "standing bent".
3. Another criterion is the support area of the body. If the body is not supported only through the feet then the segment is classified as "standing leaned".

Given a pose $F(t)$, if the condition (5) is satisfied, then the pose is "standing", where $P_3(t)$, $P_1(t)$, $P_6(t)$ and $P_4(t)$ is the positions of the left ankle, left hip, right ankle and right hip joints respectively (see Fig. 2).

$$(\angle(P_3(t)P_1(t), OY) < \varepsilon) \vee (\angle(P_6(t)P_4(t), OY) < \varepsilon), \tag{5}$$

where the threshold ε is considered to be the maximal value over the minimal values of the angles between each leg and the vertical axis during a typical running movement.

Additionally if the x- or z-joint angle of the torso is greater than another user-defined small threshold β, then the pose is classified as "standing bent" (6).

$$(F_{36}(t) > \beta) \vee (F_{38}(t) > \beta). \tag{6}$$

For defining the last variant of "standing", which is "standing leaned", suppose S is the set of body-parts that contacts the environment i.e. S is set of support body-parts. Then the "standing leaned" is recognized when S contains at least one joint except the ankles:

$$S \setminus \{J3, J6\} \neq \varnothing \tag{7}$$

Sitting. The "sitting" posture is a main body posture in which the body is supported by the buttocks rather than the feet, and the torso is upright (8). Through the height of the hip joint can be decided whether one sits on an object or on the floor. The first "sitting" condition implies that the projection of the body center of gravity lies outside the support base of the body, which is formed through the feet. No constraints are put on the legs because there are many variants of "sitting" posture according to the legs position. Legs can be vertical, crossed or on each other.

$$(F_{36}(t) < \beta) \wedge (F_{38}(t) < \beta) \text{ where } \beta \text{ is defined as in Eq. (6)} \tag{8}$$

Kneeling. "Kneeling" is also a main body posture in which at least one knee touches the ground or a horizontal surface. In addition to this condition, knee must be bent i.e.

$$(F_{12}(t) < \varepsilon) \vee (F_{27}(t) < \varepsilon), \tag{9}$$

where ε here is the half of the knee motion range. If only one knee fulfills these criteria then the "kneeling" is called unsymmetric otherwise it is called "symmetric kneeling". Also the "kneeling" conditions can be formulated as following:

$$((F_{14}(t) \approx y_p) \wedge (F_{12}(t) < \varepsilon)) \vee ((F_{29}(t) \approx y_p) \wedge (F_{27}(t) < \varepsilon)) \tag{10}$$

where y_p is the considered height of the ground.

Squatting. "Squatting" is a main human body posture, in which at least one knee joint is bent (11) without contacting the ground (10) and the corresponding ankle joint is close to or contacts the buttocks or the back of the corresponding thigh (12).

$$(F_{12}(t) < \varepsilon) \vee (F_{27}(t) < \varepsilon) \tag{11}$$

$$(F_{14}(t) \neq y_p) \wedge (F_{29}(t) \neq y_p) \tag{12}$$

$$(|P_1(t) - P_3(t)| < \delta) \vee (|P_4(t) - P_6(t)| < \delta) \tag{13}$$

where $P_1(t)$ and $P_4(t)$ are the three dimensional positions of the left and right hip joint at the frame t respectively and $P_3(t)$ and $P_6(t)$ are the three dimensional positions of the left and right ankle at the frame t respectively, ε the same as in (9) and δ is a given small threshold which can be computed from the triangle hip, knee and ankle as the length of the edge hip-ankle where the lengths of femur and tibia are known and the knee-angle is considered to be equal to ε. "Squatting" is symmetric when the both knees are bent and asymmetric when only one knee is bent.

Lying. The "Lying" posture is defined as a human body posture, in which the body is in a horizontal or resting position supported along its length. In the proposed approach this definition is restricted on the torso i.e. the torso must be horizontal and supported along its length (see Fig. 1).

$$\angle(P_7(t)P_9(t), OXZ) \approx 0 \tag{14}$$

If at least one hip lies on the floor then the body is classified as lying on the ground:

$$\left(|F_{10}(t) - y_p| \leq l\right) \vee \left(|F_{25}(t) - y_p| \leq l\right), \tag{15}$$

otherwise on an object:

$$\left(|F_{10}(t) - y_p| > l\right) \wedge \left(|F_{25}(t) - y_p| > l\right), \tag{16}$$

where l is set to be the length of the foot and used to avoid effects caused by noisy data. If the two hip joints have approximately the same height and the normal of the frontal plane points down (17), then the body is lying on the belly, else if the mentioned normal points up and the two hip joints have approximately the same height (18), then the body is lying on the back (18).

$$(F_{10}(t) \approx F_{25}(t)) \wedge (\angle(N_f, OY) \approx 180) \tag{17}$$

$$(F_{10}(t) \approx F_{25}(t)) \wedge (\angle(N_f, OY) \approx 0) \tag{18}$$

If the heights of the hips are significant different then the body is lying sideways (19).

$$|F_{10}(t) - F_{25}(t)| > \eta, \tag{19}$$

where η can be defined as the half of the distance between the two hip joints.

Four-Supported. In this posture the hands and the feet contact the ground:

$$(F_{19}(t) \approx y_p) \wedge (F_{34}(t) \approx y_p) \wedge (F_{67}(t) \approx y_p) \wedge (F_{82}(t) \approx y_p) \tag{20}$$

If the belly faces the ground (21) then the position is called "forwards four-supported", otherwise the back faces the ground (22) and the position is called in this situation "backwards four-supported".

$$\angle(N_f, OY) \approx 180 \tag{21}$$

$$\angle(N_f, OY) \approx 0 \tag{22}$$

Another variant of this posture is when at least one upper limb and at least one lower limb contact the ground at the same time:

$$\left((F_{19}(t) \approx y_p) \vee (F_{34}(t) \approx y_p)\right) \wedge \left((F_{67}(t) \approx y_p) \vee (F_{82}(t) \approx y_p)\right) \tag{23}$$

This variant allows more movements to be performed than the first variant.

Transition. The transitions between the above mentioned main postures of the human body are considered here. The start and end postures determine the name of the transition i.e. the classification of a transitional segment is depended on the two surrounding main postures. For example the segment that corresponds to the transitional phase between "sitting" posture and "standing" posture will be as "standing up" classified. In order to find transition segments in a motion stream, we segment it firstly into the above mentioned human body postures, and then each segment which could not be classified as a main human body posture is considered as a transition segment. Additionally, most transitions exhibit significant changes of the height of the root joint. This feature is utilized to assert that a segment is a transition segment.

5   Results

We segmented 10 sequences of motion capture data from the CMU Graphics Lab Motion Capture Database [14] into elementary motions automatically using our presented method. The mean sequence length is around 8200 frames. Each Sequence contains different types of human activities such as walking, running, sitting, standing idle, jumping, drinking and some exercising. Cyclic activities such as walking and running consist of many cycles while some other activities such as sitting and jumping are repeated subsequently several times. For more details about the considered motion see [14]. To evaluate the ability of our approach to detect the correct cuts we also segmented these 10 sequences manually, and then we compared the manual cuts with the automatic cuts. The segmentation precision and recall are calculated as following: precision = number of manual cuts coincided with automatic cuts/ total number of manual cuts. Recall = number of correct (coincided) automatic cuts/total number of correct cuts (manual cuts), where an automatic cut is considered to be coincided with a manual cut if the automatic cut lies within a small range around the manual cut. That is due to the variations in manual segmentation when it is performed by different humans. Figure 8 shows a graphical comparison between the manual and automatic segmentation of the 10 mentioned streams. The computed accuracy over these 10 streams is more than 95 %, while the recall score is around 96 %. The mean segmentation speed is around 2000 fps on computer running Windows 8 with AMD A4-4300 M APU processor, 2.50 GHz and 4.00 GB RAM. That means that our method can work well in real time applications.

Fig. 8. Results of segmentation 10 motion capture data streams into motion primitives. The upper bar represents the manual segmentation while the lower represents the automatic segmentation.

Another approach to test the performance of our proposed method was to show how the boundary conditions of motion segments are fulfilled. For this purpose we have defined some boundary conditions of three motions namely walking, hopping and drinking, then we have investigated how these conditions are satisfied in the segments resulted from our method.

For walking segments we have defined one boundary condition, which is that the both feet are on the ground (lowest position) at the start and end of the segment. Figure 9 shows that the cuts coincide with lowest positions of the support foot, while relative low positions of the other foot are maintained. The same boundary condition can be used for hopping motion, where the feet must be on the ground at the segment begin and segment end (Fig. 10). For a drinking segment, the used hand must be far from the head at the segment start then it goes slowly towards the head so that it has the closest position to the head at the end of the segment. Figure 11 shows that these conditions are almost fulfilled regardless of the first cut which indicates the start of a static segment because the body seems motionless while drinking (segment from $\sim$7650 to $\sim$7850).

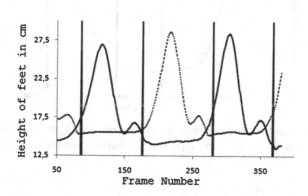

Fig. 9. Fulfillment of boundary conditions for walking motion. Vertical black lines are the segments boundaries. The solid curve is for the height of the right foot while the dashed one is for the left foot height.

We also tested our method on captured data of walking motion of a human with leg prosthesis.[1] The motion sequences could be perfectly segmented and classified. That emphasizes that our approach is invariant for pose deformations. It achieves also rotation invariance because it uses basically joint angles which are related to local frames at each joint. Additionally, the method is able to process motion capture data with different axes convention through enabling of axes reassignment which maintains the current meaning of joint angles.

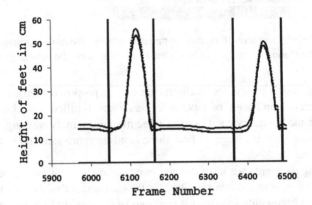

Fig. 10. Fulfillment of boundary conditions for hopping motion. Vertical black lines are the segments boundaries. The solid curve is for the height of right foot while the dashed one is for the left foot height.

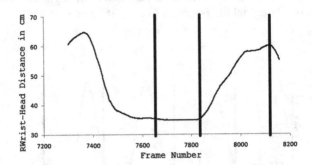

Fig. 11. Fulfillment of boundary conditions for drink motion with right arm. Vertical black lines are the segment boundaries. The curve represents the distance between the right wrist and the head joints.

---

[1] This data are captured at Chemnitz University of Technology.

6 Conclusion and Future Work

In this paper, a method for automatic semantic hierarchical segmentation by classification of motion capture data is presented. The main and secondary human body postures are utilized to reduce the search space simulating the human perception of motion segmentation, and then simple basic body parts movements are used to segment and classify more complex motions. The developed software is able to describe motion capture data streams in detail and with high accuracy in real time. Results are motion notations with number of periods (for periodic and repeated motions) and time length, for example, "walk 3 steps in 2 s, jump twice in 2.5 s then sitting for 10 s" and so on. The major drawback of the proposed method is that the classification part is hand-designed which makes it not trivial to add new motion classes to recognizable motions set. However, mean level segmentation can still be achieved without any modifications. All mentioned results were achieved with one set of thresholds. As future work, we plan to do firstly many experiments with other threshold sets, then secondly to extend our taxonomy tree so that the main body planes are used, and finally to facilitate adding new motion classes to the set of recognizable motions.

Acknowledgments. The data used in this work was obtained from motion capture.cs.cmu.edu.

References

1. Barbic, J. Safonova, A. Pan, J.Y., Faloutsos, C. Hodgins, J.K., Pollard, N.S.: Segmenting motion capture data into distinct behaviours. In: Graphics Interface, pp. 185–194 (2004)
2. Kulic, D., Nakamura, Y.: Scaffolding on-line segmentation of full body human motion patterns. In: IEEE/RSJ International Conference on Intelligent Robots and Systems, Acropolis Convention Center, France (2008)
3. Yun, S., Park, A., Jung, K.: Graph-based high level motion segmentation using normalized cuts. World Academy of Science Engineering and Technology 20 (2008)
4. Zhou, F. De la Torre, F., Hodgins, J.K.: Aligned cluster analysis for temporal segmentation of human motion. In: IEEE Conference on Automatic Face and Gestures Recognition (2008)
5. Lin, J.F., Kulic, D.: Segmentation human motion for automated rehabilitaion exercise analysis. In: 34th Annual International Conference of the IEEE EMBS (2012)
6. Gong, Dian, Medioni, Gérard, Zhu, Sikai, Zhao, Xuemei: Kernelized temporal cut for online temporal segmentation and recognition. In: Fitzgibbon, Andrew, Lazebnik, Svetlana, Perona, Pietro, Sato, Yoichi, Schmid, Cordelia (eds.) ECCV 2012, Part III. LNCS, vol. 7574, pp. 229–243. Springer, Heidelberg (2012)
7. Nakata, T.: Temporal segmentation and recognition of body motion data based on inter-limb correlation analysis. In: Proceedings of the 2007 IEEE/RSJ International Conference on Intelligent Robots and Systems San Diego, CA, Oct 29–Nov 2 (2007)
8. Müllerm, M., Röder, T.: Motion templates for automatic classification and retrieval of motion capture data. In: Eurographics/ACM SIGGRAPH Symposium on Computer Animation (2006)
9. Zhao, L., Sukthankar, G.: A semi-supervised method for segmenting multi-modal data. In: Proceedings of the International Symposium on Quality of Life Technology (2009)

10. Cho, K., Chen, X.: Classifying and Visualizing Motion Capture Sequences using Deep Neural Networks. arXiv preprint arXiv:1306.3874 (2013)
11. Lv, Fengjun, Nevatia, Ramakant: Recognition and segmentation of 3-D human action using HMM and multi-class AdaBoost. In: Leonardis, Aleš, Bischof, Horst, Pinz, Axel (eds.) ECCV 2006. LNCS, vol. 3954, pp. 359–372. Springer, Heidelberg (2006)
12. Li, C., Kulkarni, P.R., Prabhakaran, B.: Segmentation and recognition of motion capture data stream by classification. Multimedia Tools Appl. **35**, 55–70 (2007)
13. Bruderlin, A., Williams, L.: Motion signal processing. In: Proceedings of the 22nd Annual Conference on Computer Graphics and Interactive Techniques, pp. 97–104 (1995)
14. CMU Graphics Lab Motion Capture Database, Subject #86. http://mocap.cs.cmu.edu/search.php?subjectnumber=86. Accessed 24 March 2014

Content Creation and Authoring Challenges for Virtual Environments: From User Interfaces to Autonomous Virtual Characters

Ralf Dörner[1]([✉]), Marcelo Kallmann[2], and Yazhou Huang[2]

[1] RheinMain University of Applied Sciences, Wiesbaden, Germany
ralf.doerner@hs-rm.de
[2] University of California, Merced, USA

Abstract. How is content for virtual environments (VEs) created? How is behavior and motion in VEs specified? How are user interfaces designed and implemented for VEs? Authoring is a crucial aspect for using VEs successfully. This chapter addresses some of the current challenges in authoring VEs and recent research directions that are being explored in order to address these challenges. One highly relevant use case is the definition of motions to be executed by virtual characters. For this, motion modeling interfaces are presented that facilitate the process of programming the motions of virtual agents in VEs.

Keywords: Authoring process · Authoring tools · Virtual environments · Motion modeling · Virtual characters · User interfaces for virtual environments

1 Introduction

Since the first virtual environment has been created in the 1960s [59] there have been tremendous advances not only in the basic hardware and software but also in the quality and complexity of the content. While the first VEs were static, most VEs now contain animated scenes and autonomous entities. Whereas initially the specification of animation was mostly based on methods such as user-triggered keyframe animations, now the definition of animations has evolved to an abstract behavioral level e.g. by describing overall goals. This leaves the execution of low-level behavior (e.g. path finding, obstacle avoidance, object interaction) to sophisticated methods from artificial intelligence that are capable of generating complex emergent behavior. Today VEs are expected to contain not only 3D models but highly complex entities such as autonomous virtual characters who behave autonomously in complex scenarios. This evolution has led to exciting new applications in strategy games, simulation-based training, and synthetically populated scenes in movies. This chapter addresses a crucial issue that is directly affected by the rising complexity: *authoring* of virtual environments.

A Virtual Environment (VE) allows users to experience a virtual world and to feel present in it. Here, the term *virtual world* denotes the content of a VE.

G. Brunnett et al. (Eds.): Virtual Realities, LNCS 8844, pp. 187–212, 2015.
DOI: 10.1007/978-3-319-17043-5_11

Content consists of geometric 3D models of entities, their position and orientation in 3D space, other media (e.g. audio) associated with them, descriptions of their appearance and physical properties, descriptions of their behavior (e.g. in the form of simulation models) and specifications how users can interact with individual entities or the whole virtual world (e.g. navigation, selection, manipulation). Authors create the content. For instance, in a Virtual Reality training application for critical decision making such as [50] where agents engage the learner in a game-like scenario, the authors needed to create a 3D model of a virtual airport, create and animate 3D models of the agents, specify the behavior of the agents and specify the simulation of the virtual world. Usually, there are several authors involved which are required to possess different expertise. While one author needs the ability to animate a virtual human, another author might need knowledge in the application domain, e.g. to specify a training scenario. Authoring of the content is only one aspect of creating a working VE. For example, one integral part is the implementation of the underlying VR systems (e.g. the realization of image rendering, collision detection or physics simulation).

Another integral part of VEs is the user interface. With the advances in hardware, software and animated content of VEs, their *user interfaces (UIs)* also became more complex and sophisticated. Every VE has to include an interface for interaction between the user and the virtual world presented by the underlying computer system. Hence, VEs can be considered as a specific research subject and application field of human computer interaction (HCI). The HCI methodologies used for VEs differ considerably from graphical UIs that often rely on the WIMP (windows, icons, menus, pointer)-metaphor. The term *post-WIMP UIs* has been coined for UIs that make use of advanced technology, e.g. tracking technology [12]. They equip real time interactive systems with a plethora of interaction techniques stemming not exclusively from virtual reality and augmented reality, but also from gesture-based UIs, speech-based UIs, multi-touch and tangible user interfaces (i.e. a user interface where real objects called props are used as proxies for interaction). Post-WIMP UIs are becoming main stream with the advent of reasonably prized hardware such as digital cameras in smart phones and smart tablets, the Oculus Rift head mounted display [24], or the Leap Motion [23] or Microsoft Kinect [45] depth sensor. This is a novel situation for UIs that are employed by VEs which traditionally have been used only by small user groups. With more people involved and commercial products available, the developments in this area have become highly dynamic. As a result, UIs for VEs are rapidly exploring new paradigms of interaction that are increasingly more difficult to author. This also exceeds the scope of traditional 3D user interfaces [6] that have been employed in VEs.

Why is authoring important for VEs? If authoring processes do not evolve in a usable way, the potential of virtual and augmented reality might not become fully realized, and the use of VEs will remain accessible only to specialized users. There is a risk that only a small group of authors will possess the necessary skills to create content and design VEs. This would directly impact the costs of creating a VE; the sinking hardware costs would not compensate the increasing authoring costs. But the consequences would be not only purely economic.

Many applications need flexible authoring solutions. For instance, in the training application example it is important that trainers are able to modify and adapt the content or UI to their trainees' needs [13]. This calls for the need of dynamically updating the content in a way accessible to the non-specialized user. All VEs are the result of an authoring process, hence VEs in general can benefit from advances in authoring methodologies.

Given its importance, authoring was a topic of the 2013 Dagstuhl seminar Virtual Realities. We report some of the current challenges in the area of authoring identified in the seminar and some of the recent research directions that are being explored in order to address these challenges. We focus on content creation and authoring of UIs for VEs. In the next section, we start by discussing the challenges of recent approaches for authoring tools and processes, and we also discuss the specific challenge of designing immersive interfaces for modeling motions for autonomous virtual characters, which represents a highly relevant example for the next generation type of content creation. In Sects. 3 and 4 we discuss novel solutions for approaching these authoring challenges. This is followed by a conclusion.

2 Challenges

The creation of content and UIs that today's VEs require comprises a whole range of authoring activities, from usual multimedia content, to 3D interaction, and even motion specification for simulated autonomous entities. What challenges need to be addressed in order to provide adequate support for these activities? We start by characterizing eight of today's challenges in authoring post-WIMP UIs before we focus on challenges in authoring motions for virtual characters. While promising approaches exist, those challenges are still serious obstacles for using VEs in many real world applications.

2.1 Authoring Post-WIMP User Interfaces

For the creation of post-WIMP UIs, eight challenges were highlighted in the Dagstuhl seminar. We refer to them as the design guideline challenge, standardization challenge, emulation challenge, visibility challenge, authoring process challenge, tool challenge, event aggregation and abstraction challenge, and uncertainty challenge.

The *design guideline challenge* is to collect and to compile experiences and best practice in creating post-WIMP UIs and transform these pieces of information into operational guidelines for interaction techniques to be successfully used in each context and in each use case. User interfaces for virtual environments and generally user interfaces that rely on the post-WIMP paradigm are usually more difficult to design, implement and test than graphical user interfaces (GUIs). One reason is that post-WIMP UIs offer more options how to design a certain interaction. The design space for interaction techniques not only comprises keyboard entries, mouse movements and mouse clicks but for example in-the-air gestures, multi-touch gestures on a surface, speech commands, manipulation of props or movements of the head. Since GUIs have been used much more extensively than post-WIMP UIs, this design space has not been explored as thoroughly; much more experience is available about the design of GUIs and GUI authors have become more proficient by using a limited set of interaction techniques repeatedly. Consequently, there are fewer UI designers accustomed to post-WIMP UIs. Equipping UI designers with the necessary knowledge shows two sides of the design guideline challenge: the deduction of suitable guidelines and processes how to inform authors about these guidelines and support them in their application.

The *standardization challenge* is to agree on suitable common standards for post-WIMP UIs. No established set of interaction techniques comparable to GUI widgets (e.g. radio buttons or sliders) is available. This is not only a problem for UI designers, but also the users often need to familiarize themselves with the interaction techniques they encounter in different VEs. Which standards will emerge? Who will be able to define de facto standards such as the pinch gesture that was made well-known by Apple? While researchers are usually not in the position to set standards, especially de facto standards, they can make valuable contributions in suggesting standards, providing evidence to assess and evaluate standardization proposals, and catalyzing the standardization process.

The *emulation challenge* is to provide the authors with an authoring environment that allow them to test the UI easily on the target platform and switch between the author's view and the user's view. In addition, the authors need to be equipped with methodologies for rapid prototyping to conduct user tests in the early stages of the development (such as paper prototyping that is used for quick GUI prototyping). A reason for this is that the hardware platform the author uses can be significantly different from the target platform. While an author uses a software tool with a GUI in order to create a GUI, an author often does not work in a CAVE or uses body tracking in order to realize a post-WIMP UI. The target platform is used only occasionally for testing, making a WYSIWYG (what you see is what you get) approach impractical. The question is how to emulate aspects of post-WIMP UIs as well as necessary while still providing a comfortable authoring environment and support the author to effortlessly put themselves in the user's position.

The *visibility challenge* is to identify metaphors that are helpful for authoring entities in a user interfaces without visual representation. For authoring GUIs, GUI builders are commonplace and often integrated in development environments such as Eclipse or Visual Studio. GUI builder tools are similar to each other; they offer GUI components to the author together with means for changing parameters of the components (e.g. color, size), combining and arranging them to form a UI. This way, a WYSIWIG approach is realized where the author can inspect the current state of the UI easily and also demonstrate it to users in order to receive a feedback from them. With post-WIMP UIs, however, this approach is not feasible. One reason is that not all components of the UI (e.g. gestures) possess a graphical representation. For example, a thumbs-up gesture could be used to navigate forward in a VE. While there could be a kind of explanatory text or pictorial information present that illustrate to the user how the gesture is to be performed or remind them that this gesture can be used for navigation, this type of graphical representation is often omitted (e.g. in order to save screen space or to avoid distraction). As a result, a WYSIWIG view gives the author no clue that there is a certain component present in the UI. In GUIs, standard mouse interactions such as the double click have also no visual representation in the UI. But their number is small and they can be enumerated easily. In post-WIMP UIs, a plethora of such interaction techniques might be present.

The *authoring process challenge* is to define appropriate author roles and a workflow outlining the cooperation of authors. Ideally, the creation of a UI is an interdisciplinary effort. During the creation of a GUI, sometimes authors with technical background and programming knowledge and authors with skills in the arts and design work together. In the post-WIMP case, there is even more need to divide the work between several authors with different skill sets [1,3,4]. This is due to the increased complexity of the authoring task. For instance, interaction techniques are more difficult to realize [4,32]. The authoring process needs to provide common ground for the authors to work together seamlessly and to reduce friction. By limiting the prerequisites for an author role, it should also enable new groups of potential authors to contribute to the UI creation (e.g. authors from the application domain who are able to adapt the UI within certain limits).

The *tool challenge* is to support the different authors adequately. Because the tools should allow the author to easily adopt the user's point of view and they should solve the emulation challenge, they need to have post-WIMP UIs themselves. On the one hand, this makes the tools harder to build. On the other hand, post-WIMP interaction techniques might have the potential to make a significant contribution to mastering the tool challenge. Since a new authoring process is needed for post-WIMP UIs, the tools available for GUI creation are not sufficient.

The *event aggregation and abstraction challenge* is to provide events to the application UI programmer on an adequate abstraction and aggregation level. The underlying complexity of the sensor data and its fusion should be hidden from this author role. A significant difference between WIMP and post-WIMP UIs are the number of events that need to be processed in order to react on a user's action. Many sensors (e.g. gyroscopic sensors, depth cameras, tracking devices, pressure sensors) are employed in post-WIMP UIs. They are able to deliver complex information about users (e.g. the pose of different body parts of a user), sometimes more than 1000 times per second. This is in contrast to an occasional 'key pressed' event in GUIs. But the problem is not only the amount of events that need to be processed in real time in order to avoid a lag and to not jeopardize usability. Events need to be aggregated since they may need to be interpreted in context to each other [40]. For instance, the semantics of a hand gesture could differ if there is a certain voice interaction within a time limit. Moreover, the application UI programmer might find it overwhelming to evaluate hundreds of pieces of information on how users held different parts of their fingers over the time in order to identify whether one of the users performed a 'high-five gesture' or not. Reacting on a single event that has been aggregated from low level events and that states which user performed this gesture is preferable.

The *uncertainty challenge* is to inform the UI programmer about the probability that a specific event has occurred and to equip the author with strategies how to handle the uncertainties. While it can be determined with nearly 100 % certainty whether a key was hit on the keyboard or not, this is often not the case with other input devices. Uncertainty might be introduced e.g. due to noise, sampling errors, and sensitivity of sensors to changes in environmental conditions or users making ambiguous gestures.

That these challenges do present obstacles in today's authoring of VEs does not mean that these challenges are exclusive for VEs. For example, the standardization challenge was already present before graphical user interfaces established themselves. But the challenges may raise in VEs and solutions found to those challenges in GUI authoring or authoring of 3D user interfaces may not be simply transferable to post-WIMP UIs. While the uncertainty challenge, for instance, is also an issue in GUI authoring (e.g. do two mouse clicks of the user constitute a double-click or were they meant to be separate clicks), the higher number and complexity of events in post-WIMP user interfaces aggravate this challenge.

2.2 Authoring Motions for Virtual Characters

While the many challenges listed in the previous section address a broad range of needs when designing user interfaces, specific authoring metaphors have still to be developed for types of content that are not easily defined with usual tools. One important example is the definition of motions to be executed by virtual characters.

Improved tools for programming virtual characters are increasingly important in many applications of virtual environments. The challenges described in the previous section still apply to the several sub-problems involved, for ex: definition of agent behaviors, placement and customization of scenarios, etc. However, one particular new challenge that emerges is to design new approaches, techniques and algorithms that can enable new paradigms of user interaction to become effective user interfaces. While such a challenge can be classified as part of the tools challenge, the involved processes and techniques can become significantly complex to address modern still-emerging applications and solutions, such as the problem of programing motions of virtual agents by demonstration. We use this particular problem to illustrate the high complexity that can be involved in a particular challenge of our overall challenge classification.

The process of programming the motion of virtual agents by direct demonstration is highly important because it opens a complex task to the generic user. An effective interface will enable the creation of virtual characters that perform motions as needed in a given application. Due to the great need of variations and precise control of actions and gestures in many scenarios, modeling and parameterization of realistic motions for virtual agents become key problems to be addressed.

Common solutions to motion modeling rely on either hand-crafted motions [19,58,61] with commercial modeling tools or algorithmically synthesizing gestures with algorithmic procedures such as Inverse Kinematics [27,30]. However it remains difficult to achieve both controllable and realistic results, and every attempt to solve the problem purely algorithmically will require specific adaptations and models for every new action and situation being modeled.

On the other hand, motion blending techniques with motion capture data [31,47,51,52] provide powerful interpolation approaches for parameterizing pre-defined example animations according to high-level characteristics. While intensive research has been dedicated to find suitable interpolation schemes and/or motion style controls, less attention has been given to the development of techniques that enable intuitive interfaces for building suitable motion databases interactively, and that can well cover the simulated workspace with dedicated blending and parameterization procedures. This is especially important for tasks that require parameterizations with respect to spatial constraints within the environment. For instance, the interactive construction of real-time motion controllers has been proposed before [10], but without the inclusion of immersive interfaces for interactive edition and visualization of the obtained models during the creation process.

The obvious approach to this challenge is to develop motion modeling interaction metaphors with mechanisms that are similar to how people would demonstrate motions to each other. Such modeling by demonstration approach is necessary for achieving accessible interfaces that allow generic users to define new motion content. Furthermore, given the recent developments in effective and low-cost 3D sensing (for example with the Kinect) and 3D vision, modeling by demonstration can now be seen as a highly feasible approach to any system.

The recently introduced immersive modeling solution by Camporesi et al. [8] implements an interactive motion modeling approach via direct demonstration using an immersive multi-tile stereo visualization system with full-body motion capture capabilities. The system can be operated in two distinct phases: in the *modeling phase* the expert, who has the specialized knowledge of how to correctly perform the required motions, will demonstrate the needed motions to our system interactively. Later, in the *training phase*, by relying on the database of motions previously collected from the expert, the virtual human trainer is then able to reproduce the motions in interactive sessions with apprentice users learning the training subject, with the ability to reproduce the motions in respect to arbitrary target locations inside the environment.

While this overall approach has the right elements for being very effective, achieving intuitive interactive modeling interfaces has been critical for proving the system to be useful in concrete applications. In particular for the motion modeling phase, intuitive interfaces are important to allow expert trainers to focus on the motions being demonstrated rather than on irrelevant details. A good set of tools for inspection, parameterization and testing are also very important in order for users to effectively build suitable motion databases. Existing motion capture interfaces hardly offer any of these features, and in most

Fig. 1. Example configurations for full-body motion demonstration platforms, from a fully immersive system (left) to a desktop-based environment (right). In both scenarios the demonstrated motions are captured from a reduced marker set placed on the user and tracked by an optical multi-camera tracking system. The motions are then retargetted in real-time to the avatar in order to allow interactive construction of the motion databases to be used by the virtual character [8]. Several variations on these example configurations are possible and customization should be explored according to the goals of a given specific application (see for instance Table 1).

cases the user is required to work tedious hours in front of a computer using the keyboard and mouse to perform post-processing operations after many motion capture session.

The needed technology for achieving such types of systems is currently available. As an example Fig. 1 exemplifies two prototype configurations being tested at the UC Merced Motion Capture and Visualization facility. It is now the right time to start identifying the principles of a new class of interaction operators and procedures that can achieve intuitive full-body motion demonstration, coverage inspection, parametrization, motion refinement, etc. Section 4 summarizes some of the approaches being investigated in this area.

3   Authoring Tools and Processes for Post-WIMP User Interfaces

We present some approaches how to address all the challenges identified in Sect. 2.1. We do not restrict ourselves to 3D and spatial user interfaces [6]. These can be considered a sub-class of the more general post-WIMP UIs. Related to this, we do not require VEs to be fully immersive with using 3D input and output devices. Elements of 2D UIs can become part of a VE [38]. In addition, VEs can be presented as desktop VR, i.e. on a 2D display (e.g. a tabletop display) and still achieve a characteristic goal of a VE: making the user feel present in the virtual environment [44]. As a result, while being able to address authoring issues for VEs, the approaches presented are not exclusively applicable to the authoring of VEs. As post-WIMP UIs are becoming more main stream (see Sect. 1), this could enable research in authoring of VEs to take advantage of the resources and the developments in the area of post-WIMP UIs in general.

We start by providing an example of an authoring process, before we discuss frameworks and tools that have been proposed in the literature. Finally, we review some middleware solutions for the challenges.

3.1   An Example of an Authoring Process

One modern example of an authoring process for post-WIMP UIs was presented at the Dagstuhl seminar Virtual Realities: the EMIL authoring process [42] depicted in Fig. 2. It follows the software engineering approach of an object-oriented application framework [16]. The basic idea is to provide an application framework that is initially "empty" and needs to be filled with reusable components that are collected in a component library. Components foster reuse. This is not only economical and supports robustness but it is a strategy with regard to the standardization challenge. In addition, there are always two author roles involved when using a component: the author who created it and the author who used it to fill the application framework. Hence, the usage of components fosters the division of work between authors who may possess different skill sets. Consequently, there are two different tools in EMIL: the component authoring tool and the application authoring tool. In EMIL, a component represents an interaction (e.g. a multi-touch gesture, a GUI widget or the interaction facilities of a prop).

Application frameworks in EMIL are tailored to a specific application (e.g. for financial counseling in a bank). They all have a base framework in common that is built on some middleware (e.g. Adobe Flash). It offers an abstract interface for handling user interaction and also for accessing the operating system and the hardware. The base framework implements a mechanism that allows an easy insertion of a component and its linking to the framework. Different author roles are involved in creating the base framework and extending it to application frameworks. All frameworks are always executable. This is in contrast to approaches where components are considered building blocks that need to be assembled first before runnable software is formed. Thus, the current state of the application can always be demonstrated and tested with users even in the very early project stages since every project starts with an empty but working application. Involving users in all stages of UI development and progressing in an iterative manner is characteristic for user-centered design (ISO standard human-centered design for interactive systems ISO 9241-210), today's standard for authoring UIs in general.

EMIL uses a component approach not only for developing software but also for collecting information and fostering organizational learning. Therefore, every interaction component is equipped with a meta-data component. While in the application framework, the meta-data component executes code in order to collect information automatically, e.g. it counts how often an interaction component was used, it records user errors that were detected or it measures lag times. The knowledge browser is a tool that allows to import this data and to visualize it to an author. Moreover, with this tool an author is able to prepare an information

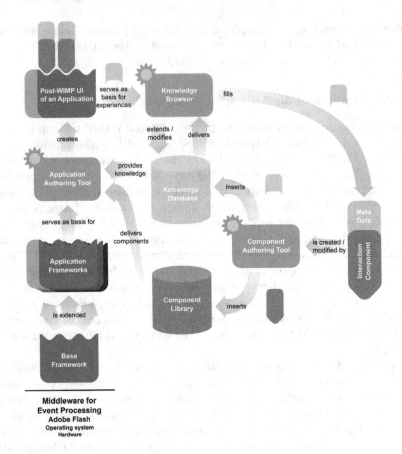

Fig. 2. The EMIL authoring framework for post-WIMP user interfaces

sheet about this component in the form of an interaction pattern [56]. For example, the author can add videos of user tests were the interaction component was tested or give advice for using this component (e.g. concerning the prerequisites for using the component or other components that have been used successfully in combination with the component). These patterns can be arranged hierarchically in order to form an interaction pattern language analogous to [49]. In the knowledge browser, the author can create a new pattern or augment an existing one that was already stored in the knowledge database. In the application authoring tool, the author who is filling the application framework with interaction components can access the knowledge data base in order to search for and to identify interaction components that are potentially suitable for a given task. On the contrary, this author could also choose an interaction component first. Since this component possesses meta-data, the author would be able to access without searching all the experience already gathered by using this interaction component in other projects. Thus, the access to the knowledge about an interaction component is integrated seamlessly in the authoring process. Using an

Fig. 3. (a) Collaboration of authors when using EMIL rapid prototyping (b) Usage of mobile devices for an author-specific view [42]

interaction component multiple times and collecting and refining its meta-data leads to the emergence of design guidelines. This is a strategy to address the design guideline challenge.

Component based approaches only pay off if the components are reused frequently and if there is a critical mass of components available in the library. Considering the diversity of post-WIMP UIs, this might pose a problem. One solution adopted in EMIL is to introduce a specific iteration at the beginning of the iterative development process. This iteration is executed not on the target platform of the post-WIMP UI to be created but on a carefully chosen platform that supports a whole class of post-WIMP UIs, e.g. interactive surfaces or virtual environments. Thus, components and application frameworks created for this class can be reused in different projects in order to illustrate and discuss different UI design alternatives by building prototypes rapidly. During the evaluation of EMIL, this was demonstrated to a team of experts in order to collect qualitative feedback. This team consisted of a UI designer, a programmer and a concept designer from an advertising agency versed in creating post-WIMP UIs for interactive surfaces. They highlighted the ability of this approach for quick design - test cycles with higher quality as even sophisticated interaction techniques can be tried out realistically (e.g. in contrast to a paper prototype). Particularly, they liked that authors involved in the design process can use this prototyping platform to collaboratively assemble and modify the results of their work directly (see Fig. 3a). Providing each participant with a mobile device is an approach to allow each author to have an individual author's view of the UI (see Fig. 3b). For this, a magic lens metaphor [5] can be used. This means that the user can apply a visual filter to reveal additional information. It can be implemented by using Augmented Reality methodologies [39].

Moreover, the experts saw an application area in project acquisition where customized prototypes could be used to convince a potential customer of the advantages of post-WIMP UIs [42]. The prototypes can also be used for analyzing the user requirements and for first user testing. The resulting well specified UI can then be realized on the target platform. This is a step towards meeting the emulation challenge.

3.2   Frameworks and Tools

In the literature, several frameworks and tools have been presented specifically for
the authoring of virtual reality and augmented reality applications. For example,
AMIRE [1] is a component-based framework for authoring augmented reality. It
draws from the idea of 3D components [14] that combine graphical representation
and behavior. APRIL [33] is a framework for creating augmented reality presentations. Sinem and Feiner describe an authoring framework for wearable augmented
reality [57]. These frameworks, however, focus on solutions for their specific application field. Moreover, the literature contains reports about methodologies that
can be applied to authoring, for example Lee et al. [34] show that it is beneficial to
perform the authoring of a VE in an augmented reality environment. Case studies
(e.g. [63]) that highlight some of the challenges in authoring are rare.

For authoring post-WIMP UIs several frameworks have been proposed. Some
are targeted at certain authoring aspects. For instance, the focus of the OpenIn-
terface (OI) Framework [42] lies on the flexible usage of several input channels
for realizing multi-modality. OI is based on components. These can be used in an
authoring application where the author manipulates a graphical representation
of the user interface based on a data flow graph. Other frameworks focus on
specific methodologies. For example, the Designer's Augmented Reality Toolkit
(DART) [43] is a framework supporting design activities in early project stages
of creating user interfaces employing methodologies from Augmented Reality. In
addition, DART aims to assist authors in a smooth transition from low-fidelity
prototypes to final products. One of DART's key ideas is to provide behaviors
that can be easily attached to content. DART is one of the few approaches
where the authoring process is taken explicitly into consideration. More often,
not processes but tools are conceived. A tool always shapes an authoring process
indirectly.

Many authoring tools used for creating post-WIMP UIs are either used by
programmers or by artists. For programmers, text based integrated development
environments (IDEs) are commonplace, e.g. Microsoft's Visual Studio [46] or
Eclipse [15]. Some tools for non-programmers are available which often employ
visual programming techniques [28]. A typical metaphor used is that of a wiring
diagram known from electrical engineering. Following the component idea, a set
of building blocks is made available. They possess input and output slots and
the author's task is to connect them. Examples for such tools are Virtools [62]
and Quest3D [48]. Some promising results for such authoring tools are reported,
for instance [21] describes an AR authoring tool targeted at non-programmers
where tasks can be carried out more accurately and in less than half of the
time compared to standard IDEs. The work of Broll et al. shows that visual
prototyping can be useful for prototyping VEs [7]. However, these tools are not
used widely.

Some IDEs offer functionality for authoring post-WIMP UIs. For example,
Apple's Xcode [2] is more than a standard GUI builder. It offers some typical multi-touch gestures that can be connected to the GUI. The connections
are visualized resulting in a better overview [37]. Some IDEs can be extended by

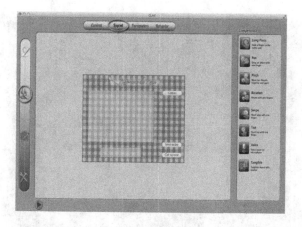

Fig. 4. Screenshot of the CLAY authoring tool [20]

plugins. For instance, Gesture Studio [40] is a plugin that introduces new authoring metaphors or paradigms to Eclipse, e.g. programming-by-example [53] where the system is trained to recognize gestures by examples provided by the author. However, all these authoring tools are limited to a subset of post-WIMP interaction techniques. A small number of tools are tailored for creating VEs, for example Autodesk's VRED. In addition, tools initially intended for computer game development, e.g. Unity 3D [60] or the sandbox editor of CryEngine3 [11], are also equipped with specific functionality for creating the user interface of VEs.

Only few tools offer comprehensive post-WIMP authoring. Squidy [29] is a tool supporting visual programming under a unified working space. It uses a metaphor based on data flow diagrams as well as a zooming metaphor to provide information about components of the UI on several levels of detail. However, Squidy focuses on technical issues such as the seamless connection of several input and output devices. For example, it is not even possible to create a GUI. A zooming metaphor is also supported by ZOIL (Zoomable Object-Oriented Information Landscape) [65], a software framework for creating distributed post-WIMP UIs. The work in the literature highlights the shortcomings of traditional IDEs and the advantages of providing a dedicated authoring tool for post-WIMP UIs. Still, tools are lacking that are able to address the whole range of post-WIMP interaction techniques. The specific requirements of different authoring roles and the need for supporting collaboration between authors are sometimes not addressed at all.

CLAY (Cross Layer Authoring Tool) [20] explicitly acknowledges that there are different author roles. It distinguishes several layers where each layer represents the work space of one author role. In CLAY, these author roles are programmer, GUI designer, post-WIMP UI designer and end user, i.e. the tool can not only be used during the development of the UI but also for configuration and adaptation after deployment. A slider is used to switch between the layers (see Fig. 4). The slider can also be set between two layers. Transparency is used to blend between these layers making it feasible to view two layers in parallel.

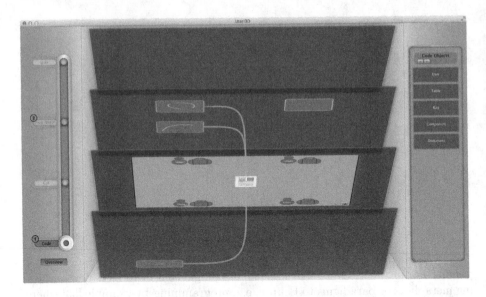

Fig. 5. The overview mode in Utari3D

Using the same tool and not switching between tools, it is therefore possible to visualize the interfaces and dependencies between the work spaces of different authors, e.g. programmers working on the code layer can see for which GUI widgets (on the GUI layer) and which gestures (on the post-WIMP layer) their methods are used as a callback. This supports collaboration between authors who are assigned to different authoring tasks while working on creating the same post-WIMP UI. Pursuing the idea of a single tool supports a movement back and forth as the slider to switch between layers can be moved in two directions. This is more suitable for user-centered design, where results of an evaluation (e.g. a user test on the user layer) need to be fed back to all layers. For example, the need to change a gesture can impact the code. Supporting the different author roles with a single tool can solve problems due to incompatibilities and the need for data exchange between traditional tools. In CLAY, the authors place entities (e.g. widgets or graphical representation of gestures) on the layers and may combine them to form more complex entities. They can also change individual parameters of the entities. CLAY is based on a matrix metaphor, i.e. functionality is arranged in a tabular layout analogous to a matrix. The rows represent different layers, e.g. a code layer or a post-WIMP layer; the columns represent topics, e.g. content, layout, parameters, or behavior. For example, the author can select a cell in the table representing the layout of the GUI layer. In this cell, all according functionality is made available. While this metaphor helps to reduce complexity (since it organizes the functionality and sorts it for different author roles such as a GUI designer), it uses much screen space and can only show connections between two neighboring layers.

Utari3D (Unified Tool for Authoring Realtime Interaction in 3D) is also relying on layers. In contrast to CLAY, it is based on a 3D metaphor and utilizes a specifically shaped 3D space where layers are arranged in parallel. The 3D metaphor provides affordances for possible interactions of the author. In addition, it suggests visualizations. Authors can use a slider to move the layers back and forth. Transparency is used to blend from one layer to the next. In addition, authors can change to a pre-set camera position that allows for a birds-eye view of the layers (see Fig. 5). In the space between the layers, dependencies are visualized. For each switch, a transition animation is used. Utari3D has been used in a user test where several experts built a post-WIMP UI. The evaluation shows that the test users had no difficulty grasping the metaphor. Indeed, these users appreciated an overarching metaphor tying together multiple tools for authoring; this is more than just plug-in tools together. The 3D space offers more degrees of freedom to place the camera. Hence, the authors can adopt different views, e.g. look at layers perpendicularly and compare two layers or use the overview mode where they can look in between the layers from a bird's eye perspective. Animating the camera or transforming the layers' position and orientation, smooth transitions can be made between the views. Similar approaches are used for example in Apple's iOS 7 where all browser tabs can be viewed in a 3D space or the cover flow metaphor that allows for browsing music. There is no sudden break by switching between tools which might be confusing and makes it difficult to understand dependencies from entities in one tool to entities in a separate tool. The metaphor can be extended to use 3D layers which is particularly relevant to author the spatial aspects of a VE. Authoring approaches for specific tasks that have proven to be successful and that are used by many authors today (e.g. text-based authoring of program code or visual layout of GUI widgets) can be integrated seamlessly in Utari3D as it is used only for a high level of abstraction. For instance, Utari3D does not impose that every authoring aspect needs to be accomplished graphically and that the use of visual programming techniques is mandatory on the code level. The users in the test appreciated that familiar authoring processes have been complemented and not replaced. Thus, the tools presented do not only address the authoring process challenge, but also the tool challenge.

3.3 Middleware Solutions

In order to address the event aggregation and abstraction challenge and uncertainty challenge often middleware solutions are proposed. Several approaches have been already explored. For instance, the Midas [55]/Mudra [25] system supports the processing of event streams from different sources ranging from low-level, simple raw data streams to higher-level, complex semantic events. It employs a fact base and also a declarative language to specify how facts, i.e. events, are automatically processed. However, this approach has several drawbacks. First, with every event the fact base needs to be constantly updated. As input events are usually short lived and transient in nature this approach requires additional maintenance functions which have to be added to the fact base. Second, the processing rules are realized using the inference engine CLIPS

[54], an expert system tool. The inference engine is also not designed for continuous evaluation and thus has to be also modified. Third, the interface to the application layer does not support selection of events based on application defined rules (such as complex Boolean expressions). This is a prerequisite to deal with large amounts of events on different abstraction levels. Lastly, this approach has difficulties in reaching an acceptable performance. Instead of a fact base, [18] used a multi-agent architecture [64] for analyzing all input modalities to find out what the user actually wants to accomplish. While this might be a general approach (such as the Open Agent Architecture [9]), this work focuses on speech input that is accompanied by other types of sensor data in order to resolve ambiguous situations. It remains questionable if this can be transferred to other kinds of post-WIMP interactions. The approaches mentioned above are domain specific approaches to the challenges in the field of HCI. A more general approach is taken by complex event processing (CEP). The term CEP refers to the detection, analysis, and general processing of correlated raw or simple events and their transformation in more abstract and meaningful complex events [41]. CEP is based on the concept of the event driven architecture (EDA), in which loosely coupled components communicate by emitting and consuming events. The methodologies of CEP and EDAs have rarely been applied to interactive systems [22].

UTIL [35] is a middleware that is based on CEP, in particular the interaction event processing architecture [36] and the CEP engine Esper. It applies CEP to interactive systems and provides an abstraction between code of an application's UI and the input devices of a system. It also provides an interaction layer that manages the access of applications to any event from the event processing layer. This middleware can be used for instance as a foundation for the EMIL base framework (see Fig. 2). UTIL offers several benefits. Detection, aggregation, fusion and selection of input events is based on a declarative specification (using the Event Processing Language EPL). This declarative approach facilitates the specification of post-WIMP interactions on a high level of abstraction. Moreover, it lets the CEP engine perform the actual processing and maintenance of current and past events. This abstraction also makes it possible to benefit from optimizations and other improvements the engine can perform without changing the application's code. Continuous queries enable applications to precisely specify which kinds of events are expected. This allows reducing the amount of post-processing within user interface code to a minimum, thus possibly improving the software quality. It is also feasible to write rules that determine the uncertainty of an aggregated event based on the uncertainty of its base events.

UTIL was evaluated in a representative usage scenario [35]. In this scenario, 4,384 raw input events and 27 rules were used, implementing various gesture-based interaction techniques. In order to also measure the impact of the event delivery, 1,000 unspecific queries for all events on the interaction layer were added. For each raw event passed into the middleware, the time it took the middleware to accept the next event was measured. This round-trip time includes all query evaluations as well as calling all registered event listeners. For the evaluation, a notebook computer (MacBook Pro with an 2.66 GHz Intel Core 2 Duo with 4 GB of RAM) was used. An average roundtrip time of 12.35 μs per event with a standard deviation of 4.8 μs was measured, i.e. an average event throughput of 80,973 event/s. This can be considered sufficient for post-WIMP UIs, as input event rates typically range from hundreds to a few thousand events per second.

4   Motion Modeling Interfaces for Virtual Environments

Among the many functions a user interface may have for content preparation in virtual environments, one that has particular potential to take advantage of a post-WIMP paradigm is the process of programming the motions of virtual agents in virtual environments. With the increased availability of motion capture devices, motion modeling has the clear potential to evolve from an expert-only tedious activity relying on specialized modeling software to a modeling by direct demonstration approach accessible to most users.

Such an approach is extremely important for allowing users to update their content and achieve effective virtual characters in their simulated environments. One particularly important class of applications is the motion modeling of virtual trainers and assistants that can learn, train and assist people in interactive applications of virtual environments. In these applications, facilitating the process of motion content creation is very important. The topic of motion modeling by demonstration represents a good example of a non-traditional type of interface that modern applications are starting to address. This section discusses possible solutions to address this area.

A generic system for interactive motion modeling will have typically two distinct modes: a capture interface and a motion modeling interface. When the user demonstrates new motions on-the-fly during capture, the user can then immediately playback, crop, reject or accept each captured motion segment. This is similar to recording video sequences from a video camera and preparing the sequences for later editing. The motion modeling mode will allow the user to organize the captured motions according to the intended use.

The focus here is on the particular organization of motion segments that is suitable for motion blending and parameterization. The approach creates parameterized gestures or actions from clusters of aligned example motion segments of the same type, but with variations with respect to the spatial parameterization to be considered. For example, a gesture cluster for a certain way of pointing will typically consist of several examples of similar pointing gestures, but with each pointing motion pointing to a different location. Different motion blending techniques can be used with motion capture data in order to achieve parameterization, and a recent comparison study provides a good overview of the most popular methods [17]. The solutions presented on this chapter are based on the *inverse blending* technique [17,26].

One first issue that has to be addressed by the interactive system is to provide appropriate feedback of the coverage achieved by the current cluster of

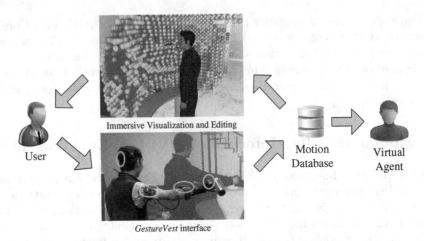

Immersive Visualization and Editing

User

Motion
Database

Virtual
Agent

GestureVest interface

Fig. 6. The main components for an interactive motion modeling by demonstration system.

motions and the employed motion blending technique. The goal is to allow the user to quickly observe the coverage of the database inside the target virtual environment with different visualization tools, and to allow the user to improve the database coverage as needed. The coverage of a database here refers to how well parameterized motions interpolated from the discrete motion examples in the current database are able to satisfy precise spatial constraints as needed in the environment. With the appropriate visualization tools the user is able to quickly switch between capture and modeling modes until the needed coverage is achieved, therefore guaranteeing correct execution in the target environment.

Figure 6 shows one example scenario where the user is modeling a pouring motion cluster with a *motion vest* motion capture interface based on inertial sensors. For the illustrated pouring action the spatial parameterization needs to well cover the target container, which can be placed anywhere on the table in the scenario. By providing a few pouring actions for key locations on the table inverse blending procedures can then precisely interpolate the given example motions towards arbitrary targets on the table.

The definition of clusters for collecting example motions is an important concept of system based on motion blending. Clusters are necessary for specifying each parameterized action or gesture. When the user selects to start a new cluster, every recorded motion becomes associated with that cluster. Motions in a cluster will be blended and therefore they have to consistently represent variations of a same type of motion. The capture process is straightforward and it just requires a button to notify start and stop signals. The user first initializes a new motion cluster, and then holds down the capture button to begin recording. A button in the WiiMote controller is used in the presented examples. The button is then released after performing the motion.

Using the WiiMote controller, the user can instantly switch from on-line capture mode to playback/editing, scroll through the already captured motions,

Fig. 7. This example interface allows the user to easily scroll through captured motions, crop out unwanted frames, and most importantly mark stroke frames to be parameterized. This image shows the user inspecting one motion segment with a simple hand movement.

delete unwanted clips from memory, mark the start and end of each motion segment to crop out unnecessary parts, and most importantly mark the stroke frames (stroke times) for each segment before populating them into clusters in the database. The stroke frame of each captured motion is then used as the point in the motion (the main stroke point) to be parameterized.

4.1 Motion Database Inspection

Since great variations can be found among different gestures and actions, an easy way to go through each motion cluster and to quickly crop lead-in/lead-out frames and annotate the motion strokes is needed. We have experimented with buttons to skip over motions captured and with an editing interaction mode where the trajectory of the user's hand is captured and mapped into a linear horizontal movement in real-time, and the movement directly controls the motion playback slider. This enables the user to quickly visualize the available motions with a simple horizontal hand movement, allowing the user to remain inside the capture area and conveniently validate and edit the motion cluster. Figure 7 shows several snapshots of the playback interface being used to analyze a recently captured pointing motion.

4.2 Workspace Coverage Visualization

The ability to enforce constraints using inverse blending greatly depends on the existing variations among the example motions being interpolated. In general, the size of motion database is proportional to the volume of the covered workspace. In order to produce quality motions satisfying many possible constraints spanning the whole workspace, it is important to determine which example motions to capture during the capture process. This will ensure that a well-built cluster of motions is formed, with good coverage of the regions of interest (ROIs) inside the workspace.

On the other hand, defining an overly fine subdivision of the constraint space with too many examples is inefficient and impractical as it requires capturing too many example motions to populate a database. Not only the database would

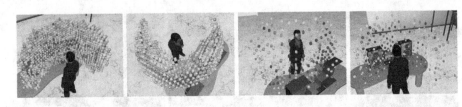

Fig. 8. Volume visualization with global workspace sampling at different sampling densities. The error threshold can be adjusted to only display regions with large errors and thus help the user to focus on improving those regions (Color figure online).

be redundant, this would also impose a huge workload on the user. Instead, since similar examples can often be interpolated to produce valid new motions with good quality, a small number of carefully selected example motions is better in providing good coverage for the ROIs in the workspace. Achieving an efficient database is also key to ensure lag-free interactivity of the system.

The approach of using a palette of colors to quantify error inside the workspace is explored here in order to intuitively guide the user during the process of adding new motions to the database. A global coverage visualization of the workspace volume can be achieved with a coarse uniform sampling of workspace points. Each point is assigned a color that quantifies the error achieved by the inverse blending routine when addressing the target point.

Consider a pointing database as example. In this case the constraint is the target locations for the finger tip to reach. The user can visualize how accurate the current cluster of motions can be parameterized to cover the entire area in front of the virtual character. This example is shown in Fig. 8. In the example, the error measures the distance between each sampled pointing target (small color cubes) and the position that can actually be reached by the finger tip, using the current database. While the visualization may be of a large portion of the workspace, the computed colors come from the interpolation errors in the current database independent of the quantity of example motions in the database.

This visualization method requires some computation time, normally a few seconds, depending on the fineness/coarseness of the sampling. After this initial computation, it can be visualized from different points of views interactively in real-time without any lag. This solution provides a good overview of the whole cluster coverage in the given environment.

4.3 Local Coverage Visualization

It is possible to observe that the global error-based volume visualization is not needed when the user is fine tuning the coverage of a small region, or when only a small local region is of interest. In addition, even if using the global cluster coverage visualization is always helpful, the pre-computation time can impose undesirable wait times when editing large motion sets since every time new motions are added to the cluster visualizer nodes have to be re-computed.

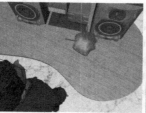

Fig. 9. The local coverage visualizer can be interactively placed over a small ROI during the motion modeling phase, enabling the user to instantly visualize the current motion cluster coverage at important locations. The user can then easily further improve the cluster as needed. The right-most image shows the user interactively placing the local coverage visualizer close to the control panel of the sound system to inspect the cluster coverage in those specific regions (Color figure online).

A possible second coverage inspection method is local and allows the user to interactively place a colored mesh geometry in the scene for precise coverage visualization in a specific region. See Fig. 9 for an example using the same pointing motion database as in Fig. 8. When switched to the local coverage visualization mode, the system renders a transparent colored mesh geometry in the approximate form of a sphere covering a small ROI inside the workspace, which follows the movement of the user's hand. In this case, the motion cluster coverage evaluation is performed only within the specific region delimited by the mesh geometry volume.

The mesh color computation is very efficient. Only the vertices of the mesh are evaluated for error computation, and the obtained color on the mesh surface comes from color interpolation with Gouraud shading. Mesh size, shape

Table 1. Analysis of possible types of applications, their main characteristics, and the design choices relevant to immersive modeling interfaces.

Types of Applications	Design Choices						
	stereo vizualization	scene in 100% scale	tracking scope	tracking precision	motion modeling	coverage visualization	challenges
high-precision procedures with object manipulation, ex: virtual surgery training	important	important	full upper-body with fingers	high precision important	direct interaction important	important	VR system alone will not provide force feedback
procedures where object manipulation is not crucial, ex: demonstration of machine operations	maybe important	maybe important	full upper-body with fingers	medium precision may be enough	both direct interaction and avatar display useful	important	need effective interface for virtual objects manipulation
generic demonstrative gestures for delivery of information, ex: giving directions or object info.	maybe important	maybe important	single arm with fingers	medium precision may be enough	both direct interaction and avatar display useful	important	current solutions should be sufficient
modeling generic motions/exercises without reference to objects, ex: exercises for physical therapy	less important	less important	full body no fingers	medium precision may be enough	modeling motions with only avatar display may be more effective	may not be needed	current solutions should be sufficient

and resolution can be easily changed during the interactive inspection by using the WiiMote controller. The user can select different mesh sizes for either fast sweeping of areas of interests, or for carefully checking small spots of interests. The local coverage visualization mode is particularly useful for close examination of coverage within small local ROIs. This mode easily takes into account any new demonstrated motions dynamically added to the database without any pre-computation lag.

5   Conclusion

The eight challenges for authoring VEs (design guideline challenge, standardization challenge, emulation challenge, visibility challenge, authoring process challenge, tool challenge, event aggregation and abstraction challenge and uncertainty challenge) identified are still serious obstacles for a more widespread use of virtual environments in various application areas. In addition to these broad challenges, there is a lack of specific authoring metaphors for addressing new emerging types of content and content creation. One highly relevant example is immersive motion modeling, i.e. the authoring of motions to be executed by virtual characters. The techniques discussed in this paper provide an overview of solutions implementing an immersive motion modeling interface.

It is important to observe that for the overall approach of immersive motion modeling to be most effective the involved design choices have to be customized according to the target application. Table 1 provides an analysis of several types of relevant applications and their respective relevant characteristics. Table 1 was built from the experience of the authors working with the described system.

Even if the described underlying algorithmic solutions based on motion blending are replaced by other methods, a user-driven motion capture based interface will need to integrate basic motion segmentation editing tools, quick motion database traversal tools, and coverage/quality of results visualization. The discussed examples only provide a first exploration of techniques into this broad realm.

Likewise, the examples for authoring processes, authoring framework and authoring tools for creating virtual environments in general and their user interfaces in particular that were presented can also be considered only first steps towards solving the wide-ranging challenges. More research efforts are necessary in this area and the novel approaches to authoring and modeling need to be employed and evaluated more extensively in field tests. One important issue for the future research roadmap is to not only examine every authoring task and authoring challenge independently but to provide authors with a consistent and coherent authoring framework.

Acknowledgements. Marcelo Kallmann and David Huang were partially supported in this work by NSF award IIS-0915665. Ralf Dörner was partially supported in this work by the German Federal Ministry of Education and Research (BMBF) grant 17043X10.

References

1. Abawi, D.F., Dörner, R., Grimm, P.: A component-based authoring environment for creating multimedia-rich mixed reality. In: Proceedings of the Seventh Eurographics Conference on Multimedia, EGMM 2004, pp. 31–40. Eurographics Association, Aire-la-Ville, Switzerland (2004). http://dx.doi.org/10.2312/EGMM/MM04/031-040
2. Apple: Xcode, January 2014. developer.apple.com/xcode
3. Bastide, R., Navarre, D., Palanque, P.: A model-based tool for interactive prototyping of highly interactive applications. In: CHI 2002 Extended Abstracts on Human Factors in Computing Systems, CHI EA 2002, pp. 516–517. ACM, New York (2002). http://doi.acm.org/10.1145/506443.506457
4. Beaudouin-Lafon, M.: Instrumental interaction: an interaction model for designing post-wimp user interfaces. In: Proceedings of the SIGCHI Conference on Human Factors in Computing Systems, CHI 2000, pp. 446–453. ACM, New York (2000). http://doi.acm.org/10.1145/332040.332473
5. Bier, E.A., Stone, M.C., Pier, K., Buxton, W., DeRose, T.D.: Toolglass and magic lenses: the see-through interface. In: Proceedings of the 20th Annual Conference on Computer Graphics and Interactive Techniques, SIGGRAPH 1993, pp. 73–80. ACM, New York (1993). http://doi.acm.org/10.1145/166117.166126
6. Bowman, D.A., Kruijff, E., LaViola, J.J., Poupyrev, I.: 3D User Interfaces: Theory and Practice. Addison-Wesley, Boston (2004)
7. Broll, W., Herling, J., Blum, L.: Interactive bits: prototyping of mixed reality applications and interaction techniques through visual programming. In: IEEE Symposium on 3D User Interfaces, 3DUI 2008, pp. 109–115. IEEE (2008)
8. Camporesi, C., Huang, Y., Kallmann, M.: Interactive motion modeling and parameterization by direct demonstration. In: Safonova, A. (ed.) IVA 2010. LNCS, vol. 6356, pp. 77–90. Springer, Heidelberg (2010)
9. Cheyer, A., Martin, D.: The open agent architecture. Auton. Agent. Multi-Agent Syst. 4(1–2), 143–148 (2001). http://dx.doi.org/10.1023/A:1010091302035
10. Cooper, S., Hertzmann, A., Popović, Z.: Active learning for real-time motion controllers. ACM Trans. Graph. (SIGGRAPH 2007) 26(3) (2007)
11. Crytech: Cryengine 3, January 2014. cryengine.com
12. van Dam, A.: Post-wimp user interfaces. Commun. ACM 40(2), 63–67 (1997). http://doi.acm.org/10.1145/253671.253708
13. Dörner, R., Grimm, P.: Etoile - an environment for team, organizational and individual learning in emergencies. In: Proceedings of the 9th IEEE International Workshops on Enabling Technologies: Infrastructure for Collaborative Enterprises, WETICE 2000, pp. 27–34. IEEE Computer Society, Washington, DC (2000). http://dl.acm.org/citation.cfm?id=647068.715502
14. Dörner, R., Grimm, P.: Three-dimensional beanscreating web content using 3d components in a 3d authoring environment. In: Proceedings of the Fifth Symposium on Virtual Reality Modeling Language (Web3D-VRML), pp. 69–74. ACM (2000)
15. Eclipse: Eclipse foundation homepage, January 2014. eclipse.org
16. Fayad, M., Schmidt, D.C.: Object-oriented application frameworks. Commun. ACM 40(10), 32–38 (1997). http://doi.acm.org/10.1145/262793.262798
17. Feng, A., Huang, Y., Kallmann, M., Shapiro, A.: An analysis of motion blending techniques. In: Kallmann, M., Bekris, K. (eds.) MIG 2012. LNCS, vol. 7660, pp. 232–243. Springer, Heidelberg (2012)

18. Flippo, F., Krebs, A., Marsic, I.: A framework for rapid development of multimodal interfaces. In: Proceedings of the 5th International Conference on Multimodal Interfaces, ICMI 2003, pp. 109–116. ACM, New York (2003). http://doi.acm.org/10.1145/958432.958455

19. Gebhard, P., Kipp, M., Klesen, M., Rist, T.: What are they going to talk about? towards life-like characters that reflect on interactions with users. In: Proceedings of the 1st International Conference on Technologies for Interactive Digital Storytelling and Entertainment (TIDSE 2003) (2003)

20. Gerken, K., Frechenhäuser, S., Dörner, R., Luderschmidt, J.: Authoring support for post-WIMP applications. In: Kotzé, P., Marsden, G., Lindgaard, G., Wesson, J., Winckler, M. (eds.) INTERACT 2013, Part III. LNCS, vol. 8119, pp. 744–761. Springer, Heidelberg (2013). http://dx.doi.org/10.1007/978-3-642-40477-1_51

21. Gimeno, J., Morillo, P., Orduna, J., Fernandez, M.: A new ar authoring tool using depth maps for industrial procedures. Comput. Ind. **64**(9), 1263–1271 (2013). http://www.sciencedirect.com/science/article/pii/S0166361513001267, special Issue: 3D Imaging in Industry

22. Hinze, A., Sachs, K., Buchmann, A.: Event-based applications and enabling technologies. In: Proceedings of the Third ACM International Conference on Distributed Event-Based Systems, DEBS 2009, pp. 1:1–1:15. ACM, New York (2009). http://doi.acm.org/10.1145/1619258.1619260

23. Homepage: Leap motion, January 2014. leapmotion.com

24. Homepage: Oculus rift, January 2014. oculusvr.com

25. Hoste, L., Dumas, B., Signer, B.: Mudra: a unified multimodal interaction framework. In: Proceedings of the 13th International Conference on Multimodal Interfaces, ICMI 2011, pp. 97–104. ACM, New York (2011). http://doi.acm.org/10.1145/2070481.2070500

26. Huang, Y., Kallmann, M.: Motion parameterization with inverse blending. In: Boulic, R., Chrysanthou, Y., Komura, T. (eds.) MIG 2010. LNCS, vol. 6459, pp. 242–253. Springer, Heidelberg (2010)

27. Kallmann, M.: Analytical inverse kinematics with body posture control. Comput. Anim. Virtual Worlds **19**(2), 79–91 (2008)

28. Kelleher, C., Pausch, R.: Lowering the barriers to programming: a taxonomy of programming environments and languages for novice programmers. ACM Comput. Surv. **37**(2), 83–137 (2005). http://doi.acm.org/10.1145/1089733.1089734

29. König, W.A., Rädle, R., Reiterer, H.: Squidy: a zoomable design environment for natural user interfaces. In: CHI 2009 Extended Abstracts on Human Factors in Computing Systems, CHI EA 2009, pp. 4561–4566. ACM, New York (2009). http://doi.acm.org/10.1145/1520340.1520700

30. Kopp, S., Wachsmuth, I.: Synthesizing multimodal utterances for conversational agents: research articles. Comput. Anim. Virtual Worlds **15**(1), 39–52 (2004)

31. Kovar, L., Gleicher, M.: Automated extraction and parameterization of motions in large data sets. ACM Trans. Graph. (Proceedings of SIGGRAPH) **23**(3), 559–568 (2004)

32. Lawson, J.Y.L., Coterot, M., Carincotte, C., Macq, B.: Component-based high fidelity interactive prototyping of post-wimp interactions. In: International Conference on Multimodal Interfaces and the Workshop on Machine Learning for Multimodal Interaction, ICMI-MLMI 2010, pp. 47:1–47:4. ACM, New York (2010). http://doi.acm.org/10.1145/1891903.1891961

33. Ledermann, F., Schmalstieg, D.: April: a high-level framework for creating augmented reality presentations. In: Proceedings of the Virtual Reality, VR 2005, pp. 187–194. IEEE (2005)

34. Lee, J.Y., Seo, D.W., Rhee, G.W.: Tangible authoring of 3d virtual scenes in dynamic augmented reality environment. Comput. Ind. **62**(1), 107–119 (2011)

35. Lehmann, S., Doerner, R., Schwanecke, U., Haubner, N., Luderschmidt, J.: Util: complex, post-wimp human computer interaction with complex event processing methods. In: Proceedings of the 10th Workshop Virtual and Augmented Reality of the GI Group VR/AR, pp. 109–120. Shaker Verlag, Aachen (2013)

36. Lehmann, S., Doerner, R., Schwanecke, U., Luderschmidt, J., Haubner, N.: An architecture for interaction event processing in tabletop systems. In: Proceedings of the First Workshop Self Integrating Systems for Better Living Environments, Sensyble 2010, pp. 15–19. Shaker Verlag, Aachen (2010)

37. Li, P., Wohlstadter, E.: View-based maintenance of graphical user interfaces. In: Proceedings of the 7th International Conference on Aspect-Oriented Software Development, AOSD 2008, pp. 156–167, ACM, New York (2008). http://doi.acm.org/10.1145/1353482.1353501

38. Lindeman, R.W., Sibert, J.L., Hahn, J.K.: Towards usable vr: an empirical study of user interfaces for immersive virtual environments. In: Proceedings of the SIGCHI Conference on Human Factors in Computing Systems, CHI 1999, pp. 64–71. ACM, New York (1999). http://doi.acm.org/10.1145/302979.302995

39. Looser, J., Grasset, R., Billinghurst, M.: A 3d flexible and tangible magic lens in augmented reality. In: Proceedings of the 2007 6th IEEE and ACM International Symposium on Mixed and Augmented Reality, pp. 1–4. IEEE Computer Society (2007)

40. Lü, H., Li, Y.: Gesture studio: authoring multi-touch interactions through demonstration and declaration. In: Proceedings of the SIGCHI Conference on Human Factors in Computing Systems, CHI 2013, pp. 257–266. ACM, New York (2013). http://doi.acm.org/10.1145/2470654.2470690

41. Luckham, D.C.: The Power of Events: An Introduction to Complex Event Processing in Distributed Enterprise Systems. Addison-Wesley Longman Publishing Co. Inc., Boston (2001)

42. Luderschmidt, J., Haubner, N., Lehmann, S., Dörner, R.: EMIL: a rapid prototyping authoring environment for the design of interactive surface applications. In: Kurosu, M. (ed.) HCII/HCI 2013, Part I. LNCS, vol. 8004, pp. 381–390. Springer, Heidelberg (2013). http://dx.doi.org/10.1007/978-3-642-39232-0_42

43. MacIntyre, B., Gandy, M., Dow, S., Bolter, J.D.: Dart: a toolkit for rapid design exploration of augmented reality experiences. In: Proceedings of the 17th Annual ACM Symposium on User Interface Software and Technology, UIST 2004, pp. 197–206. ACM, New York (2004). http://doi.acm.org/10.1145/1029632.1029669

44. McMahan, A.: Immersion, engagement and presence. In: Wolf, M.J.P., Perron, B. (eds.) The Video Game Theory Reader, pp. 67–86. Routledge, New York (2003)

45. Microsoft: Kinect homepage, January 2014. xbox.com/kinect

46. Microsoft: Microsoft visual studio, January 2014. visualstudio.com

47. Mukai, T., Kuriyama, S.: Geostatistical motion interpolation. In: ACM SIGGRAPH, pp. 1062–1070. ACM, New York (2005)

48. Quest3d: Act-3d b.v.: Quest3d, January 2014. quest3d.com/

49. Remy, C., Weiss, M., Ziefle, M., Borchers, J.: A pattern language for interactive tabletops in collaborative workspaces. In: Proceedings of the 15th European Conference on Pattern Languages of Programs, EuroPLoP 2010, pp. 9:1–9:48. ACM, New York (2010). http://doi.acm.org/10.1145/2328909.2328921

50. Richards, D., Porte, J.: Developing an agent-based training simulation using game and virtual reality software: experience report. In: Proceedings of the Sixth Australasian Conference on Interactive Entertainment, IE 2009, pp. 9:1–9:9. ACM, New York (2009). http://doi.acm.org/10.1145/1746050.1746059

51. Rose, C., Bodenheimer, B., Cohen, M.F.: Verbs and adverbs: multidimensional motion interpolation. IEEE Comput. Graph. Appl. **18**, 32–40 (1998)

52. Rose III, C.F., Sloan, P.P.J., Cohen, M.F.: Artist-directed inverse-kinematics using radial basis function interpolation. Comput. Graph. Forum (Proceedings of Eurographics) **20**(3), 239–250 (2001)

53. Rubine, D.: Specifying gestures by example. In: Proceedings of the 18th Annual Conference on Computer Graphics and Interactive Techniques, SIGGRAPH 1991, pp. 329–337. ACM, New York (1991). http://doi.acm.org/10.1145/122718.122753

54. Savely, R., Culbert, C., Riley, G., Dantes, B., Ly, B., Ortiz, C., Giarratano, J., Lopez, F.: Clips, January 2014. clipsrules.sourceforge.net

55. Scholliers, C., Hoste, L., Signer, B., De Meuter, W.: Midas: a declarative multitouch interaction framework. In: Proceedings of the Fifth International Conference on Tangible, Embedded, and Embodied Interaction, TEI 2011, pp. 49–56. ACM, New York (2011). http://doi.acm.org/10.1145/1935701.1935712

56. Seffah, A., Taleb, M.: Tracing the evolution of hci patterns as an interaction design tool. Innov. Syst. Softw. Eng. **8**(2), 93–109 (2012). http://dx.doi.org/10.1007/s11334-011-0178-8

57. Sinem, G., Feiner, S.: Authoring 3d hypermedia for wearable augmented and virtual reality. In: 2012 16th International Symposium on Wearable Computers, pp. 118–118. IEEE Computer Society (2003)

58. Stone, M., DeCarlo, D., Oh, I., Rodriguez, C., Stere, A., Lees, A., Bregler, C.: Speaking with hands: creating animated conversational characters from recordings of human performance. ACM Trans. Graph. **23**(3), 506–513 (2004)

59. Sutherland, I.E.: The ultimate display. In: IFIP 1965 International Federation for Information Processing, vol. 2, pp. 506–508 (1965)

60. Unity Technologies: Unity3d, January 2014. unity3d.com

61. Thiebaux, M., Marshall, A., Marsella, S., Kallmann, M.: Smartbody: behavior realization for embodied conversational agents. In: Seventh International Joint Conference on Autonomous Agents and Multi-Agent Systems (AAMAS) (2008)

62. Virtools: Daussault systemes: 3dvia virtools, January 2014. 3ds.com/de/products-services/3dvia/3dvia-virtools/

63. Wojciechowski, R., Walczak, K., White, M., Cellary, W.: Building virtual and augmented reality museum exhibitions. In: Proceedings of the Ninth International Conference on 3D Web Technology, pp. 135–144. ACM (2004)

64. Woolridge, M.: An Introduction ot MultiAgent Systems. Wiley, Hoboken (2002)

65. Zoellner, M., Jetter, H.C., Reiterer, H.: Zoil: a design paradigm and software framework for post-wimp distributed user interfaces. In: Gallud, J.A., Tesoriero, R., Penichet, V.M. (eds.) Distributed User Interfaces. Human-Computer Interaction Series, pp. 87–94. Springer, London (2011). http://dx.doi.org/10.1007/978-1-4471-2271-5_10

Tele-Existence

Technical Report: Exploring Human Surrogate Characteristics

Arjun Nagendran$^{(\boxtimes)}$, Gregory Welch, Charles Hughes, and Remo Pillat

Synthetic Reality Lab, University of Central Florida, Orlando, FL 32826, USA
arjun@cs.ucf.edu, welch@ucf.edu, {ceh,rpillat}@cs.ucf.edu
http://sreal.ucf.edu

Abstract. This report highlights some of the historical evolution of our research involving the characteristics that are essential for effective human-surrogate interactions. In this report, a consolidated glossary of terms related to human-surrogate interaction is described, following which an attempt at defining a consolidated space of surrogate characteristics is made. The rationale behind the space definition is to provide an easy way to categorize existing and future systems, and help identify areas in which the research community might focus its efforts.

1 Introduction

The notion of human *surrogates* has been explored in, among other places, literature, movies, computer games, and virtual reality. Research contributions from the disciplines of computer science, psychology, social science, and neuroscience help to shed light on how real human users/subjects perceive and interact with various forms of such surrogates. Today, applications of human surrogates include telepresence, military and medical training, education, and healthcare.

Though the manifestation of surrogates can range from *real humans* (e.g., standardized patients in medicine) to completely *virtual humans* (e.g., virtual patients) with computer-synthesized appearance and behavior, recent technological advances in computer graphics, robotics, and display technology are beginning to blur the line between real and virtual humans. Some researchers suggest that the advent of accurate visual portrayals of humans will soon allow the completely seamless blending of virtual and real elements and make them indistinguishable from each other [1].

Compared to real human surrogates, it is *virtual* (or *physical-virtual*) humans that we are particularly interested in. Figure 1 is intended to help illustrate the relationships between inhabiters (left), their surrogates (middle), and interacting human users/subjects (right). We use the term *virtual avatar* to indicate a surrogate with human-directed or autonomous behavior rendered on a conventional computer screen. We use the term *Physical-Virtual Avatar* (PVA) to indicate a surrogate with a physical manifestation, but virtual appearance and/or behavior. One example of a PVA is realized using cameras and digital projectors to map the appearance and motion of an inhabiter onto a life-sized animatronic human

© Springer International Publishing Switzerland 2015
G. Brunnett et al. (Eds.): Virtual Realities, LNCS 8844, pp. 215–228, 2015.
DOI: 10.1007/978-3-319-17043-5_12

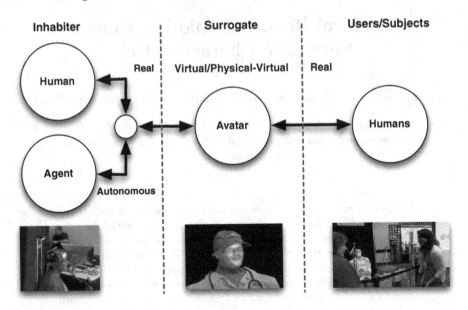

Fig. 1. The relationships between inhabiters (left), their surrogates (middle), and interacting human users/subjects (right).

(see left and middle of Fig. 1) [2]. The relationship patterns illustrated in Fig. 1 can be conceptually arranged or even "chained" to reflect different scenarios involving multiple inhabiters, surrogates, or users/subjects.

Getting started. Since at least October of 2012 we have been undertaking activities aimed at exploring the following primary questions:

- Can we define a space of characteristics that encompasses all currently known manifestations of human surrogates?
- How should the set of characteristics be chosen to provide a compromise between their generalization power and their utility towards distinguishing existing (and future) systems?
- How do the various dimensions of (or points in) said space affect human perceptions, their emotional responses, and interactions with human surrogates?

Our rationale was that satisfactory answers to these questions could offer a starting point for future research activities and potentially provide a set of application-specific recommendations. We continue the effort to explore the many factors that affect the responses of human users/subjects to various manifestations of human surrogates. In particular, one of our goals is to develop a comprehensive framework that identifies and classifies the main determinants for real humans' perceptions towards and interactions with human surrogates. A well-developed framework will prove invaluable in guiding future research directions while providing a clear structure to categorize previous contributions. We also hope to provide insights into the effectiveness of certain factors for applications employing human surrogates. This report describes a historical evolution of our research.

2   Terminology

Traditionally, two terms have been used to denote manifestations of human surrogates: avatars and agents. The distinction is based on the controlling entity, which could be either a human (avatar) or a computer algorithm (agent). The word **avatar**, in the context of computing, first appeared in the science fiction novel *Snow Crash* [3], in which avatars were introduced as virtual entities controlled by human users. More rigorously, [4] defines an avatar as "*a perceptible digital representation whose behaviors reflect those executed, typically in real time, by a specific human being*".

If a human surrogate is labeled as an **agent**, the common assumption is that its behavior is controlled by a computer program rather than a real human being. Analogous to the avatar definition, an agent is "*a perceptible digital representation whose behaviors reflect a computational algorithm designed to accomplish a specific goal or set of goals*" [4].

Since we do not want to restrict our investigation to either avatars or agents, we prefer to use the term **human surrogates** in our work. In the broadest sense, "surrogate" captures the fact that we are interested in human representations, while not being encumbered by traditional distinctions between digital and physical form as well as the nature of the agency. As elaborated in [1], our current generation might be the last one that can readily distinguish between real and virtual beings, so we believe that the generalizing terminology of surrogacy is appropriate.

A common metric of the human response to virtual environments is the feeling of "presence" or immersion that the users experience. **Presence** is a broad concept but is usually understood as the subjective experience of being in one place, even when one is physically somewhere else [5,6]. More relevant for our research interests are the concepts of co-presence and social presence, which are subsumed under the more general presence category. The feelings of co-presence and social presence that subjects experience when interacting with human surrogates are common metrics to evaluate what surrogate characteristics elicit physical and psychological responses. Due to their importance, these terms will be repeatedly used throughout the paper and we would like to provide basic definitions for them.

Co-presence was originally termed by [7] and denoted a state where "*people sensed that they were able to perceive others and that others were able to actively perceive them*". Reference [8] used the concept of co-presence in virtual environments to measure the psychological connection to and with another person. We would like to adopt this perspective and use the term to denote an acknowledgment by study participants that a human surrogate is perceived as a distinct, potentially intelligent, entity.

Social presence was first defined in relation to a medium by [9]: it is "*the degree of salience of the other person in a mediated communication and the consequent salience of their interpersonal interactions*". Reference [10] distinguishes social presence from co-presence by associating the first with the medium and the latter with the degree of psychological involvement. The authors of [11] propose an extension of the concept to Embodied Social Presence (ESP) which focuses on the embodied avatar as the center of activity in social interactions.

The definition of social presence exhibits a certain degree of overlap with co-presence, but we adopt the position of [11] that highlights the interactive component that allows human surrogates to actively influence and take part in social exchanges and thus be perceived as part of the social context. The surrogate can take cues from the environment, other surrogates, or human subjects and exert some level of influence on its surroundings.

We believe that both co-presence and social presence are valid measures of the quality of human-surrogate encounters.

3   Rationale

Virtual reality technology has been consistently used in training and educational scenarios over the last decade. The effectiveness of this technology has been the focus of researchers over several years, in order to better understand the underlying factors that influence the perceptions and interactions of the human users. Specifically, researchers have focused on several facets of the technology and the embedded surrogates, including the visual fidelity (appearance), auditory feedback, haptics (conveying force/touch information), physical manifestations (robots, 3D characters), intelligence of these systems, and so on. While several hypotheses of how human perceptions and emotional responses can be influenced have been tested during evaluation, there is no comprehensive space that encompasses all these findings.

From a purely academic perspective, a taxonomy is attractive for multiple reasons. A space of surrogate characteristics would provide an easy way for categorizing existing and future systems, while at the same time identifying regions that might merit further exploration. In addition, the variety of perspectives that have contributed to human surrogate research, e.g. psychological, technological, physiological, neurological, warrants an attempt to find generalizing principles.

Although we hope that the resulting space can be constructed as application-agnostic as possible, an appropriately defined set of axes could assist choices of technology and surrogate characteristics in relation to application-specific training and interaction needs.

Additionally, we believe that the space will provide us with a better understanding of human-surrogate interactions from a psychological perspective, which in turn should translate to the ability to provide an effective means of interaction.

4   Defining the Space

Several attempts to classify existing work in this research area have been made previously. [12] proposed the Autonomy, Interaction, and Presence (AIP) cube to describe the components of virtual reality systems. Although not exactly a taxonomy of human surrogates, it is interesting that the author emphasizes the importance of agency, i.e. Autonomy, and interactive capacity, i.e. Interaction.

In the context of mixed-reality agents, a similar effort was undertaken by [13]. A 3D cube with the axes of Agency, Corporeal Presence, and Interactive Capacity

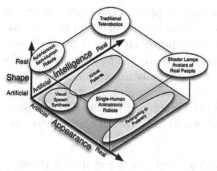

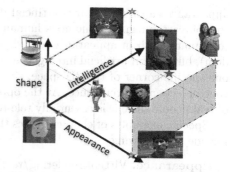

(a) Regions of existing human surrogate manifestations are highlighted through ellipses.

(b) Several instances of real systems can be placed in this 3D space. In addition, it allows us to place our own work on physical-virtual avatars.

Fig. 2. Historically, we envisioned the space of human surrogate characteristics as a 3D cube spanned by Appearance, Shape, and Intelligence. These are two early visualizations of this space defined in a top-down fashion.

mirrors some of our thinking, although the authors' choice of distinguishing characteristics is not sufficiently justified or grounded in existing literature. In addition, the authors concentrate on purely autonomous agents and combine attributes of body shape and appearance in the Corporeal Presence category.

Reference [14] discusses a framework for classifying representations of humans (avatars) in physical and virtual space. The main discriminants discussed by the authors are Form Similarity (avatar resembles human) and Behavioral Similarity (avatar behaves like controlling human), but the singular focus on avatars does not allow the classification of computer-controlled agents.

We began to express our own thoughts on the subject in research funding proposals over the past several years, introducing a 3D classification cube with Intelligence, Shape, and Appearance axes. Our thoughts stemmed from a top-down choice of characteristics based on our a priori knowledge of humans and first-hand human surrogate research. Building upon these earlier developments, we were able to position our own work within the context of other systems and use the classification system to guide our research directions [15]. Please see Fig. 2a for a visualization of the resulting 3D space and highlighted regions that correspond to particular manifestations of human surrogates. Specific instances of existing surrogate systems are positioned in the same cube in Fig. 2b.

Each axis ranges from being artificial to real, with "real" referring to being "as close as possible" to a human and "artificial" occupying the other end of the spectrum. This, in particular, must not be confused on the intelligence axis, since "artificial intelligence" strives to achieve "human-like" intelligence. Virtual avatars (flat screen display) for instance could be made to appear like a particular human, exhibit artificial intelligence, but have no real shape (i.e. physical manifestation) associated with them. A typical example could be a football player in a computer game. Note that the intelligence of this avatar can tend towards the real when controlled by a real human playing the game. Similarly, the appearance can tend towards artificial if a human-player customizes his avatar to look cartoonish. Autonomous humanoid robots can be made to look similar to humans both in appearance and shape (depending on their degrees of freedom), but exhibit artificial intelligence. Tele-robotics on the other hand occupies one specific corner of the 3D space, since it is generally associated with human control—i.e. real intelligence. At the opposite corner lie Shader-lamp avatars [2] of real people since it is essentially tele-robotics combined with real appearance.

Specific examples of characteristics that would fit into each one of these axes include the following:

- **Appearance.** Virtual rendering/real video. Real video, but from a different time period or different user. Skin color/race. Auditory playback. Olfactory simulation.
- **Shape/Corporeal Presence.** Apparent physical structure/representation, e.g. humanoid vs. non-human mobile robot. Tactile feel of surrogate. Presentation medium, e.g. flat screen TV, projection screen. The term "corporeal presence" was termed by [13] and not only includes the external shape of the surrogate, but also its capacity to occupy a physical space, hence the term might be a bit more general than simply using "shape".
- **Intelligence/Agency.** In some publications this is also referred to as "Agency" in the sense of who the controlling entity (human, AI, some hybrid) is. This might also include the realism of the exhibited behavior, which [4] mentions as a significant dimension of realism.

5   Our Testbed and Surrogate System Instances

For several years, we have been working on developing a unified system for controlling *surrogates* in virtual environments. The system's architecture utilizes the Marionette Puppetry Paradigm. It is designed to support individualized experience creation in fields such as education, training and rehabilitation. The system has evolved over a period of six years with continuous refinements as a result of constant use and evaluation. It provides an integrated testbed for evaluating human surrogates for live-virtual training and is called AMITIES^{TM} [16,17]. *Surrogates* in our virtual environments that can be controlled via AMITIES^{TM} consist of various manifestations ranging from life-size 2D flat screen displays to fully robotic entities. Figure 3 shows the different surrogate instances in our lab and the space occupied by them in the hypothetical 3D cube of characteristics shown in Fig. 2 of this article. For example, visually simulated 2D surrogates via flat-panel displays have real intelligence (human-in-the-loop) and scale. They have virtual shape and appearance. A good instance of this manifestation and its effective use is described in Sect. 5.2 of this article. Similarly, all surrogate instances described henceforth can be tied back to the 3D space illustrated in Fig. 2 as well as comply with the illustration of human-surrogate relationships depicted in Fig. 1. In particular, one can envision each of these surrogates occupying the central band in Fig. 1, while an inhabiter (Real Intelligence) or an agent (Artificial Intelligence) controls their actions (left of the figure) when interacting with human subjects

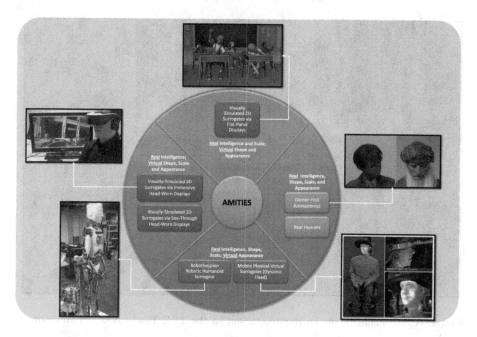

Fig. 3. The integrated testbed consisting of several manifestations of *surrogates* controlled by the unified AMITIES™ architecture.

(right side of the figure). Use cases for each surrogate in our lab and the underlying framework used to drive them are described in the following sections.

5.1 AMITIES™

AMITIES™ stands for *Avatar-Mediated Interactive Training and Individualized Experience System.* This is a framework to interactively control avatars in remote environments and serves as the central component that connects people controlling avatars (inhabiters), various manifestations of these avatars (surrogates) and people interacting with these avatars (participants). A multi-server-client architecture, based on a low-demand network protocol, connects the participant environment(s), the inhabiter station(s) and the avatars. A human-in-the-loop metaphor provides an interface for remote operation, with support for multiple inhabiters, multiple avatars, and multiple participant-observers.

Custom animation blending routines and a gesture-based interface provide inhabiters with an intuitive avatar control paradigm. This gesture control is enhanced by genres of program-controlled behaviors that can be triggered by events or inhabiter choices for individual or groups of avatars. This mixed (agency and gesture-based) control paradigm reduces the cognitive and physical loads on the inhabiter while supporting natural bi-directional conversation between participants and the virtual characters or avatar counterparts, including ones with physical manifestations, e.g., robotic surrogates. The associated system affords the delivery of personalized experiences that adapt to the actions and

Fig. 4. A screenshot of the surrogate student in the TLE TeachLivE™ Lab environment

interactions of individual users, while staying true to each virtual character's personality and backstory.

In addition to its avatar control paradigm, AMITIES™ provides processes for character and scenario development, testing and refinement. It also has integrated capabilities for session recording and event tagging, along with automated tools for reflection and after-action review.

5.2   TLE TeachLivE™ Lab

The TLE TeachLivE™ Lab [18,19] is an Avatar-Mediated Interactive Simulator that is currently being used by over 55 universities and four School Districts across the US to assist in Teacher Skills Training and Rehearsal. This Virtual-Reality based simulation is used by teachers, both pre-service and in-service, to learn or improve their teaching skills through the processes of rehearsal and reflection.

The TLE TeachLivE™ Lab includes a set of pedagogies, subject matter content and processes, seamlessly integrated to create an environment for teacher preparation. The technological affordances of the system allow teachers to be physically immersed in a virtual classroom consisting of several students that exhibit a wide variety of appearances, cultural backgrounds, behaviors and personalities commonly observed in specific age groups. The environment delivers an avatar-based simulation intended to enhance teacher development in targeted skills at any level (middle school/high school etc.). In fact, studies have shown that a single discrete behavior, e.g., asking high-order questions, can be improved in just four 10-min sessions in the simulated classroom. Moreover, this improvement continues at an even faster pace once the teacher returns to her or his classroom. Teachers have the opportunity to experiment with new teaching ideas in the lab without presenting any danger to the learning of real students in a classroom. Moreover, if a teacher has a bad session, he or she can re-enter the virtual classroom to teach the same students the same concepts or skills. Beyond training technical teaching skills, the system helps teachers identify issues such as recondite biases, so they can develop practices that mitigate the influence of these biases in their teaching practices.

AMITIES™ supports the users' needs for realism and the researchers' needs for quantitative and qualitative data. The integrated after-action review system provides objective quantitative data such as time that avatars talk versus time that a user talks, and subjective tagging ability so events such as the type of dialogue can be noted and subsequently reviewed by researchers (data analysis), coaches (debriefing) and users (reflection).

The TLE TeachLivE™ Lab has been used for teacher preparation since 2009, with over 10,000 teachers having run-through the system in academic year 2013-14. It is estimated that each of these teachers interacts with nearly 50 students resulting in an effective outreach of nearly 500,000 students. The surrogates used in the TLE TeachLivE™ Lab are an example of real intelligence and scale; virtual shape and appearance.

5.3 Physical-Virtual Avatar

The Physical-Virtual Avatar (PVA) was conceived and developed at the University of North Carolina at Chapel Hill in 2008–2009 by Greg Welch, Henry Fuchs, and others [2] and has since been replicated at both the University of Central Florida and Nanyang Technological University. This surrogate has a face-shaped display surface mounted on a pan-tilt-unit, stereo microphones, a speaker, and three wide-angle HD cameras to capture the environment in front of the avatar (each camera maps directly to one of the three large-screen displays in the inhabiter station). The pan-tilt-unit is programmed using a closed-loop velocity controller to match the current pose of the tracked inhabiter's head while live imagery from the inhabiter is projected on the display surface. This gives the inhabiter the ability to interact with multiple people through a physical 3D presence at the remote location.

The entire surrogate-side system is mounted on a motorized cart, and powered by an on-board battery. Video from the three cameras as well as the inhabiter's face imagery can be streamed over the wireless network. In addition, the PVA can operate in a "synthetic mode" where its appearance can be changed to reflect any virtual character on the fly. The wireless mode of operation of this unit allows inhabiters to control the motorized cart and freely navigate in the remote environment. AMITIES™ is used to control the PVA in its "synthetic" mode. It allows inhabiters to jump between various manifestations during interaction - for instance, an inhabiter can choose to inhabit a character in the TLE TeachLivE ™ Lab at one instant and immediately switch to inhabit the PVA

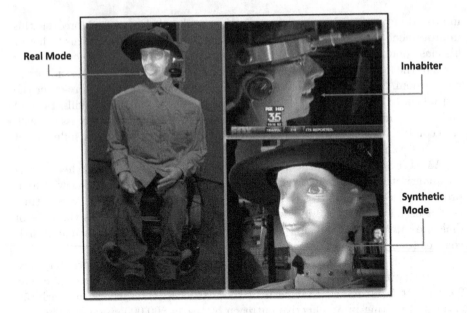

Fig. 5. The Physical-Virtual Avatar can operate in "real" or "synthetic" modes when inhabited.

at the next instant. The PVA is an example of real intelligence, scale and shape with virtual appearance.

5.4 Robothespian

The Robothespian is a humanoid robot developed by Engineered Arts, UK. It consists of a hybrid actuation system with pneumatic fluidic muscles and electric actuation. This surrogate has a total of 24 independently controllable degrees of freedom. As previously mentioned, the AMITIES™ paradigm has been developed to support inhabiting of robotic avatars including the Robothespian. This instantiation uses a master-slave relationship, where a virtual surrogate on a display screen is controlled by the inhabiter. This virtual surrogate behaves as a master and the Robothespian behaves as a slave by mimicking the master as closely as possible (both in space and time).

The Robothespian features a rear-projected head and supports appearance changing in real-time. Inhabiters can switch between virtual surrogate masters and the Robothespian's facial imagery will change to reflect this switch. In addition, each master surrogate can have very specific behaviors. The Robothespian is opaque to this behavioral uniqueness of each master and simply follows commands given to it by a specific master. This architecture allows different behaviors of the Robothespian to be associated with the same inhabiter's intent, simply by switching the master controlling it. For instance, culturally varying gestures such as "Hello" can be programmed into three different masters. Each time a master is chosen by an inhabiter, the culturally appropriate version of

Fig. 6. The Robothespian Humanoid Robot is one of our surrogates that can change appearance and physically gesture while interacting with people in the environment.

"Hello" is faithfully reproduced at the Robothespian's end. The Robothespian is another example of a surrogate with real intelligence, scale and shape and having virtual appearance.

5.5   Animatronics

Three animatronic humans (fully pneumatic) complete our collection of human surrogates used for live-virtual training. They are manufactured by Garner-Holt Productions. Two of these animatronic figures are young boys while the third is an older man. The old man has more degrees of freedom than the young boys. The appearance of these animatronics is very realistic since they have customized rubber/synthetic skin on them to represent the middle-eastern culture. While this is an advantage to explore the effect of "realism" in surrogates, there is the drawback that changing appearance becomes much harder (unlike projected systems featured in most of our other surrogates). The motion of the animatronic figures is also quite realistic. The level of control on different joints depends on whether the actuators support binary operation (on/off) or position-based responses. We are currently adapting these animatronics to be driven by the AMITIES™ paradigm. The animatronics (when driven using AMITIES) are an example of real intelligence, shape, scale and appearance since they resemble a real human very closely in all aspects.

Fig. 7. The Young Boy (left) and the Old Man (right) are two of our three very realistic-looking animatronic surrogates.

6   Conclusion and Future Work

We believe that this document begins laying the foundation for developing a comprehensive framework that identifies and classifies the main determinants for real humans' perceptions towards and interactions with human surrogates.

We began this year with a plan for exploring a "space" of surrogate characteristics. Through an extensive literature review and bottom-up categorization, we distinguished a number of fine-grained characteristics that appear to be strongly correlated with the quality of human-surrogate interaction. In addition to this bottom-up approach, we also posited a substantially smaller set of high-level characteristics in a top-down fashion: appearance, shape/corporeal presence, and intelligence/agency. These were conceived through our prior knowledge of humans and previous research results with which we were already familiar. Future work in this area includes consolidating the characteristics from both top-down and bottom-up approaches.

While this initial "space" exploration was useful, we are most excited now about developing a broader framework that will expand the original "space" exploration to include psychological, environmental, and other aspects that affect real humans' perceptions towards and interactions with human surrogates. Our original "space" of surrogate characteristics could conceptually be contained within the "Surrogate" section of that framework.

Such a framework will keep evolving, as will our database of relevant work (publications, studies, etc.), and both will guide the development of a research roadmap that describes future research directions for exploring interesting aspects of the framework. From a practitioner's perspective, we hope that our work will also be a tool to provide application-specific recommendations of which characteristics are most pertinent to meet individual training and interaction needs.

Acknowledgements. The material presented in this publication is based on work supported by the Office of Naval Research (ONR) Code 30 (Program Manager - Dr. Peter Squire) (N00014-12-1-0052, N00014-14-1-0248 and N00014-12-1-1003), the National Science Foundation (CNS1051067) and the Bill & Melinda Gates Foundation. Any opinions, findings, and conclusions or recommendations expressed in this material are those of the authors and do not necessarily reflect the views of the sponsors. The authors would like to thank all team members of SREAL at the Institute for Simulation and Training at UCF.

References

1. Badler, N.I.: Virtual beings. Commun. ACM **44**(3), 33–35 (2001)
2. Lincoln, P., Welch, G., Nashel, A., State, A., Ilie, A., Fuchs, H.: Animatronic Shader Lamps Avatars. Virtual Reality **15**(2–3), 225–238 (2011)
3. Stephenson, N.: Snow Crash, 1st edn. Bantam Books, New York (1992)
4. Bailenson, J.N., Blascovich, J.J.: Avatars. In: Bainbridge, W.S., ed.: Encyclopedia of Human-Computer Interaction. 1st edn, pp. 64–68. Berkshire Publishing Group, Great Barrington (2004)
5. Barfield, W., Zeltzer, D., Sheridan, T., Slater, M.: Presence and performance within virtual environments. In: Barfield, W., Furness, T.A. (eds.) Virtual Environments and Advanced Interface Design, pp. 473–513. Oxford University Press, USA (1995)
6. Witmer, B.G., Singer, M.J.: Measuring presence in virtual environments: a presence questionnaire. Presence: Teleoperators Virtual Environ. **7**(3), 225–240 (1998)
7. Goffman, E.: Behavior in Public Places: Notes on the Social Organization of Gatherings. The Free Press, New York (1963)
8. Nowak, K.L., Biocca, F.: Presence: Teleoperators Virtual Environ. **12**(5), 481–494 (2003)
9. Short, J., Williams, E., Christie, B.: The Social Psychology of Telecommunications. Wiley, New York (1967)
10. Nowak, K.: Defining and differentiating copresence, social presence and presence as transportation. In: International Workshop on Presence (PRESENCE) (2001)
11. Mennecke, B.E., Triplett, J.L., Hassall, L.M., Conde, Z.J.: Embodied social presence theory. In: 43rd Hawaii International Conference on System Sciences (HICSS), pp. 1–10. IEEE (2010)
12. Zeltzer, D.: Autonomy, interaction, and presence. Presence: Teleoperators Virtual Environ. **1**(1), 127–132 (1992)
13. Holz, T., Campbell, A., O'Hare, G., Stafford, J., Martin, A., Dragone, M.: MiRA - mixed reality agents. Int. J. Hum. Comput. Stud. **69**(4), 251–268 (2011)
14. Bailenson, J.N., Yee, N., Merget, D., Schroeder, R.: The effect of behavioral realism and form realism of real-time avatar faces on verbal disclosure, nonverbal disclosure, emotion recognition, and copresence in dyadic interaction. Presence: Teleoperators Virtual Environ. **15**(4), 359–372 (2006)
15. Nagendran, A., Pillat, R., Hughes, C.E., Welch, G.: Continuum of virtual-human space : towards improved interaction strategies for physical-virtual avatars. In: ACM International Conference on Virtual Reality Continuum and Its Applications in Industry (VRCAI), pp. 1–10 (2012)
16. Nagendran, A., Pillat, R., Kavanaugh, A., Welch, G., Hughes, C.: Amities: avatar-mediated interactive training and individualized experience system. In: Proceedings of the 19th ACM Symposium on Virtual Reality Software and Technology, pp. 143–152. ACM (2013)

17. Hughes, C., Dieker, L., Nagendran, A., Hynes, M.: Semi automated digital puppetry control (2013) US Provisional Patent, SL: 61/790,467, Date Filed: 15 March, 2013
18. Dieker, L.A., Rodriguez, J.A., Lignugaris/Kraft, B., Hynes, M.C., Hughes, C.E.: The potential of simulated environments in teacher education: Current and future possibilities. Teacher Educ. Spec. Educ.: J. Teach. Educ. Div. Counc. Except. Child. **37**(1), 21–33 (2014)
19. TLE TeachLivE™ Lab, 6 April 2014. http://sreal.ucf.edu/teachlive/

Telexistence

Past, Present, and Future

Susumu Tachi (✉)

Professor Emeritus, The University of Tokyo, Tokyo, Japan
tachi@tachilab.org

Abstract. Telexistence technology allows for highly realistic sensation of existence in remote places without actual travel. The concept was originally proposed by the author in 1980, and its feasibility has been demonstrated through the construction of alter-ego robot systems such as the TELExistence Surrogate Anthropomorphic Robot (TELESAR) and TELESAR V, which were developed under national large-scale projects on "Robots in Hazardous Environments" and "CREST Haptic Telexistence Project," respectively, as well as the HRP super-cockpit biped robot system developed under the "Humanoid Robotics Project." Mutual telexistence systems, such as TELESAR II & IV, capable of generating the sensation of being in a remote place in local space using the combination of an alter-ego robot and retro-reflective projection technology (RPT) has been developed, and the feasibility of mutual telexistence has been demonstrated. In this paper, the past, present, and future of telexistence technology is discussed.

Keywords: Telexistence · Mutual telexistence · Telepresence · Teleoperation · Master-slave system · Virtual reality · Augmented reality · Retro-reflective projection technology (RPT) · TELESAR · TWISTER

1 Introduction

Telexistence is a fundamental concept that refers to the general technology that allows human beings to experience real-time sensation of being in a place different from their actual location and interact with such remote environment, which can be real, virtual, or a combination of both [1]. It also refers to an advanced type of teleoperation system that allows control operators to perform remote tasks dexterously with the perception of being in a surrogate robot working in a remote environment. Telexistence in the real environment through a virtual environment is also possible.

Sutherland [2] proposed the first head-mounted display system that led to the birth of virtual reality in the late 1980s. This was the same concept as telexistence in computer-generated virtual environments. However, Sutherland's system did not include the concept of telexistence in real remote environments. The concept of providing an operator with a natural sensation of existence in order to facilitate dexterous remote robotic manipulation tasks was called "telepresence" by Minsky [3] and "telexistence" by Tachi [4]. Telepresence and telexistence are very similar concepts proposed independently in the USA and in Japan, respectively. However, telepresence

© Springer International Publishing Switzerland 2015
G. Brunnett et al. (Eds.): Virtual Realities, LNCS 8844, pp. 229–259, 2015.
DOI: 10.1007/978-3-319-17043-5_13

does not include telexistence in virtual environments or telexistence in a real environment through a virtual environment.

The concept of telexistence was proposed by the author in 1980 [4], and it was the fundamental principle of the eight-year Japanese national large scale "Advanced Robot Technology in Hazardous Environment" project, which began in 1983, together with the concept of "Third Generation Robotics." Theoretical considerations and the systematic design procedure of telexistence were established through the project. An experimental hardware telexistence system was developed and the feasibility of the concept was demonstrated.

In this paper, the development of telexistence technology and telexistence systems is historically reviewed; its present status is summarized, and future prospective is discussed.

2 Telexistence

2.1 What Is Telexistence?

In telexistence, the requirements to create an environment where a person effectively exists are as follows: (1) it must be composed of a natural three-dimensional space; (2) the person must be able to act freely in it, and interaction with the environment must occur naturally in real time; and (3) self-projection into the environment must occur. These are analogous to the three elements of virtual reality (VR): life-size spatiality, real-time interaction, and self-projection.

To control a robot utilized for telexistence, the movements and internal status of the person controlling the robot are measured in real time and intent is estimated. Such estimated intent is transmitted to the robot and its motion control system is driven directly. In particular, the artificial eyes, neck, hands, and feet of the robot are controlled to faithfully reproduce the movements of the person. Concurrently, information from the artificial sensory organs of the robot is transmitted directly to the corresponding sensory organs of the person.

For example, if the person turns in a certain direction to see, the robot faces the same direction; moreover, the image of the scene in that direction, where there might be people present, is formed as an actual image on the person's retina. If the person brings their hand before their eyes, the hand of the robot appears in the person's visual field in place of their own hand, with exactly the same positional relationship. In this manner, it is possible for the person to perform tasks by capturing the relationship between their hand and the object or with the surrounding space based on similar scenarios from the person's past experience. The robot transmits its sense of contact with the object as tactile stimulation to the person's hand, and the person might experience a sensation similar to having touched the object directly.

Thus, telexistence refers to the technology of working or communicating from a remote location while providing a highly realistic sense of being present in another environment. The practical use of this technology is being promoted in the fields of medical care, space exploration, and deep-sea investigation; furthermore, the use of a robot as a person's alter ego is being studied.

Telexistence liberates humans from conventional space-time constraints and allows them to exist effectively in an environment that is beyond space, time, or both. It is a technique that can make humans ubiquitous by using a robot. Incidentally, the term ubiquitous means "being or seeming to be everywhere at the same time: omnipresent". The term "ubiquitous computing" was created by Mark Weiser of Xerox Palo Alto Research Center (PARC) in 1993, and it refers to the concept of being able to use a computer anywhere at any time. In contrast, telexistence is the concept of making humans, rather than computers, ubiquitous.

Using telexistence, it is possible to manipulate a robot in a remote location as one's other self, experience the working environment of the robot with a realistic sensation through its sight, sound, and touch sensory receptors, and act freely in that environment. Furthermore, it is possible to enter the artificial environment generated by a computer and act in it with the perception of actually being present at that location.

In addition to creating the perception of being in a remote location, telexistence helps to enhance the capability of the person. For example, humans are not capable of seeing objects obscured by darkness or smoke; however, by using the robot's infrared or ultrasonic sensors, the obscured objects can be perceived. If the robot's sensor information obtained by remote presence is presented in actual space utilizing the augmented reality method, it is possible to act even in darkness or smoke by controlling the robot in actual space. This is referred to as augmented telexistence.

Figure 1 displays the structure of an actual environment, a virtual environment, and telexistence in the actual environment via the virtual environment. The human side of the system remains exactly the same, irrespective of whether telexistence is in the actual environment or in the virtual environment. The current status of the person and his/her intent are estimated; accordingly, the alter ego robot in the actual environment or the virtual human in the virtual environment is controlled at will. As the alter ego robot or the virtual human acts in the actual or virtual environment, interaction with the respective environment proceeds, and the results received through the sensory organs of the alter ego robot or the virtual human are integrated and realistically presented to the corresponding human sensory organs. Other telexistence users can also participate in the environment; accordingly, their interactions are also transmitted.

2.2   Design Concept of Telexistence

Figure 2 gives the configuration of a basic telexistence system and a concrete method for the configuration of a visual display that provides a sense of self-presence. Figure 2(I) shows the principle of the recording and reproduction of light wave fronts in a holographic manner, as conceived in the past. In other words, a closed surface is created so as to surround the remote place, and the wave fronts entering that area are recorded at multiple points on the enclosure surface.

These wave fronts are then transmitted to the location of the local observer and are subsequently reconstructed using a reproduction device on a similar enclosure surface surrounding the observer. However, this method alone makes it difficult to realize telexistence for the following reasons [5, 6]:

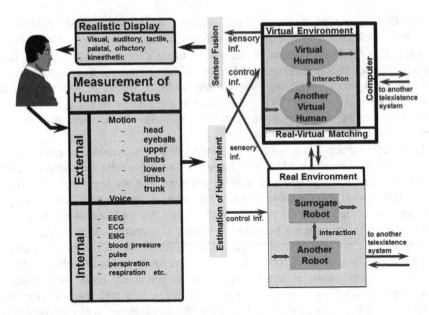

Fig. 1. Telexistence in a real environment, a virtual environment, and a real environment via the virtual environment. (I) Estimation of the user's state (including the external state represented by user movements and tone of voice, as well as the internal state represented by electroencephalograms and electrocardiograms) and evaluation of the human decision making process; (II) interaction between the robot and the natural environment and/or interaction between the virtual human and the virtual environment; and (III) presentation to the user of the process described in (II) and results with a sense of presence in real time.

(1) If the recording and reproduction device were designed to reconstruct the actual environment, they would be too large to be practical. In addition, in holography, the recording and reproduction of real-time information cannot be achieved with the technology that is presently available

(2) Although the display of a distant background scene can be approximated by a large two-dimensional screen, technically, it is extremely difficult to achieve a three-dimensional reproduction of nearby objects in actual size and in real time without such objects being occluded by real objects

(3) In particular, the actual sense of presence cannot be achieved if the hands of the operator are located at a place different from those of the robot. In telexistence, the hands of the robot must be visible at the place where those of the human operator ought to appear. However, the realization of such a state is generally difficult when using the abovementioned holographic method

As a consequence, it is not possible to utilize this conventional method to acquire a true sense of presence, i.e., the sense of being inside the robot or at the place where the robot is located, which would be produced by the realization of the appropriate relationship between the background scene, the task at hand, and the hands of the robot.

Figure 2(II) shows the proposed method for configuring telexistence on the basis of robot technology and human sensory structure. According to the method described

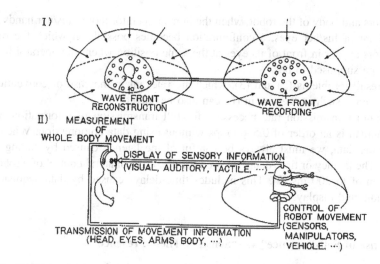

Fig. 2. Principle of telexistence: (I) principle for the recording and reproduction of light wave fronts in a holographic manner; (II) principle for configuring telexistence on the basis of robot technology and human sensory structure [5, 6].

in (I), an attempt is made to reproduce all wave fronts simultaneously. However, this is unnecessary in view of the working mechanism of the human visual perception system. The basis of human visual perception is a pair of images focused on the retinas, and the wave fronts perceived by a person as retinal images at any given instant of time constitute only part of the total wave fronts. These wave fronts change in real time with the movements of the person's head and eyes. The person then creates, inside his/her brain, a three-dimensional world based on two images that change with time, and projects it back to the place where the objects really exist.

As a result, if it is possible to measure a person's head and eye movements faithfully and in real time, to move the head and the eyes of the robot in line with those movements, to transmit to the human side the pair of images created in the visual input device of the robot at that time, and to recreate these images on the person's retinas accurately and without a time delay using a suitable display device, that person can then receive retinal images equivalent to those seen directly by the robot. In other words, by using these images, the person can create inside his/her brain a three-dimensional world equivalent to the one seen directly from the place where the robot is located, and then project it again into the real world.

Thus, by scanning partial wave fronts continuously using a human motion measurement device and a system that consists of a display device and a slave robot, a recording and reproduction device can be produced that is small enough to be realistically configured; therefore, problem (1) presented above can be solved.

In addition, this method creates a state in which visual information obtained from direct observation on the human side is shielded, and instead, visual information from the remote robot is displayed as though the human operator were at the same place where the robot is located. Moreover, because the movement of human hands, arms, and torso is measured faithfully, and because this information is used to move the manipulators and body of the robot, when the human operator moves his/her hands and arms in front of his/her eyes, a configuration becomes possible in which the robot manipulators appear in front of its eyes at the same position where the operator hands and arms are supposed to be.

As a result, problems (2) and (3), which are relevant in the case of conventional display systems, such as the one in (I), can also be solved.

Maximum transmission rate necessary for full transmission of information from robot to human is an order of 0.5–6 Gbps without using data compression. When we compress the data, we must always be careful of the latency caused by coding and decoding. The latency or time delay allowed for the direct bilateral control of a robot is a maximum of to 200 ms [7]. This includes time delays caused by data acquisition, transmission, and display.

2.3 "Sense of Self-Presence" vs. "Sense of Their Presence"

The perception of actually positioning oneself in a certain place is referred to as the "sense of self-presence," or "sense of self-existence." This is the "sense of realism." The audio stereo system that creates a listening effect similar to being in a concert hall might be referred to as a system filled with realism. This is auditory realism. Virtual reality and telexistence provide the system user with a realistic sensation visiting the environment generated by the computer and/or an actual remote environment. In realism, the senses of vision, hearing, touch, smell, taste, and body balance are all ideally aligned, and studies are being conducted to facilitate ultimate realism in virtual reality and telexistence.

Thus, realism is a word frequently used to describe the capabilities of sound reproduction equipment such as the stereo or the telephone, and visual reproduction technology such as film, television, and the videophone. In these cases, realism denotes the sensation perceived by the system user.

There is also a sensation referred to as the "sense of their presence," or simply the "sense of presence." The sense of their presence is the perception of the definite existence of people or objects. This term existed before the invention of telephones, stereos, or movies. There are innumerable examples of phrases such as "he has no sense of presence" used in the real world. In particular, regardless of a person being present as an entity, the people around the person might not notice his/her presence, and there might be occasions when his/her presence is ignored. In contrast, when the person is more than a mere physical entity and his/her presence is noticeable, he/she is said to have a strong presence, or that they are "larger than life."

The "sense of self-presence," i.e., the perception of being present in the place experienced by the user and the "sense of their presence," i.e., the presence of the user perceived by people nearby are illustrated in Fig. 3.

With the widespread use of videoconferencing, the lack of sense of presence of a person on the screen was perceived as a limitation, similar to the real world. The lack of sense of presence is considered natural, given the absence of a physical entity. However, the reasons that a sense of presence cannot be created using only pictures and sounds remain unsolved. Researchers are attempting to integrate a sense of self-presence and

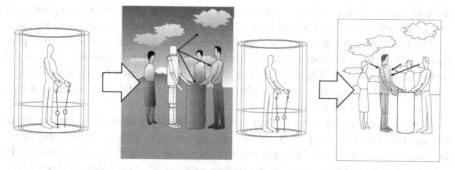

Fig. 3. Sense of self-presence: system user has a sensation of being present in a place (left), and Sense of their presence: people nearby perceive the presence of the system user (right).

sense of their presence, currently missing in typical teleconference systems, into virtual reality and telexistence systems, and to achieve the ultimate sense of presence, along with a sense of realism.

Sense of self-presence and sense of their presence are described below utilizing a videoconferencing system as an example. Suppose that there is a large screen in the conference room and one person is participating in the conference from a distant place. The person participating from the distant place sees the image of the camera installed in the conference room on the monitor placed in his room. Because the present system is usually two-dimensional, the sense of self-presence is obtained to some extent, and it is not exactly similar to being at the remote location. This is what is perceived by the system user from the distant place.

At the other location, the people gathered in the meeting room look at the screen and welcome the participant from the distant place, and at that time, everybody notices him. A certain type of a sense of his presence is created at that time. However, the person on the screen might be forgotten when the discussion among the people who are actually gathered in the conference room becomes impassioned. In this situation, the sense of his presence becomes extremely weak.

To summarize, the sense of self-presence or self-existence is perceived by the system user, and it is a sensation of being present in a generated or remote environment. In contrast, the sense of their presence or sense of their existence is not what is perceived by the system user, but by the people around the system user with regard to the user's presence.

In this case, what is it that conveys a sense of presence or sense of existence? If the sense of presence in the real world is analyzed as an example, a higher possibility of having an impact on the people who are nearby generally results in a higher sense of presence. The sense of presence is as high as the degree or effectiveness of the potential for interaction. Between a stone that is stable on the floor and one that might fall at any moment, the latter has a higher sense of presence. If a wasp, a poisonous snake, or a lion is in one's immediate vicinity, its sense of presence is high. In a similar way, objects that make a loud noise, are colorful, or move have a high sense of presence. People who are quiet and yet convey a sense of presence also have a dignity and an aura about them. When all the people in an environment perceive, for some reason, a sense of danger, fear, or enjoyment because of the presence of an object or a person, an interaction occurs and the possibility of being affected heightens the sense of presence.

The reason that the sense of presence is greater in a live performance or in a play than in television or in films originates from the feeling that it is possible to touch the viewer at any moment. The difference in the sense of presence between watching a game of sumo from a gallery where a giant sumo wrestler can fall, and watching it on a big screen TV, is quite evident.

In order to create the sense of their existence in media, it is obviously important to convey that which is not present in the existing images, such as a complete three-dimensional feeling with multi-view support, the sense of smell, and other stimuli. In addition, it is necessary to provide a structure to allow the possibility of direct inter-action with the generated object or person, and in particular, one that can detect danger.

In this context, among insufficient sensations, the sense of touch is, at present, more likely to contribute to the creation of the sense of presence. However, the sense of presence can be conveyed even if contact does not actually occur. In other words, there is a high sense of presence of something frightening that could cause harm.

If telexistence is achieved, operators will perceive the distant environment as the actual environment; they will be able to talk, hear, and act similar to the actual environment and relate with the people at the distant environment as a real person, without any sense of incongruity. However, this is not the case with individuals who are in the environment where the person appears by telexistence. If a robot in a person's vicinity moved as a human being and generated a human-like voice, it would be incongruous.

Accordingly, it is not desirable to establish a setting where people would interact or work together. Thus, it becomes important for the person appearing through telexistence to be depicted pictorially and clearly. Moreover, if this image is fitted onto the body or head of a robot and projected on a TV screen, the image remains unchanged on the viewing side, and it is unlikely to create the feeling of the person being present.

The user of a telexistence device can act with a sense of self-presence or self-existence, with the perception of having entered into a robot and integrated into the remote environment. This is achievable because the user senses that the surrounding environment and the people in it have an awareness of his/her physical existence in the environment. More succinctly, there is a sense of realism. However, the people looking at the robot perceive the presence of the robot, not the presence of the user. Accordingly, the sense of their presence is lacking.

For example, consider a caregiving situation utilizing a telexistence system. Similar to the previous case, in reality, a human being is providing care, not the automatic robot. However, because the person receiving care only sees the robot, he/she does not feel the presence of the human caregiver. In this case, if the caregiver appears to the person receiving care as being within the robot, it is possible to persuade the latter to believe that he/she is actually being cared for by the human caregiver. If a three-dimensional image of the operator is projected on the robot, the person receiving care would see the robot not as a mere mechanical device, but as the actual caregiving person, who is the operator.

This is the concept of the next generation telexistence that has both the sense of self-existence and the sense of their existence, or "mutual telexistence."

Mutual telexistence also enables a number of people to gather through telexistence in an actual location using plural alter-ego robots through a network. Furthermore, dispensing with the robot, a virtual environment can be created in which each person will enter using a telexistence booth near his/her home. In this booth, the virtual environment is observed through his/her avatar with the sense of self-existence in the virtual environment. At the same time, each person's image is captured in real time and projected on his/her corresponding avatar in the virtual environment, thus creating the sense of their presence. It will then be possible for people to converse with each other while watching facial expressions, similar to having a face-to-face conversation. This system will become a highly evolved videophone.

3 Short History of Telexistence

3.1 How Telexistence Was Conceptualized and Developed

Human beings have long desired to project themselves in remote environments, i.e., to experience the sensation of existing in a place different from the one they really exist in, at the same time. Another goal has been to amplify human muscle power and sensing capability using machines while maintaining human dexterity with a sensation of actually performing a given task.

In the late 1960s, a research and development program was planned to develop a powered exoskeleton that an operator could wear similar to a garment. The concept for the Hardiman exoskeleton was proposed by General Electric Co.; an operator wearing the Hardiman exoskeleton would be able to command a set of mechanical muscles that would multiply his/her strength by a factor of 25, yet, in this union of man and machine, he/she would feel the object and forces almost as though he/she were in direct contact with it.

However, the program was unsuccessful because: (1) wearing the powered exoskeleton was potentially quite dangerous in the event of machine malfunction; and (2) autonomous mode was difficult to achieve and everything had to be performed by a human operator. Thus, the design proved impractical in its original form.

However, with the advance of science and technology, it has become possible to realize this dream with a different concept. The concept of projecting ourselves using robots, computers, and a cybernetic human interface is referred to as telexistence. This concept allows human operators to perform remote manipulation tasks dexterously with the perception that he/she exists in an anthropomorphic robot in a remote environment. Telexistence realizes a virtual exoskeleton human amplifier, i.e., a human can work with his/her power multiplied without actually being inside the exoskeleton. Because a human operator is not inside the robot, he/she is safe even in the event of malfunction. An exoskeleton robot can be replaced by an intelligent robot so that the robot is used autonomously when the operator is not telexisting into it. Thus, telexistence solves the aforementioned two problems of an exoskeleton human amplifier.

Figure 4 illustrates the emergence and evolution of the concept of telexistence. Teleoperation emerged in Argonne National Laboratory soon after World War II to manipulate radioactive materials. In order to work directly in the environment rather than remotely, an exoskeleton human amplifier was invented in the 1960s as described previously, whereas the concept of supervisory control was proposed by T. B. Sheridan in the 1970s to add autonomy to human operations. In the 1980s, the exoskeleton human amplifier evolved to telexistence, i.e., into the virtual exoskeleton human amplifier. This virtual system also integrated supervisory control in order to include the concept of a telexistence human-intelligent robot system. Fundamental studies for the realization of telexistence systems were conducted under the national large scale project "Advanced Robot Technology in Hazardous Environment," which was an eight-year research and development program launched in 1983 for the development of a system that avoids the need for humans to work in potentially hazardous working environments, such as nuclear power plants, underwater, and disaster areas. Figure 5 shows a human-intelligent robot system that performs essential work in hazardous working environments.

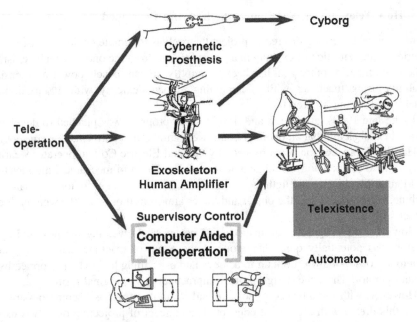

Fig. 4. Emergence and evolution of telexistence. Cyborg, telexistence, and automaton originated form teleoperation, which emerged soon after World War II.

Each independent, mobile, intelligent robot assumes part of the overall work and operates in conjunction with other robots in severe environments. Instructions are provided to these robots by a human operator stationed in a control module. A supervisory controller is responsible for the allocation of work, as well as for planning and scheduling, and the intelligent mobile robots send it reports concerning work progress. Such information is organized by the supervisory controller, and it is then transmitted to the operator by voice or by visual or tactile information. If the operator instructs in a language similar to natural language, these instructions are transmitted to the respective robots through speech recognition equipment and the supervisory controller.

The respective robots recognize the task description and perform using their own intelligence and knowledge.

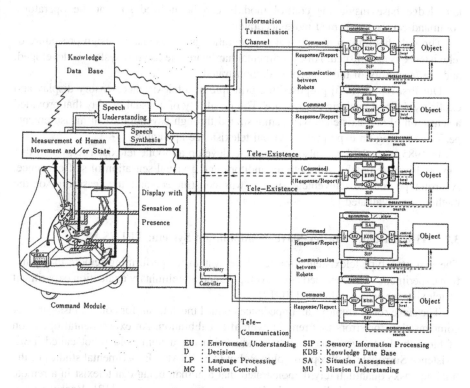

EU : Environment Understanding SIP : Sensory Information Processing
D : Decision   KDB : Knowledge Date Base
LP : Language Processing   SA : Situation Assessment
MC : Motion Control   MU : Mission Understanding

Fig. 5. Telexistence system architecture. The system consists of intelligent mobile robots, their supervisory controller, a command module to control robots with a sensation of self-presence and a sensory augmentation system that allows an operator to use the robot's ultrasonic, infrared, and additional, otherwise invisible, sensory information with the computer-generated pseudo-realistic sensation of presence. In the command module, realistic visual, auditory, tactile, kinesthetic, and vibratory displays are provided [8].

Information in the robots' intelligence system is an important source of operation and can be monitored by the operator at any time. Moreover, safety is checked at three levels: by the intelligent robot, by the supervisory controller, and by the operator; thus, safety is greatly improved.

When an intelligent robot encounters difficult work that it cannot manage, the operation mode of the robot is switched to remote control mode either at the robot's own request or at the judgment of the operator. At that time, instead of a conventional remote control system, an advanced type of teleoperation system, called telexistence, is used. This enables the operator to control the robot as though he/she were inside the robot. In this case, each subsystem of the intelligent robot works similar to a slave-type robot that is directly and accurately controlled by the operator.

The operator can also utilize the robot's sensor information about radiation, ultraviolet rays, infrared rays, microwaves, ultrasonic, and extremely low frequency waves. The operator can effectively use this information to expand human ability. The knowledge base inside the control module can be utilized so that the operator's command can be performed more accurately.

Through this project, theoretical consideration and systematic design procedure of telexistence is established. An experimental hardware telexistence system is developed, and the feasibility of the concept is demonstrated.

Our first report [5, 6] proposed the principle of a telexistence sensory display and explicitly defined its design procedure. The feasibility of a visual display that provided a sensation of self-existence was demonstrated through psychophysical measurements performed using an experimental visual telexistence apparatus.

In 1985, a method was also proposed to develop a mobile telexistence system that can be driven remotely with both an auditory and a visual sensation of self-existence. A prototype mobile televehicle system was constructed, and the feasibility of the method was evaluated [9].

3.2   TELExistence Master-Slave Manipulation System: TELESAR

The first prototype telexistence master-slave system for performing remote manipulation experiments was designed and developed, and a preliminary evaluation experiment of telexistence was conducted [10–12].

The slave robot employs an impedance control mechanism for contact tasks and for compensating for errors that remain even after calibration. An experimental operation of block building was successfully conducted using a humanoid robot called TELExistence Surrogate Anthropomorphic Robot (TELESAR). Experimental studies of the tracking tasks quantitatively demonstrated that a human being can telexist in a remote environment using a dedicated telexistence master-slave system [12]. Because measurements are performed using goniometers and potentiometers and all programs are written in C, the system is operated at an extremely high speed cycle time of 3 ms, even when the operation is conducted as impedance control mode. Virtually, no delay is observed. Human operators perceive as though they were inside the robots. Figure 6 illustrates a telexistence master-slave manipulation system.

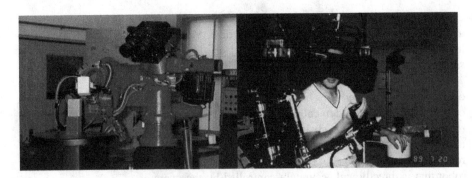

Fig. 6. TELESAR (left) and telexistence master system (right).

3.3   Augmented Telexistence

Telexistence can be divided into two categories: telexistence in a real environment that actually exists at a distance and is connected via a robot to the place where the operator is located, and telexistence in a virtual environment that does not actually exist, but is created by a computer.

The former can be referred to as "transmitted reality;" the latter as "synthesized reality." Synthesized reality can be classified as a virtual environment that represents the real world, and that which represents an imaginary world. Combining transmitted reality and synthesized reality, which is referred to as mixed reality, is also possible, and it has great significance for real applications. This is referred to as augmented telexistence to clarify the importance of a harmonic combination of real and virtual worlds.

Augmented telexistence can be used in several situations, for instance, controlling a slave robot in an environment with poor visibility. An experimental augmented tel-existence system was constructed using mixed reality. An environment model was also constructed from the design data of the real environment. When augmented reality is used to control a slave robot, modeling errors of the environment model must be calibrated. A model-based calibration system using image measurements was proposed for matching the real environment with a virtual environment.

An experimental operation in an environment with poor visibility was successfully conducted using TELESAR and its virtual dual. Figure 7 illustrates the virtual telex-istence anthropomorphic robot used in the experiment [13, 14].

A quantitative evaluation of the telexistence manipulation system was conducted by tracking tasks using the telexistence master-slave system. Through these experimental studies, it was demonstrated that a human being can telexist in a remote environment and/or a computer-generated environment using a dedicated telexistence system.

Through these research and development programs, it has become possible to telexist between places with dedicated transmission links, such as optical fiber com-munication links, as has been demonstrated by the above experiments. However, it is still difficult for everyone to telexist freely through commercial networks, such as the Internet or the next generation worldwide networks, and more efforts are anticipated.

Fig. 7. Operational virtual TELESAR.

3.4   R-Cubed

In order to realize a society wherein everyone can freely telexist anywhere through a network, the Japanese Ministry of International Trade and Industry (MITI) and the University of Tokyo proposed a long-range national research and development program that was dubbed R-Cubed (R^3) in 1995. R^3 means real-time remote robotics. The concept of this program is the research and development of technologies that allow human operators to telexist freely by integrating robots, virtual reality, and network technology.

Figure 8 illustrates an example of an R^3 robot system. Each robot site has a server as its local robot. The type of robot varies from a humanoid (high end) to a movable camera (low end). A virtual robot can also be a local controlled system.

Each client has a teleoperation system. The system can be a control cockpit with master manipulators and a head-mounted display (HMD) or a CAVE Automatic Virtual Environment (CAVE) at the high end. It is also possible to use an ordinary personal computer system as a control system at the low end. In order to assist low-end operators with controlling remote robots through networks, R-Cubed Manipulation Language/R-Cubed Transfer Protocol (RCML/RCTP) was developed.

An operator accesses the web site that describes robot information in the form of hypertext and icon graphics using a WWW browser. Clicking an icon downloads a description file that is written in the RCML format, onto the operator's computer and launches the RCML browser. The RCML browser parses the downloaded file to process the geometrical information, including arrangement of the degrees of freedom of the robot, controllable parameters, available motion ranges, sensor information, and other pertinent information.

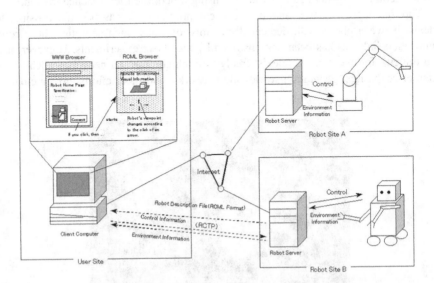

Fig. 8. Diagram for RCML and RCTP processes. Robots and control devices are placed virtually everywhere in the world and connected by Internet. Any user can use any robot when the robot is in use.

The browser decides the type and number of devices required to control the remote robot. Then, it generates a graphical user interface (GUI) panel to control the robot, in addition to a video window that displays the images "as seen" by the robot and a monitor window that allows operators to observe the robot's status from outside the robot. The operator can employ a device such as a six-degree-of-freedom (DOF) position/orientation sensor instead of the conventional GUI panel to indicate the robot-manipulator's endpoint [15].

3.5   Humanoid Robotics Project (HRP)

On the basis of the R^3 program and after conducting a two-year feasibility study called Friendly Network Robotics (FNR) from April 1996 until March 1998, a National Applied Science & Technology Project called "Humanoid and Human Friendly Robotics," or "Humanoid Robotics Project (HRP)" was launched in 1998. This was a five-year project toward the realization of an R^3 Society by providing humanoids, control cockpits, and remote control protocols.

A novel robot system capable of assisting and cooperating with people is necessary for any human-centered system to be used for activities such as the maintenance of nuclear plants or power stations, construction work, aid supply in the case of emergencies or disasters, and care of elderly people. However, if we consider such systems from both technical and safety perspectives, it is clearly impossible to develop a completely autonomous robot system for these objectives.

Therefore, robot systems should be realized using a combination of autonomous control and teleoperated control. By introducing telexistence techniques through an advanced type of teleoperated robot system, a human operator can be provided with information about the robot's remote environment in the form of natural audio, visual, and force feedback, thus invoking a feeling of existence inside the robot [13].

Thus, in phase 1 of the project, a telexistence cockpit for humanoid control was developed (Fig. 9), and the telexistence system was constructed using the developed humanoid platform.

A Computer Graphics (CG) model of the robot in the virtual environment is depicted and updated according to the current location and orientation received from the sensors located on the real robot. The model is displayed on the bottom-right screen of the surround visual display, and by augmenting the real images captured by the camera system; this assists the operator with robot navigation of the robot. Because the series of real images presented on the visual display are integrated with the movement of the motion base, the operator perceives a real-time sensation of stepping up and down.

To the best of our knowledge, this was the world's first successful experiment of controlling a humanoid biped robot using telexistence [16].

3.6   Mutual Telexistence: TELESAR II

A new prototype of a mutual telexistence master-slave system was designed and developed [17, 18]. The mutual telexistence master-slave system is based on RTP and

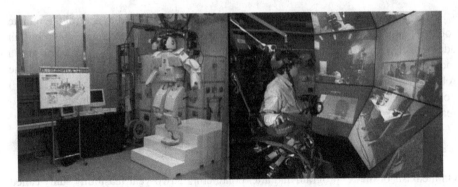

Fig. 9. HRP humanoid biped robot (left) and telexistence cockpit (right).

is composed of three subsystems: slave robot TELESAR II, master cockpit, and viewer system, as shown in Fig. 10.

The robot constructed for this communication system is called "TELESAR II." In order to use this system for telecommunication, we designed the robot by focusing on reproducing human-like realistic movements. TELESAR II has two human-sized arms and hands, a torso, and a head. Its neck has two DOFs, which can rotate around its pitch and roll axes. Two CCD cameras are placed inside its head for stereoscopic vision. The robot also has four pairs of stereo cameras located on top of its head for a three-dimensional surround display to benefit the operator. A microphone array and a speaker are also employed for auditory sensation and verbal communication. Each arm has seven DOFs, and each hand has five fingers with a total of eight DOFs.

To control the slave robot, we developed a master cockpit for TELESAR II. The cockpit consists of two master arms, two master hands, a multi-stereo display system, speakers and a microphone, and cameras for capturing the images of the operator in real time. In order for the operator to move smoothly, each master arm has a six-DOF structure so that the operator's elbow is free of constraints. To control the redundant seven DOFs of the anthropomorphic slave arm, a small orientation sensor is placed on the operator's elbow. Therefore, each master arm can measure seven-DOF motions for each corresponding slave arm, whereas force is transmitted back from each slave arm to each corresponding master arm with six DOFs.

The master arm is lightweight, and its impedance is controlled so that the operator perceives to be inside the slave robot. It is important for the master to transmit the exact amount of force to the operator, and for the slave robot to maintain safe contact with humans in remote environments. The impedance-control-type master-slave system adopted by us can achieve this force presentation. Moreover, safety compliant contact can be maintained with humans because the slave is subjected to impedance control. The motion of the robot's head is synchronized with the motion of the operator's head; these motions are measured using a head tracker in the master cockpit.

The most distinctive feature of the TELESAR II system is the use of an RPT viewer system. Both the motion and visual image of the operator are important factors to determine in order for the operator to perceive existence at the place where the robot is working. In order to view the image of the operator on the slave robot such that the

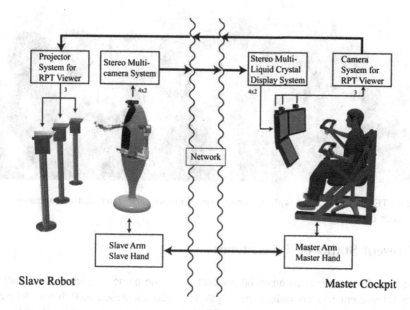

Fig. 10. Schematic diagram of TELESAR II master-slave manipulation system.

operator is inside the robot, the robot is covered with a retro-reflective material, and the image captured by the camera in the master cockpit is projected on the TELESAR II. TELESAR II acts as a screen, and a person seeing through the RPT viewer system observes the robot as though it were the operator because of the projection of the real image of the operator on the robot.

The face and chest of TELESAR II are covered with a retro-reflective material. A ray incident from a particular direction is reflected in the same direction as the surface of the retro-reflective material. Because of the characteristics of retro-reflective materials, an image is projected on the surface of TELESAR II without distortion. Because many RPT projectors are used in different directions, and different images are projected corresponding to the cameras located around the operator, the corresponding images of the operator can be viewed.

Figure 11 (left) illustrates an example of the projected images of an operator on its surrogate robot TELESAR II, and Fig. 11 (right) shows the operator who is telexisting in the TELESAR II robot.

The slave hand consists of five fingers with five finger-shaped haptic sensors. Each haptic sensor comprises a transparent elastic body, two layers of blue and red markers, and a CCD camera; it can measure the distribution of both the magnitude and direction of force. The master hand follows a compact exoskeleton mechanism called "circuitous joint," which covers the large workspace of the operator's finger. It can provide an encounter-type force feedback to the operator. The encounter-type force feedback avoids unnecessary contact sensations and allows unconstrained motion of the operator's fingers. Each fingertip has an electrocutaneous display unit attached to it in order to present tactile sensation to each finger of the operator in order to realize haptic telexistence.

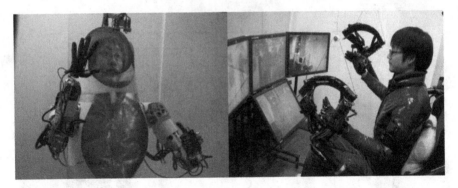

Fig. 11. TELESAR II robot with the projection of an operator (left), and the operator at the telexistence controls (right).

4 Present Status of Telexistence

There have been several commercial products with the name of telepresence, such as Teliris telepresence videoconferencing system, Cisco telepresence, Polycom telepresence, Anybots QB telepresence robot, Texai remote presence system, Double telepresence robot, Suitable Beam remote presence system and VGo robotic telepresence. Current commercial telepresence robots controlled from laptops could provide an increased sense of presence on the side of the robot, but the remote user might have a poor sense of self-presence.

An android that quite resembles its master is called a Geminoid [19]. Although it has a strong sense of the master's presence, it can only be used by the one whose face is used to make the robot. When the robot is used remotely, it is necessary to send the robot in advance. Because one of the merits of telexistence is to exist remotely without traveling, telexistence robots should be designed to be capable of being used by anyone so that it is not necessary to send the robot in advance. Study on automatic face replacement for an android has been conducted to solve this problem with some success [20]. However, three seconds are required to display the face, and real-time face expression cannot be transmitted. Research toward ideal telexistence is being conducted, such as research for transmitting the sense of presence of an operator through projections of the operator's facial image on the model of a human head in real time [21].

However, all these efforts have not achieved both a sense of self-presence and a sense of their presence as described in Sect. 2.2 in order to be mutual telexistence systems. Although ideal telexistence should provide haptic sensations, conventional telepresence systems provide mostly visual and auditory sensations with, at most, only incomplete haptic sensations. In this section, recent research aimed at mutual telexistence and haptic telexistence by the author and his team is introduced.

4.1 Face-to-Face Telexistence Communication Using TWISTER Booths

Telexistence Wide-angle Immersive STEReoscope (TWISTER) is designed as a telecommunication system that uses a virtual environment as a place for communication, thereby allowing highly realistic telecommunication between multiple persons. The system is designed to fulfill three conditions: (1) the virtual environment should have highly realistic audiovisual properties; (2) face-to-face communication should allow eye contact; and (3) participants in the virtual environment should possess a body, and should feel that the body belongs to them. We designed and built such a system and verified its utility.

In particular, to TWISTER's omnidirectional, three-dimensional naked eye display, we added a three-dimensional facial image acquisition system that captures expressions and line of sight, and a user motion acquisition system that captures information about arm and hand position and orientation; moreover, we constructed an integrated system whereby communication occurs via an avatar in a virtual environment. We then evaluated the system to verify that it fulfilled the established conditions. Furthermore, the results of having two participants engage in TWISTER-to-TWISTER telecommunication verified that participants can engage in telecommunication in the shared virtual environment under mutually equivalent conditions [22].

We used TWISTER V as a display to present audiovisual images of the virtual environment. As with TWISTER IV, TWISTER V displays binocular images using 36 LED display units, each with separate LED arrays for the left and right eyes. These are equally spaced along a circle with 1 m radius centered on the user, and rotated at high speed (1.7 rps) around the user. Persistence of vision creates a three-dimensional effect regardless of the viewing angle, and given that parallax images are presented by a rotating parallax barrier mechanism, glasses and other paraphernalia are not necessary to experience the three-dimensional effect.

TWISTER V has a 3162 × 600 pixel display resolution, and a 60 fps refresh rate. Users can move their upper body freely within the rotating part. Figure 12 (left) shows TWISTER V's exterior, and Fig. 12 (center) shows the full circumference of the interior as seen from below. Because images are displayed using persistence of vision during rapid rotation, the cylindrical surface upon which the LED units are affixed can be made transparent, allowing a clear view of the user within (Fig. 12 (right)).

Fig. 12. TWISTER V: (left) general view, (center) view from inside, and (right) user seen from outside.

TWISTER V is equipped with speakers that allow presentation of fully inclusive sound from the bottom of the rotating part. Six speakers are located at a 60° interval along the periphery, allowing for sound directionality. This allows environmental sounds within the virtual environment and user utterances to be adjusted and presented as sounds within the space along the full periphery.

Figure 13 shows the conceptual diagram of mutual telexistence using TWISTER. This omnidirectional three-dimensional audiovisual system uses TWISTER and peripheral speakers to share virtual environment information. The movement acquisition system uses optical motion capture, a data glove, and a joystick, and information about the user hand and arm positioning and orientation is used to calculate avatar movements that are sent to the system. Information other than user facial images and utterances are collected, and differential information between the virtual environments is mutually transmitted using the User Datagram Protocol (UDP) to reflect changes in the virtual environment.

The three-dimensional facial imaging system has a mobile camera unit and a headset microphone. The mobile camera unit uses avatar positional relationships from the virtual environment to determine required camera movements, and controls self-propelled stereo cameras so that they are appropriately positioned. Captured user facial images are sent directly via a network to the virtual environment of other users. User utterances acquired by the headset microphone are sent via the network to the peripheral speakers of the user and others in the virtual environment, where they are presented along with environmental sounds.

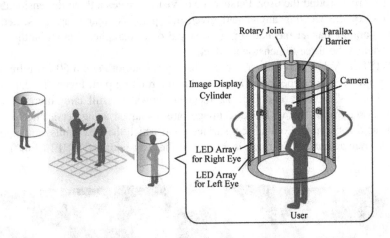

Fig. 13. Conceptual image of mutual telexistence using TWISTER.

We performed a communications experiment to test the telecommunication system, ensuring that the established requirements were sufficiently fulfilled to allow smooth communications in a shared virtual environment. The experiment was performed between two remote users engaged in one-on-one communications using TWISTER. The users were located at the University of Tokyo Hongo Campus (Hongo, Tokyo) and the Keio University Hiyoshi Campus (Hiyoshi, Yokohama). The network between the two TWISTER systems was over a dedicated 10 GB Ethernet line. Six participants were involved (three at each location), all ranging in age from 20 to 29. Two pairs of participants between the locations used the system in turn for approximately 30 min each, and one pair used it for approximately 2 h.

Figure 14 (left) shows the display of a facial image onto an avatar face area, as seen from the front. Figure 14 (center) shows the projection as seen from the side, which is presented as an appropriate three-dimensional profile image (cf. Fig. 14 (left)). Figure 14 (right) shows the position of the stereo camera and the facial image on the avatar with TWISTER external illumination adjusted so that both the stereo camera and the facial image can be seen. The stereo camera overlaps with the avatar's eye position so that line of sight naturally aligns. We verified that an avatar with physicality similar to a human can be used in a virtual environment for free movement, gestures, and transport of virtual objects such as glasses.

Fig. 14. Facial image on avatar in telexistence communication: (left) front view of the face image, (center) side view of the face image, (right) stereo camera overlapping with the eyes on the facial image, which assures eye contact of the two users.

Figure 15 shows the results of telecommunication in the integrated system. Figure 15 (left) is an image of the TWISTER booth located at Keio University and Fig. 15 (right) shows the booth at the University of Tokyo. We confirmed that the basic flow of the experiment can be conducted without significant problems.

Fig. 15. TWISTER to TWISTER communication: (left) a view from TWISTER V at Keio University, (right) a view from TWISTER IV at the University of Tokyo.

Subjective evaluation of the system from experiment participants was unanimous in reporting that interactions in the virtual environment invoked sensations similar to performing interactions in the real world. One participant reported the experience as being not so similar to having one's body transported to a virtual environment, but rather as though the TWISTER booth itself had been transported. We interpret this as meaning that entering the virtual environment in clothing similar to a space suit invoked a sensation of near immersion. Demonstrative pronouns frequently used in the real world such as "there" and "this" were naturally understood, leading to opinions that communication is easily performed. Such qualitative results are further indications that telecommunication that includes physicality and transmission of intent was realized.

4.2   Mobile Mutual Telexistence Communication System: TELESAR IV

Figure 16 shows a conceptual sketch of mobile mutual telexistence using TWISTER and a surrogate robot. User A can observe remote environment [B] using an omnistereo camera mounted on surrogate robot A'. This provides user A with a panoramic stereo view of the remote environment displayed inside the TWISTER booth. User A controls robot A' by using the telexistence master-slave control method. Cameras B' and C' mounted on the booth are controlled by the position and orientation of users B and C relative to robot A', respectively. Users B and C can observe different images of user A projected on robot A' by wearing their own Head Mounted Projector (HMP) to provide the correct perspective. Since robot A' is covered with retroreflective material, it is possible to project images from both cameras B' and C' onto the same robot while having both images viewed separately by users B and C.

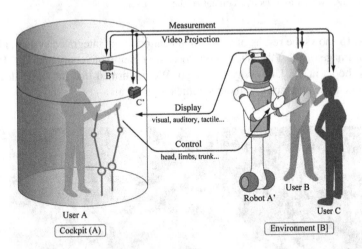

Fig. 16. Conceptual sketch of mobile mutual telexistence system using TWISTER as a cockpit.

The mobile mutual telexistence system, TELESAR IV, which is equipped with master-slave manipulation capability and an immersive omnidirectional autostereoscopic three-dimensional display with a 360° field of view known as TWISTER, was developed in 2010 [23]. It projects the remote participant's image onto the robot using RPT. Face-to-face communication was also confirmed, as local participants at the event were able to see the remote participant's face and expressions in real time. It was further confirmed that the system allowed the remote participant to not only move freely about the venue by means of the surrogate robot but also perform some manipulation tasks such as a handshake and other gestures. Figure 17 shows a general view of the system.

Fig. 17. General view of TELESAR IV system.

The TELESAR IV system consists of a telexistence remote cockpit system, telexistence surrogate robot system, and RPT viewer system. The telexistence remote cockpit system consists of the immersive 360° full-color autostereoscopic display known as TWISTER, a rail camera system installed outside TWISTER, an omnidirectional speaker system, an OptiTrack motion capture system, a 5DT Data Glove 5 Ultra, a joystick, and a microphone.

The telexistence surrogate robot system consists of an omnidirectionally mobile system, the 360° stereo camera system known as VORTEX, a retroreflective screen, an omnidirectional microphone system, a robot arm with a hand, and a speaker. The RPT viewer system consists of a handheld RPT projector, head-mounted RPT projector, and OptiTrack position and posture measurement system.

Stereo images captured by the 360° stereo camera system VORTEX are fed to a computer (PC1) mounted on the mobile robot. Real-time compensation and combination of the images are performed to transform these into 360° images for TWISTER. The processed images are sent to TWISTER and unprocessed sound from the omnidirectional microphone system is sent directly to the corresponding speaker system in TWISTER.

Cameras are controlled to move along the circular rail and to imitate the relative positions of the surrogate robot and the local participants at the venue. The images of the remote participant taken by these cameras outside TWISTER are fed to a computer (PC3) and sent to another computer (PC2) mounted on the mobile surrogate robot. These images are sent to the handheld and head-mounted projectors once they are adjusted using the posture information acquired by the position and posture measurement system (OptiTrack), which consists of seven infrared cameras installed on the ceiling of the venue. These processed images are in turn projected onto the retroreflective screen atop the mobile robot. The voice of the remote participant is also sent directly to the speaker of the mobile surrogate robot.

The joystick is located inside TWISTER and is controlled by the left hand of the remote participant. The data of the joystick are fed to PC3 and sent to PC1 via the network. Based on the information received, PC1 generates and executes a motion instruction to have the mobile surrogate robot move in any direction or turn freely on the spot; i.e., omnidirectional locomotion is possible. Using the motion capture system (OptiTrack) installed on the ceiling of TWISTER, the position and posture of the right arm of the remote participant are obtained. The position and posture data are also fed to PC3 and sent to PC2 via the network. Based on the received data, PC2 controls the robot arm to imitate the arm motion of the remote participant. In addition, hand motion data acquired by the 5DT Data Glove 5 Ultra are sent to the hand of the surrogate robot to imitate the hand motion of the remote participant.

A remote participant inside TWISTER joined a gathering by means of his surrogate robot and moved freely in a room with two local participants, who were able not only to see his face in real time through handheld and head-mounted RPT projectors but also to communicate with him naturally. The local participant in front of the robot saw the full face of the remote participant, while the local participant on the right side of the robot saw his right profile at the same time. The remote participant was able not only to see and hear the environment as though he were there but also to communicate face-to-face with each local participant. Moreover, he was able to shake hands and express his feelings with gestures, as shown in Fig. 18. Total latency of the visual-auditory system was less than 100 ms including data acquisition, transmission, and rendering. The total control cycle time of the robot was around 60 ms including measurement of the human operator, transmission, and control of the robot's arm and hand.

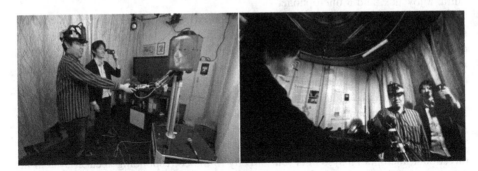

Fig. 18. Demonstration of TELESAR IV system at work.

4.3   Telexistence Avatar Robot System: TELESAR V

TELESAR V (TELExistence Surrogate Anthropomorphic Robot) is a telexistence master–slave robot system that was developed to realize the concept of telexistence. TELESAR V was designed and implemented with the development of a high-speed, robust, full upper body, mechanically unconstrained master cockpit, and 53 degrees-of-freedom (DOF) anthropomorphic slave robot. The system provides an experience of our extended "body schema," which allows a human to maintain an up-to-date representation in space of the positions of his/her various body parts. Body schema can be used to understand the posture of the remote body and to perform actions with the belief that the remote body is the user's own body. With this experience, users can perform tasks dexterously and perceive the robot's body as their own body through visual, auditory, and haptic sensations, which provide the most simple and fundamental experience of telexistence. The TELESAR V master–slave system can also transmit fine haptic sensations such as the texture and temperature of a material from an avatar robot's fingers to a human user's fingers [24, 25].

As shown in Figs. 19 and 20, the TELESAR V system consists of a master (local) and a slave (remote). A 53-DOF dexterous robot was developed with a 6-DOF torso, a 3-DOF head, 7-DOF arms, and 15-DOF hands. The robot also has Full HD (1920 × 1080 pixels) cameras for capturing wide-angle stereovision, and stereo microphones are situated on the robot's ears for capturing audio from the remote site. The operator's voice is transferred to the remote site and output through a small speaker installed in the robot's mouth area for conventional verbal bidirectional communication. On the master side, the operator's movements are captured with a motion-capturing system (OptiTrack) and sent to the kinematic generator PC. Finger bending is captured to an accuracy of 14 DOF with the "5DT Data Glove 14."

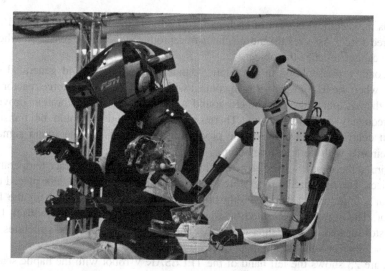

Fig. 19. General view of TELESAR V master (left) and slave robot (right).

The haptic transmission system consists of three parts: a haptic scanner, a haptic display, and a processing block. When the haptic scanner touches an object, it obtains haptic information such as contact force, vibration, and temperature. The haptic display provides haptic stimuli on the user's finger to reproduce the haptic information obtained by the haptic scanner. The processing block connects the haptic scanner with the haptic display and converts the obtained physical data into data that include the physiological haptic perception for reproduction by the haptic display. The details of the scanning and displaying mechanisms are described below [26–29].

First, a force sensor inside the haptic scanner measures the vector force when the haptic scanner touches an object. Then, two motor-belt mechanisms in the haptic display reproduce the vector force on the operator's fingertips. The processing block

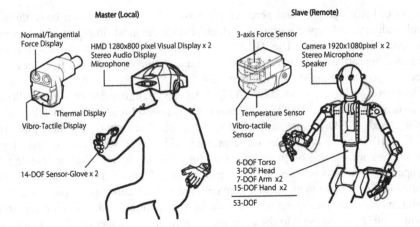

Fig. 20. TELESAR V system configuration.

controls the electrical current of each motor to provide the target torques based on the measured force. As a result, the mechanism reproduces the force sensation when the haptic scanner touches the object.

Second, a microphone in the haptic scanner records the sound generated on its surface when the haptic scanner is in contact with an object. Then, a force reactor in the haptic display plays the transmitted sound as a vibration. This vibration provides a high-frequency haptic sensation. Therefore, the information should be transmitted without delay. For this purpose, the processing block transfers the sound signals by using circuits with no transformation.

Third, a thermistor sensor in the haptic scanner measures the surface temperature of the object. The measured temperature is reproduced by a Peltier actuator placed on the operator's fingertips. The processing block generates a control signal for the Peltier actuator. The signal is generated based on a PID control loop with feedback from a thermistor located on the Peltier actuator. Figures 21 and 22 show the structures of the haptic scanner and the haptic display, respectively.

Figure 23 shows the left hand of the TELESAR V robot with the haptic scanners, and the haptic displays set in the modified 5DT Data Glove 14.

Fig. 21. Structure of haptic scanner.

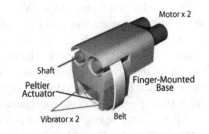

Fig. 22. Structure of haptic display.

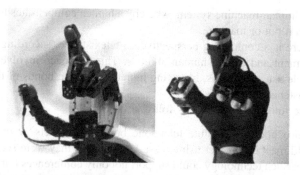

Fig. 23. Slave hand with haptic scanners (left) and master hand with haptic displays (right).

Figure 24 shows TELESAR V conducting several tasks such as picking up sticks, transferring small balls from one cup to another cup, producing Japanese calligraphy, playing Japanese chess (shogi), and feeling the texture of a cloth.

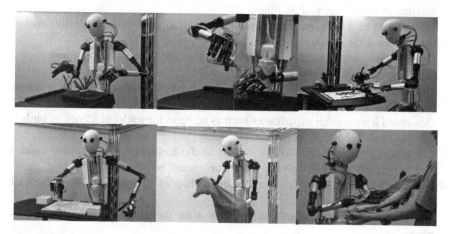

Fig. 24. TELESAR V conducting several tasks transmitting haptic sensation to the user.

5 Future Perspective of Telexistence

Telexistence technology has a broad range of applications such as operations in dangerous or poor working conditions within factories, plants, or industrial complexes; maintenance inspections and repairs at atomic power plants; search, repair, and assembly operations in space or the sea; and search and rescue operations in the event of a disaster as well as repair and reconstruction efforts in the aftermath of such a disaster. It also has applications in areas of everyday life, such as garbage collection and scavenging, civil engineering, agriculture, forestry, and fisheries industries; medicine and welfare; policing; exploration; leisure; and substitutes for test pilots and test drivers. These applications of telexistence are inclined toward the concept of conducting operations as a human-machine system, whereby a human compensates for features that are lacking in a robot or machine.

Further, there is a contrasting perspective on telexistence, according to which it is used to supplement and extend human abilities. This approach involves the personal utilization of telexistence, that is, liberating humans from the bonds of time and space by using telexistence technology.

We propose future applications as follows:

- If telexistence booths substitute telephone booths on streets or in offices, many people could meet each other using these booths, as if they were seeing each other face-to-face. Such technology could support not only conferences but also situations wherein many people walk around freely, such as cocktail parties.
- For the purpose of easy management, companies whose production sites are distributed overseas could link their branch offices and factories and treat them as though they were virtually located at one place.
- Advanced medical care could be provided worldwide by employing such a transmission system in operating rooms.
- The virtual presence of doctors would facilitate the provision of emergency medical services at early stages of an illness.
- In the event of a disaster, search and rescue operations would be possible without any concerns for ensuing disasters.
- One could immediately return from a remote location to one's office or home with a real-time sensation of existence.
- One could meet with family, relatives, and friends at remote places in a manner similar to a face-to-face meeting.
- One could have special experiences such as being in the midst of a flock of birds by using a small robot bird as his/her surrogate.
- Life-altering experiences such as looking at the earth from outer space, which is now physically possible only for astronauts, could be offered to everyone.
- One could enjoy real shopping at a remote shop as if he or she were physically present at the shop.
- One could travel to seldom-visited places with the sense of existence at those places.
- Life-sized space designs and evaluation tools would be available to architects.

6 Conclusion

Telexistence technology was historically reviewed, current advancements in telexistence, including mutual telexistence and haptic telexistence, were studied, and future perspective of telexistence were outlined.

Telexistence is a concept that allows humans to be emancipated from the restrictions of time and space and that allows them to exist at a "location" defined by inconsistent time and space, or a virtual space. Telexistence is the concept of making humans, rather than computers, ubiquitous. It differs from telepresence: the former also includes telexistence within or through virtual environments.

It is important to distinguish two key elements for telexistence: the "sense of self-presence" and the "sense of their presence". This paper described technologies that improve both of these elements towards the next generation of "mutual telexistence".

In particular, the TELESAR surrogate anthropomorphic robot was controlled from a cockpit that provides a sensory immersive (audiovisual and haptic) interface via gloves and tactile actuators. Many generations of the system have been constructed, including TWISTER, the improved version of the cockpit. One distinguishing feature of TELESAR is Retroreflective Projection Technology (RPT) system. Under this concept, a robot is covered with a retroreflective material, and viewers on the robot's side use head-mounted projectors to display the correct image of the interacting user, according to their perspective.

Acknowledgement. This study on telexistence has been conducted in collaboration with many former and current students, affiliates, and staff members of the Tachi Laboratory at the University of Tokyo and Keio University, including H. Arai, T. Maeda, Y. Inoue, K. Yasuda, T. Sakaki, E. Oyama, Y. Yanagida, N, Kawakami, I. Kawabuchi, M. Inami, D. Sekiguchi, H. Kajimoto, H. Nii, Y. Zaitsu, Y. Asahara, K. Sogen, S. Nakagawara, R. Tadakuma, K. Watanabe, K. Minamizawa, M. Furukawa, K. Sato, T. Yoshida, S. Kamuro, T. Kurogi, K. Hirota, M. Nakayama, Y. Mizushina and C. L. Fernando. This work is partly supported by JST-CREST and Grant-in-Aid for Scientific Research (KAKENHI). The author declares under his sole responsibility that the experimental protocol was compliant with International Ethics Regulations.

References

1. Tachi, S.: Telexistence, World Scientific (2009). ISBN-13 978-981-283-633-5
2. Sutherland, I.E.: A head-mounted three dimensional display. In: Proceedings of the Fall Joint Computer Conference, pp. 757–764 (1968)
3. Minsky, M.: Telepresence. Omni **2**(9), 44–52 (1980)
4. Tachi, S., Tanie, K., Komoriya, K.: Evaluation Apparatus of Mobility Aids for the Blind, Japanese Patent 1462696, filed on 26 December 1980; An Operation Method of Manipulators with Functions of Sensory Information Display, Japanese Patent 1458263, filed on 11 January 1981
5. Tachi, S., Abe, M.: Study on tele-existence (I). In: Proceedings of the 21st Annual Conference of the Society of Instrument and Control Engineers (SICE), pp. 167–168 (1982). (in Japanese)
6. Tachi, S., Tanie, K., Komoriya, K., Kaneko, M.: Tele-existence (I): design and evaluation of a visual display with sensation of presence. In: Proceedings of the 5th Symposium on Theory and Practice of Robots and Manipulators (RoManSy 1984), Udine, Italy, pp. 245–254. Kogan Page, London, June 1984
7. Anderson, R.J., Spong, M.W.: Bilateral control of teleoperators with time delay. IEEE Trans. Autom. Control **AC-34**(5), 494–501 (1989)
8. Tachi, S.: Human-robot systems in the third generation robots. In: Australia-Japan Technological Science Seminar on Robotics, Melbourne, Australia, pp. 1–21 (1987)
9. Tachi, S., Arai, H., Morimoto, I., Seet, G.: Feasibility experiments on a mobile tele-existence system. In: The International Symposium and Exposition on Robots (19th ISIR), Sydney, Australia, November 1988

10. Tachi, S., Arai, H., Maeda, T.: Development of an anthropomorphic tele-existence slave robot. In: Proceedings of the International Conference on Advanced Mechatronics (ICAM), Tokyo, Japan, pp. 385–390, May 1989
11. Tachi, S., Arai, H., Maeda, T.: Tele-existence master slave system for remote manipulation. In: IEEE International Workshop on Intelligent Robots and Systems (IROS 1990), pp. 343–348 (1990)
12. Tachi, S., Yasuda, K.: Evaluation experiments of a tele-existence manipulation system. Presence 3(1), 35–44 (1994)
13. Oyama, E., Tsunemoto, N., Tachi, S., Inoue, Y.: Experimental study on remote manipulation using virtual reality. Presence 2(2), 112–124 (1993)
14. Yanagida, Y., Tachi, S.: Virtual reality system with coherent kinesthetic and visual sensation of presence. In: Proceedings of the 1993 JSME International Conference on Advanced Mechatronics (ICAM), Tokyo, Japan, pp. 98–103, August 1993
15. Tachi, S.: Real-time remote robotics toward networked telexistence. IEEE Comput. Graph. Appl. 18, 6–9 (1998)
16. Tachi, S., Komoriya, K., Sawada, K., Nishiyama, T., Itoko, T., Kobayashi, M., Inoue, K.: Telexistence cockpit for humanoid robot control. Adv. Rob. 17(3), 199–217 (2003)
17. Tachi, S., Kawakami, N., Inami, M., Zaitsu, Y.: Mutual telexistence system using retro-reflective projection technology. Int. J. Humanoid Rob. 1(1), 45–64 (2004)
18. Tachi, S., Kawakami, N., Nii, H., Watanabe, K., Minamizawa, K.: TELEsarPHONE: mutual telexistence master slave communication system based on retro-reflective projection technology. SICE J. Control Meas. Syst. Integr. 1(5), 1–10 (2008)
19. Nishio, S., Ishiguro, H., Hagita, N.: Geminoid: teleoperated android of an existing person. In: Humanoid Robots: New Developments, pp. 343–352. I-Tech Education and Publishing, Vienna, Austria, June 2007
20. Maejima, A., Kuratate, T., Pierce, B., Morishima, S., Cheng, G.: Automatic face replacement for a humanoid robot with 3D face shape display. In: Proceedings of the 12th IEEE-RAS International Conference on Humanoid Robots, Osaka, Japan, pp. 469–474, 2012
21. Lincoln, P., Welch, G., Nashel, A., Ilie, A., State, A., Fuchs, H.: Animatronic shader lamps avatars. In: 8th IEEE International Symposium on Mixed and Augmented Reality, pp. 27–33 (2009)
22. Watanabe, K., Minamizawa, K., Nii, H., Tachi, S.: Telexistence into cyberspace using an immersive auto-stereoscopic display. Trans. Virtual Reality Soc. Jpn. 17(2), 91–100 (2012). (in Japanese)
23. Tachi, S., Watanabe, K., Takeshita, K., Minamizawa, K., Yoshida, T., Sato, K.: Mutual telexistence surrogate system: TELESAR4 - telexistence in real environments using autostereoscopic immersive display. In: Proceedings of the IEEE/RSJ International Conference on Intelligent Robots and Systems (IROS), San Francisco, USA (2011)
24. Tachi, S., Minamizawa, K., Furukawa, M., Fernando, C.L.: Telexistence - from 1980 to 2012. In: Proceedings of IEEE/RSJ International Conference on Intelligent Robots and Systems (IROS2012), Vilamoura, Algarve, Portugal, pp. 5440–5441 (2012)
25. Fernando, C.L., Furukawa, M., Kurogi, T., Hirota, K., Kamuro, S., Sato, K., Minamizawa, K., Tachi, S.: TELESAR V: TELExistence surrogate anthropomorphic robot. In: ACM SIGGRAPH, Los Angeles (2012)
26. Minamizawa, K., Fukamachi, S., Kajimoto, H., Kawakami, N., Tachi, S.: Gravity grabber: wearable haptic display to present virtual mass sensation. In: 34th International Conference on Computer Graphics and Interactive Techniques (ACM SIGGRAPH 2007), Emerging Technologies, San Diego, USA (2007)

27. Minamizawa, K., Kakehi, Y., Nakatani, M., Mihara, S., Tachi, S.: TECHTILE toolkit – a prototyping tool for design and education of haptic media. In: Proceedings of Laval Virtual VRIC 2012, Laval, France (2012)
28. Kurogi, T., Nakayama, M., Sato, K., Kamuro, S., Fernando, C.L., Furukawa, M., Minamizawa, K., Tachi, S.: Haptic transmission system to recognize differences in surface textures of objects for telexistence. In: Proceedings of IEEE Virtual Reality 2013, pp. 137–138 (2013)
29. Fernando, C.L., Furukawa, M., Minamizawa, K., Tachi, S.: Experiencing one's own hand in telexistence manipulation with a 15 DOF anthropomorphic robot hand and a flexible master glove. In: Proceedings of the 23rd International Conference on Artificial Reality and Telexistence (ICAT), Tokyo, Japan, pp. 20–27 (2013)

Author Index

Printed in the United States
By Bookmasters